HTML 4.01
Weekend Crash Course™

HTML 4.01
Weekend Crash Course™

Greg Perry

IDG Books Worldwide, Inc.
An International Data Group Company
Foster City, CA • Chicago, IL • Indianapolis, IN • New York, NY

HTML 4.01 Weekend Crash Course™
Published by
IDG Books Worldwide, Inc.
An International Data Group Company
919 E. Hillsdale Blvd., Suite 400
Foster City, CA 94404
www.idgbooks.com (IDG Books Worldwide Web site)

ISBN: 0-7645-4746-1
Printed in the United States of America
10 9 8 7 6 5 4 3 2 1
1B/QZ/QY/QQ/FC
Distributed in the United States by IDG Books Worldwide, Inc.
Distributed by CDG Books Canada Inc. for Canada; by Transworld Publishers Limited in the United Kingdom; by IDG Norge Books for Norway; by IDG Sweden Books for Sweden; by IDG Books Australia Publishing Corporation Pty. Ltd. for Australia and New Zealand; by TransQuest Publishers Pte Ltd. for Singapore, Malaysia, Thailand, Indonesia, and Hong Kong; by Gotop Information Inc. for Taiwan; by ICG Muse, Inc. for Japan; by Intersoft for South Africa; by Eyrolles for France; by International Thomson Publishing for Germany, Austria, and Switzerland; by Distribuidora Cuspide for Argentina; by LR International for Brazil; by Galileo Libros for Chile; by Ediciones ZETA S.C.R. Ltda. for Peru; by WS Computer Publishing Corporation, Inc., for the Philippines; by Contemporanea de Ediciones for Venezuela; by Express Computer Distributors for the Caribbean and West Indies; by Micronesia Media Distributor, Inc. for Micronesia; by Chips Computadoras S.A. de C.V. for Mexico; by Editorial Norma de Panama S.A. for Panama; by American Bookshops for Finland.

For general information on IDG Books Worldwide's books in the U.S., please call our Consumer Customer Service department at 800-762-2974. For reseller information, including discounts and premium sales, please call our Reseller Customer Service department at 800-434-3422.
For information on where to purchase IDG Books Worldwide's books outside the U.S., please contact our International Sales department at 317-596-5530 or fax 317-572-4002.
For consumer information on foreign language translations, please contact our Customer Service department at 800-434-3422, fax 317-572-4002, or e-mail rights@idgbooks.com.
For information on licensing foreign or domestic rights, please phone +1-650-653-7098.
For sales inquiries and special prices for bulk quantities, please contact our Order Services department at 800-434-3422 or write to the address above.
For information on using IDG Books Worldwide's books in the classroom or for ordering examination copies, please contact our Educational Sales department at 800-434-2086 or fax 317-572-4005.
For press review copies, author interviews, or other publicity information, please contact our Public Relations department at 650-653-7000 or fax 650-653-7500.
For authorization to photocopy items for corporate, personal, or educational use, please contact Copyright Clearance Center, 222 Rosewood Drive, Danvers, MA 01923, or fax 978-750-4470.

Library of Congress Cataloging-in-Publication Data
Perry, Greg M.
    HTML 4.01 weekend crash course / Greg Perry.
        p.   cm.
    Includes index.
    ISBN 0-7645-4746-1 (alk. paper)
    1. HTML (Document markup language)
I. Title.
QA76.76.H94 P47   2000
005.7'2--dc21   00-057550

 is a registered trademark or trademark under exclusive license to IDG Books Worldwide, Inc. from International Data Group, Inc. in the United States and/or other countries.

ABOUT IDG BOOKS WORLDWIDE

Welcome to the world of IDG Books Worldwide.

IDG Books Worldwide, Inc., is a subsidiary of International Data Group, the world's largest publisher of computer-related information and the leading global provider of information services on information technology. IDG was founded more than 30 years ago by Patrick J. McGovern and now employs more than 9,000 people worldwide. IDG publishes more than 290 computer publications in over 75 countries. More than 90 million people read one or more IDG publications each month.

Launched in 1990, IDG Books Worldwide is today the #1 publisher of best-selling computer books in the United States. We are proud to have received eight awards from the Computer Press Association in recognition of editorial excellence and three from Computer Currents' First Annual Readers' Choice Awards. Our best-selling ...For Dummies® series has more than 50 million copies in print with translations in 31 languages. IDG Books Worldwide, through a joint venture with IDG's Hi-Tech Beijing, became the first U.S. publisher to publish a computer book in the People's Republic of China. In record time, IDG Books Worldwide has become the first choice for millions of readers around the world who want to learn how to better manage their businesses.

Our mission is simple: Every one of our books is designed to bring extra value and skill-building instructions to the reader. Our books are written by experts who understand and care about our readers. The knowledge base of our editorial staff comes from years of experience in publishing, education, and journalism — experience we use to produce books to carry us into the new millennium. In short, we care about books, so we attract the best people. We devote special attention to details such as audience, interior design, use of icons, and illustrations. And because we use an efficient process of authoring, editing, and desktop publishing our books electronically, we can spend more time ensuring superior content and less time on the technicalities of making books.

You can count on our commitment to deliver high-quality books at competitive prices on topics you want to read about. At IDG Books Worldwide, we continue in the IDG tradition of delivering quality for more than 30 years. You'll find no better book on a subject than one from IDG Books Worldwide.

John J. Kilcullen
John Kilcullen
Chairman and CEO
IDG Books Worldwide, Inc.

*Eighth Annual
Computer Press
Awards ≥1992*

*WINNER
Ninth Annual
Computer Press
Awards ≥1993*

*WINNER
Tenth Annual
Computer Press
Awards ≥1994*

*Eleventh Annual
Computer Press
Awards ≥1995*

IDG is the world's leading IT media, research and exposition company. Founded in 1964, IDG had 1997 revenues of $2.05 billion and has more than 9,000 employees worldwide. IDG offers the widest range of media options that reach IT buyers in 75 countries representing 95% of worldwide IT spending. IDG's diverse product and services portfolio spans six key areas including print publishing, online publishing, expositions and conferences, market research, education and training, and global marketing services. More than 90 million people read one or more of IDG's 290 magazines and newspapers, including IDG's leading global brands — Computerworld, PC World, Network World, Macworld and the Channel World family of publications. IDG Books Worldwide is one of the fastest-growing computer book publishers in the world, with more than 700 titles in 36 languages. The "...For Dummies®" series alone has more than 50 million copies in print. IDG offers online users the largest network of technology-specific Web sites around the world through IDG.net (http://www.idg.net), which comprises more than 225 targeted Web sites in 55 countries worldwide. International Data Corporation (IDC) is the world's largest provider of information technology data, analysis and consulting, with research centers in over 41 countries and more than 400 research analysts worldwide. IDG World Expo is a leading producer of more than 168 globally branded conferences and expositions in 35 countries including E3 (Electronic Entertainment Expo), Macworld Expo, ComNet, Windows World Expo, ICE (Internet Commerce Expo), Agenda, DEMO, and Spotlight. IDG's training subsidiary, ExecuTrain, is the world's largest computer training company, with more than 230 locations worldwide and 785 training courses. IDG Marketing Services helps industry-leading IT companies build international brand recognition by developing global integrated marketing programs via IDG's print, online and exposition products worldwide. Further information about the company can be found at www.idg.com.   1/26/00

Credits

Acquisitions Editor
Greg Croy

Project Editor
Terri Varveris

Technical Editor
Scott Kinney

Copy Editors
Robert Campbell
Sarah Kleinman
Mildred Sanchez

Proof Editor
Neil Romanosky

Project Coordinator
Danette Nurse
Louigene A. Santos

Permissions Editor
Jessica Montgomery

Media Development Specialist
Laura Carpenter

Media Development Managers
Stephen Noetzel
Heather Dismore

Graphics and Production Specialists
Robert Bihlmayer
Jude Levinson
Michael Lewis
Victor Pérez-Varela
Ramses Ramirez

Quality Control Technician
Dina F Quan

Book Designer
Evan Deerfield

Illustrators
Brent Savage
Gabriele McCann

Proofreading and Indexing
York Production Services

About the Author

Greg Perry is the author of more than 65 computer books and has sold more than 2 million copies of books worldwide. Perry has written on topics ranging from operating systems, to programming languages, to end-user applications. Before becoming a full-time author and speaker, Perry worked as a Supervisor over financial systems at a Fortune 500 company before moving from industry to teaching at the college level. In addition to writing, Perry enjoys studying financial investing, traveling, and speaking on numerous computer and travel subjects.

For Mr. Leo Laporte,
the computer tutor
above all the other teachers.

Preface

Welcome to *HTML 4.01 Weekend Crash Course*. So why another HTML book among countless HTML books? The *Weekend Crash Course* series is designed to give you quick access to the topics you want to learn. You won't find a ton of reference material in this book. Instead, you will find the material you need to get the job done.

You are about to experience the joy of delivering Web content within Web pages that you design, create, and edit. No longer will you be sidelined as an Internet user only; you will now be part of the game, making your own Web sites using the language that started it all: HTML.

Who Should Read This Book

This crash course is designed to provide you with a set of short lessons that you can grasp quickly — in one weekend. The book is for two audience categories:

1. Those who want to learn HTML fast. You may need to learn HTML for employment or you just want to create Web pages at home. Perhaps you are taking a course in HTML and need a quick supplement. If you are entirely new to programming, rest easy because the 30 sessions assume no prior knowledge of programming. As long as you've used the Internet to surf the World Wide Web, you are ready to learn and write HTML.

2. Those who have some knowledge of HTML, but who have not written HTML code in a while. HTML 4.01 offers improvements over earlier versions and this course refreshes your knowledge, brings you up to date, and gives you back the confidence needed to use HTML.

To get the most out of this book, you should be an experienced Internet user. I didn't spend very much time writing basic how-to information on using a browser or on surfing Web pages. In fact, I assume that you know how to do the following:

- Log onto the Internet
- Surf the Web
- Locate information you want to see on the Web
- Use an editor (if you've used a word processor, you can use an editor)

What You Need to Have

To make the best use of this book, you need:

- An Internet account.
- An editor, such as Windows Notepad. Although a word processor works like an editor, you need the more simple features that an editor provides. A helpful Mac editor is included in this book's CD-ROM.
- A desire to learn HTML so that you can edit and create your own Web pages.

Any computer system with which you can log onto the Internet works. HTML does not require heavy processing power. If you can view Web pages, you can create your own Web pages with HTML. You can use a modem connection or a faster connection, such as a T1, T3, cable modem, or DSL connection. The faster your connection, the quicker your HTML code is loaded and working on your Web sites. However, a slow connection does not hinder your ability to learn and use HTML effectively.

I recommend that you use a high-resolution video driver (800×600 is okay, but 1024×768 is ideal). A standard 600x480 VGA resolution will do in a pinch, but the low resolution generally limits what you can see at one time on the screen.

What Results Can You Expect?

Is it *possible* to learn HTML in a single weekend? Yes, it is. Unlike other kinds of programming languages, HTML is simple and provides immediate feedback. You don't have to send your code through a process that converts it to something not readable by humans. The computer understands the same HTML that you write. Therefore, a conversion stage between you and the machine, called the *compilation process*, is not needed. This results in faster learning of HTML because less of a wall separates you from the computer.

This text is not a reference book. It does not teach you every aspect of every HTML command. Sometimes, you learn only enough about a command to make it work in the way that the majority of programmers use that command. Also, you do not have to tackle highly specific HTML commands that are rarely, if ever, used.

In addition to learning the HTML language, you also learn the context of its use. You do not learn just the mechanics. You learn why a certain HTML command works better than another; why a certain Web page design dictates that you approach the HTML code differently from usual; and why some Web page design elements work while others do not. You learn about color combinations, graphic formats, what appeals to the user's eyes, how to write to different kinds of hardware, and you get a glimpse into future HTML-based technology that is likely to change the way you create Web pages.

Weekend Crash Course's Layout and Features

This book follows the standard Weekend Crash Course layout and includes the standard features of the series so that you can be assured of mastering HTML within a solid weekend. Readers should take breaks throughout. We've arranged things so that the 30 sessions last approximately one-half hour each. The sessions are grouped within parts that take two or three hours to complete. At the end of each session, you'll find "Quiz Yourself" questions, and. at the end of each part, you'll find part review questions. These questions let you test your knowledge and practice exercising your newfound skills. (The answers to the part review questions are in Appendix A.) Between sessions, take a break, grab a snack, refill that beverage glass or cup, before plunging into the next session!

Layout

This Weekend Crash Course contains 30, one-half-hour sessions organized within six parts. The parts correspond with a time during the weekend, as outlined in the following sections.

Part I: Friday Evening

In this part, I set the stage for the rest of the book. You'll learn about the reason for HTML. You will learn about the format of HTML code and the interaction between the user's Web page and the HTML code that you write.

Part II: Saturday Morning

This part consists of six sessions that take you further into the world of HTML programming and its purpose. You learn how to add text to and format pictures on your Web pages. You also master the inclusion of hyperlnks, the links that connect Web content.

Part III: Saturday Afternoon

In this afternoon session, you take your HTML programming to a new level by embedding email links into your Web pages. You see how to use tables to format your Web pages into advanced and consistent content that presents your information effectively. In addition to tables, you also learn how to create forms on our Web pages so that you can retrieve information from visitors.

Part IV: Saturday Evening

Here, you learn the next step in Web page production. Now that you understand how to develop Web pages, you now begin to explore how to market and target your Web page content. You learn how to lay out your Web pages to make your site more appealing to the visitors who view your site.

Part V: Sunday Morning

This begins a two-part section where you follow the development of a family Web site from beginning to end. You do not start with HTML coding because effective Web pages begin in the design room. Once you have the design firmly in mind, you begin the HTML coding process. As you follow along, you develop the Web site and see how its genesis becomes a finished product.

Part VI: Sunday Afternoon

In this part, you finish the family Web site's production and explore some ways to improve the site's design and efficiency. In addition, you learn how to correct potential problems that can occur as well as how to stay on top of maintenance that is so critical in Web site development.

Features

First, as you're go through each session, look for the following time status icons that let you know how much progress you've made throughout the session:

30 Min.   **20 Min.**   **10 Min.**   **Done!**
To Go   **To Go**   **To Go**

The book also contains other icons that highlight special points of interest:

 This is a flag to clue you in to an important piece of information that you should file away in your head for later.

 This gives you helpful advice on the best ways to do things, or a tricky technique that can make your HTML programming go smoother.

 Never fail to check these items out because they provide warnings that you should consider.

 This states where in the other sessions related material can be found.

Other Conventions

Apart from the icons you've just seen, only three other conventions appear:

1. To indicate a menu choice, I use the ⇨ symbol, as in:

   ```
   Choose File⇨Open to display a list of files.
   ```

2. To indicate programming code or an Internet address within the body text, I use a special font like this:

   ```
   The Web site appears at http://www.idg.com/ and
   displays the corporate Web presence.
   ```

3. To indicate a programming example that's not in the body text, I use this typeface:

   ```
   <p><font face=Arial>Italy ice cream,</font></p>
   <p><font face=Times New Roman>called
   gelato,</font></p>
   <p><font face=Arial>is the richest, creamiest
   ice cream in the world.</font></p>
   <p><font face=Times New Roman>Buon Apitito!</font></p>
   ```

Accompanying CD-ROM

This Weekend Crash Course includes a CD-ROM in the back. The CD-ROM contains a skills assessment test, source code for the longer examples in the book, text editors, Netscape Navigator, Internet Explorer, and more. For a complete description of each item on the CD-ROM, see Appendix B.

Reach Out

The publisher and I want your feedback. After you have had a chance to use this book, please take a moment to register this book on the http://my2cents. idgbooks.com Web site. (Details are listed on the my2cents page in the back of this book.) Please let us know of any mistakes in the book or if a topic is covered particularly well. Please write to:

```
zucchi77@hotmail.com
```

You are ready to begin your weekend crash course. Stake out a weekend, stockpile some snacks, cool the beverage of your choice, set your seats in their upright positions, fasten your belt, and get ready to learn HTML the easy way. Turn the page and begin learning.

Acknowledgments

I am extremely grateful to Joe Wikert and Greg Croy, men whom I've worked with since the early days of my writing career. It's like "old home week" when we talk. By giving me the opportunity to write my first title for IDG, they show a lot of trust for which I'm extremely thankful.

The editor who wins the award for the most patience with my writing and with me is Terri Varveris. Terri, you are the best! Your suggestions are precise and they make the book so much better. Terri, I don't give you much good to work with but you *still* turn my words into readable text! In addition, Mildred Sanchez, Sarah Kleinman, and Robert Campbell, all worked together to make this the best possible HTML book on the market.

Mr. Scott Kinney stays busy with his premiere, world-renown news and discussion service Web site, MyRightStart.com, yet he still made time to perform the technical editing for this book. Mr. Kinney is a leader in the Web industry, as well as being the commercial art field's chief CEO with Kinney Creative, and it's an honor to have a man of his caliber work on my writing.

Of course, my most gratitude remains with my loving and supportive bride, Jayne. My parents, Glen and Bettye Perry, continue to support my work in every way.

Contents at a Glance

Contents

HTML 4.01
Weekend Crash Course™

☑ **Friday**

☐ Saturday

☐ Sunday

Part I – Friday Evening

PART

I

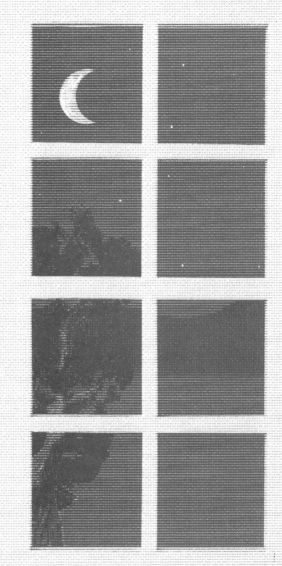

Friday Evening

HTML and the Web

Session Checklist

✔ Learn the job of the HTML programmer

✔ Understand what HTML is and its purpose

✔ Recognize how text editors and other programs work to help create HTML

**30 Min.
To Go**

Do you want to become an HTML programmer? If so, you must tackle HTML (Hypertext Markup Language). Fortunately, HTML 4.01 is more powerful than the versions that came before it, as well as much simpler to learn than typical computer programming languages such as C or Visual Basic. As this week-end crash course proves, you can go from knowing nothing about HTML to designing and producing Web pages in one short weekend.

As you will see in this session, the HTML language has gone through several improvements and each revision serves to make Web pages more interactive with the user and to present data more effectively. That data can be text, graphics, sound, video, or a combination of all four. Although today's HTML differs quite a bit from the first version, the majority of the original language elements are still in use.

Some people say that you don't need HTML anymore, and that too many graphical Web page design tools exist that make HTML unnecessary. To set your mind at ease considering that you've now spent the money for this course, you won't find any serious Web designer who doesn't work with HTML almost daily. In addition, as you will soon learn, the Web would not and could not even exist without HTML.

Become an HTML Programmer!

An HTML programmer designs, produces, and maintains Web pages. As you know from surfing the Web already, most Web sites are not single Web pages but collections of pages. A Web site consists of a series of related Web pages that users traverse, backwards and forwards, in virtually any order.

The HTML programmer's job changes almost daily. A programmer might find himself or herself performing one or more of the following HTML-related tasks daily:

- Designing new Web pages for their clients who want to present information on the Web

- Learning new HTML extensions, tools, and tricks that help get the Web-mastering job done faster and more accurately

- Maintaining existing Web sites by editing the code to correct problems and to present fresh material

The more often you put fresh material on a Web site, the more likely users are to return to the site.

The term *maintenance* refers to the process of changing and updating existing Web sites to keep their content fresh, and correcting mistakes found in them. Those mistakes might be typical computer *bugs* that keep the Web site from operating exactly right or may be nothing more than a spelling mistake or a color-blending problem from a bad graphic image.

Perhaps you want to create Web pages for your company's business. Perhaps you want to put your family news on the Internet so friends and family around the world will be able to see the news. Perhaps you want to make money — a *lot* of money — and the Internet is the hottest place for that right now. HTML programmers are in great demand, and that demand seems to be increasing. So don your thinking caps because a whole new skill set is about to be yours in fewer than 30 hours.

What Exactly Is HTML?

The name *HTML* stands for *Hypertext Markup Language*. That's a mouthful. Many people who create Web pages and work in HTML often forget what the letters stand for. The term's hypertext portion refers to the cross-links, also called hyperlinks, between Web pages. The term's markup language portion refers to the commands that format the Web pages that the users see. Knowing how to write and use HTML is the goal, not remembering the archaic abbreviation.

 The term *HTML language* is as redundant as *ATM machine* and *PIN number*. Literally, *HTML language* means *Hypertext Markup Language language*. Redundant or not, *HTML language* is often the phrase used, even by experienced HTML programmers.

The Internet is more than just a bunch of Web pages. The Internet consists of Web pages, e-mail, text, voice, video chat sessions, and an assortment of other tasks that often hide behind the scenes from typical Internet users. Amidst the array of Internet components, a Web page comprises the most important piece of the Internet because a Web page is the user interface to the information that resides on the Internet. Close to one billion Web pages comprise the World Wide Web (WWW). Virtually every Web page that you've ever visited has two things in common:

- They contain formatted text and graphic images.
- They are created, in whole or in part, using the HTML language.

It may surprise you to learn that HTML is a language that has absolutely no formatted text or graphic images. The HTML language consists solely of unformatted text. That text, however, contains instructions, called *tags* or *command tags,* that define exactly how formatted text and graphics appear on Internet Web pages. In other words, HTML determines how a Web page browser displays the information your HTML-based Web pages produce.

In other computer languages, the term *program* means a set of instructions that makes the computer perform a specific task, such as payroll processing. A Web page's HTML set of tag commands is usually referred to as *HTML code*. HTML is more of a formatting language than a programming language. Some extensions in recent versions of HTML can be considered tiny programs, but the term *program* is rarely used for HTML code.

HTML's background

**20 Min.
To Go**

HTML's genesis is interesting. Unlike the origin of many computer languages, understanding HTML requires knowing a little about the necessity that brought about the HTML language in the first place.

HTML is only about a decade old and for most of that decade, HTML simply formatted text pages viewable by only a few browsing programs. The original goal of HTML was to present textual information that would enable users to jump, or hyperlink, between areas of interest. In addition, HTML offered a method for formatting text sent between computers. Today, HTML's latest incarnation, currently at version 4.01, not only formats text but also presents graphics and manages forms of data between computers. The HTML convention is so widely used that online help systems, *intranets* (networked computers tied together at single locations as opposed to being connected solely to the World Wide Web), CD-ROM interfaces, and other uses of HTML are commonplace. As sites such as FreeBooks.com (http://www.freebooks.com/) demonstrate, you can download complete books formatted in the HTML language that you can, in turn, open and read directly from within your Internet browsing program such as Netscape Navigator, Internet Explorer, or UNIX browsers.

The true beauty of HTML is that any computer with a Web browser can read and interpret HTML code on incoming Web pages. Before the standardized HTML (which is not yet a *true* industry standard because of all the HTML extensions floating around), a computer could receive only data from a similar machine, or straight text data only. Given that HTML is straight, unformatted text, simple transfer protocols still enable any kind of computer to read and display a Web page properly.

Before the Internet became popular, one would send different kinds of files over a network connection. You might send a text file to a friend and then send a graphics file. Perhaps you downloaded a sound file from an electronic bulletin board system (a *BBS*). Today, you can still download files in various formats, but, in addition, you receive an HTML-based file when you view a Web page. One of the advantages of sending HTML over a connection, as well as individual data files, is that the HTML code ties all the other data elements together by formatting them into a readable and useable Web page.

If you or a user of your Web pages uses a browser that does not support HTML version 4.01, but instead supports a lower version, that older browser should, but does not always, ignore the newer and unrecognized HTML language commands in your Web page. Although some browsers may display error messages, most simply ignore the HTML command, resulting in your Web page looking different from your expectations. The vast majority of users use Internet Explorer or Netscape Navigator. These two browsers, depending on how current the version is, provide excellent support for the HTML language and its extensions.

HTML tags format data

You're already more than a third through this first session, and you haven't seen one line of HTML code. It is time! With only 30 hours of training, the sooner you learn HTML code, the better. Listing 1-1 contains HTML code that produces the top portion of a Web page. At this point, the HTML code may look rather foreboding. HTML code is comprised of a series of commands called *tags* that describe the look of the resulting Web page.

Listing 1-1
The top portion of a Web page created with HTML

```
<html>

<head>
<body bgcolor="#ffffff"
background="http://www.idgbooks.com/images/menu/background.gif"
leftmargin=8 topmargin=8> <table width=600 cellspacing=0
cellpadding=0 border=0> <tr><td width=130 valign=top> <table
width=110 align=left cellpadding=0 cellspacing=0>

<tr><td colspan=2 valign=top align=center><a    href="/cgi-
bin/gatekeeper.pl?uidg14112:%2F"  ><img border=0
src="http://www.idgbooks.com/images/logo.alt.gif" width=80
height=110></a></td></tr>
```

Continued

Listing 1-1 *Continued*

```
<tr><td colspan=2><img height=30
src="http://www.idgbooks.com/images/spacer.gif" ></td></tr>

<tr><td></td><td colspan=2><img height=4
src="http://www.idgbooks.com/images/spacer.gif" ></td></tr>
<tr><td background="http://www.idgbooks.com/images/buttonbk.gif"
valign=middle align=left><a class="nav"  href="/cgi-
bin/gatekeeper.pl?uidg14112:%2Fmismt%2Findex.html"  ><img
name="b19" border="0"
src="http://www.idgbooks.com/images/arrow.gif" ></a></td><td
background="http://www.idgbooks.com/images/buttonbk.gif"
valign=middle align=left><a class="nav"  href="/cgi-
bin/gatekeeper.pl?uidg14112:%2Fmismt%2Findex.html"  ><font
face="Times Roman" size=2
color=#ffffff><b>MIS Press<br>M&amp;T Books</b></font></
a></td></tr>
```

Figure 1-1 shows you what Listing 1-1's HTML code produces inside a browser window. The result is *much* more appealing and fancier than the HTML code. That's actually the beauty of HTML; the better trained you are in HTML, the more appealing your resulting Web pages will look and the more users will return to your sites — and the more in demand you will be as an HTML programmer.

Don't expect to understand much of the connection between the HTML code, called *source code,* in Listing 1-1, and the results shown in Figure 1-1. At this point, your job is to understand the purpose of HTML and not worry about the meaning of the individual command tags. HTML tells the receiving browser how to locate and format any type of data found on the Internet, including text, graphics, sound, and video.

You never have to purchase a new version of HTML. Unlike typical programming languages such as Visual Basic, which you must update as each new language version is released, you can create Web pages that contain all the latest and greatest HTML extensions with simple tools that come with Windows. The browser that reads HTML code determines which new language extensions the user experiences when a Web page you create appears on the user's screen.

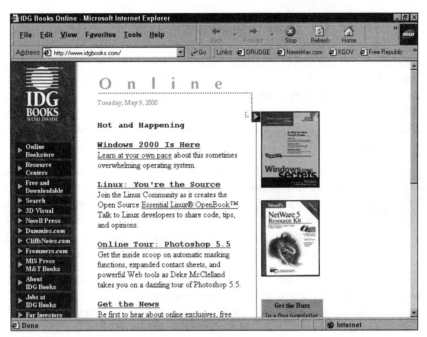

Figure 1-1
The Web page appears clean and well-formatted thanks to proper
HTML code.

Obviously, if Listing 1-1 is a complete and accurate set of HTML code that produces a Web page, you only need a text editor, perhaps one such as the UNIX vi editor or Notepad (that comes with Windows), to enter and write HTML code. A huge number of HTML programmers rely on simple text editors such as these to enter and write HTML code. Although other programs exist, as you'll see later in this session, text editors, such as Notepad, are always available on any Windows computer.

If you're wondering where the fancy formatted text and graphics are in Listing 1-1's HTML code, the mystery is that *no* formatted text and graphics ever appear inside the actual HTML code. The Web browser must read the code in Listing 1-1 before your users will see results. In other words, when a Web browser is sent a file containing HTML code, instead of displaying that actual code, the browser interprets the commands inside the file and acts accordingly.

**10 Min.
To Go**

Text Editors and Other Programs

As mentioned in the previous section, Notepad (found on the Windows Programs ⇨ Accessories menu) is a useful tool for creating HTML code on Windows machines. (Mac users often use SimpleText and Stickies or BBEdit for HTML coding.) These programs are called *editors* or *text editors*. A text editor is like a poor-man's word processor. With a text editor, you can enter and edit text. However, the text editor does not format lines, sentences, or paragraphs, and often ignores spelling errors.

Programmers who write text-based programs need their editors to retain line breaks and not wrap lines, as word processors do. In addition, features such as automatic spelling correction would change many programming commands to words that are meaningless to the computer trying to run the program. Simple text editors are the tools of the trade for text-based programming.

Before the Web came along, programs such as Notepad were going the way of monochrome PC monitors. Why would *anyone* use a text editor in the world of graphical user interfaces (*GUIs*)? For PC users, with Windows coming on the scene, straight text was on its way out, and more feature-packed word processors such as Word filled the void. Text editors could not handle the programmer's new responsibilities that required interfacing graphics and text.

Fortunately, Microsoft kept Notepad in its Windows bag of tricks for one version longer than most would think necessary. While Windows 3.1 was making its way onto the world's computer desktops, a little-known network called the Internet was leveling the pathways to build the information superhighway. The concrete used for that information superhighway was the earliest version of HTML, which required nothing more than a simple text editor.

As more and more people began using the Internet, more and more programmers learned HTML. These programmers had a choice to make: Either spend money on commercial text editors or use the freebie, such as Notepad, that came with every PC in the world. Needless to say, Notepad saw new life, and Web programmers are still using Notepad and its cousins on other kinds of computers today. Figure 1-2 shows a Notepad editing session at work on an HTML Web document.

```
Office 9 Preview Notes.htm - Notepad                                    _ 8 X
File   Edit   Search   Help
<a href="/Dispatch/Entry/0,65,,00.html?st.ne.nav.subscribe"><span style="color: black"><font colo
<a href="http://registration.cnet.com/MemberServices/1,9,,00.html?webAbbrev=ne&from=http://www.ne
<a href="/Staff/index.html?st.ne.nav.con"><span style="color: black"><font color="#000000" face="
<a href="/Help/Item/0,24,2,00.html?st.ne.nav.help"><span style="color: black"><font color="#00000
<p>

<font size="-1" face="Arial, Helvetica"
color="#006600"><strong>ABOUT CNET</strong></font><br>
<a href="http://www.cnet.com/Company/index.html"><span style="color: black"><font color="#000000"
<a href="http://www.cnet.com/Company/ss01.html"><span style="color: black"><font color="#000000"
<a href="http://www.cnet.com/Company/ss02.html"><span style="color: black"><font color="#000000"
<a href="http://www.cnet.com/Company/ss03.html"><span style="color: black"><font color="#000000"
<a href="http://www.cnet.com/Company/ss04.html"><span style="color: black"><font color="#000000"
<a href="http://www.cnet.com/Company/ss05.html"><span style="color: black"><font color="#000000"
<a href="http://www.cnet.com/Company/ss06.html"><span style="color: black"><font color="#000000"
<a href="http://www.cnet.com/Company/ss07.html"><span style="color: black"><font color="#000000"
<a href="http://www.cnet.com/Company/ss08.html"><span style="color: black"><font color="#000000"
<a href="http://www.cnet.com/Content/Builder/web.builder/"><span style="color: black"><font color
<p>

<font size="-1" face="Arial, Helvetica"
color="#006600"><strong>CNET SERVICES</strong></font><br>

<a href="http://www.cnet.com/?st.ne.nav.cnet"><span style="color: black"><font
color="#000000" face="arial, helvetica" size="-2">CNET.COM</font></span></a><font size="+1"> 
<a href="http://www.computers.com/?st.ne.nav.co"><span style="color: black"><font color="#000000"
<a href="http://www.cnet.com/Content/Builder/?st.ne.nav.bl"><span style="color: black"><font color
<a href="http://www.gamecenter.com/?st.ne.nav.gc"><span style="color: black"><font color="#000000"
<a href="http://www.download.com/??st.ne.nav.dl"><span style="color: black"><font color="#000000"
<a href="http://www.shareware.com/?st.ne.nav.sw"><span style="color: black"><font color="#000000"
<a href="http://www.browsers.com/?st.ne.nav.br"><span style="color: black"><font color="#000000"
<a href="http://www.activex.com/?st.ne.nav.ax"><span style="color: black"><font color="#000000" f
<a href="http://www.search.com/?st.ne.nav.se"><span style="color: black"><font color="#000000" fa
<a href="http://www.snap.com/index.html?st.ne.nav.sp"><span style="color: black"><font color="#00
<p>
```

Figure 1-2
Notepad is a near-perfect and simple tool for writing HTML code.

Editors such as vi and Notepad are extremely simple. Their beauty is also their flaw because that simplicity does lack features that would be nice for HTML programmers, such as a spelling checker for specific HTML code tags or automatic indention of sections of HTML code that go together to make the code more readable. These simple text editors are ignorant of HTML or any other programming language and offer no HTML-specific features.. Commercial editors, on the other hand, offer specific features, and that is why so many tools exist on the market today for HTML programming and Web authoring. In spite of the heavy competition, a huge number of HTML programmers still utilize Notepad and other simple text editors for quick edits and sometimes for their entire programming process.

Microsoft Word has made a complete circle in its support for HTML. Word is not a great word processor for writing straight HTML text, but Word is nice for formatting text and laying out graphics on a page. You can save a Word document in HTML format and then edit the HTML code to make the Web page look exactly the way you want it to look.

One reason HTML programmers began to use other, commercial editors, such as FrontPage 2000 and Dreamweaver, is that they do *not* begin with the textual HTML code. For example, Figure 1-3 shows a screen shot of a Web page, created with FrontPage. Where's the HTML code?

Figure 1-3
A screen shot of a Web page created with FrontPage does not display code.

Development programs such as FrontPage 2000 and Dreamweaver are graphical in nature. Initially, you design Web pages graphically by specifying where text and graphics will appear, by drawing lines and boxes with the editing tools, and by importing data that you want to appear in your Web page. As you design your Web page, FrontPage 2000 and the other graphical-development tools write the HTML code in the background. At any point, you can click your mouse to see the HTML code behind the Web page you are creating.

Figure 1-4 shows the HTML code used for the Web page in Figure 1-3. In this case, the page's author had to do absolutely nothing to write the HTML code. As a matter of fact, some programmers use programs such as Dreamweaver or FrontPage 2000 to design Web pages, and they never write or look at a single line of HTML code the entire time, from design to the Internet.

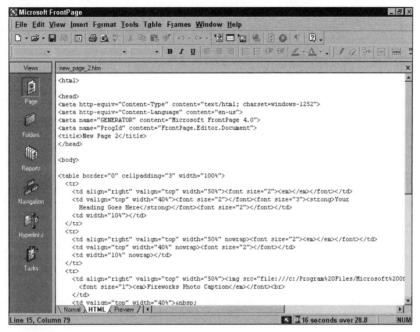

Figure 1-4
FrontPage writes the HTML code in the background as you design the Web page.

At this point, perhaps you are confused, and if so, for good reason. The first part of this session stressed the need for you to learn HTML, and now you're seeing tools that seem to eliminate the need to know HTML. The pros *all* know HTML, regardless of the fact that they mostly all use graphical development systems such as Dreamweaver for much of their Web page development. The reason is simple: With power comes lack of flexibility. Although these development tools contain super tools for placing your general Web page elements and text, they *rarely* do exactly what you want them to do.

With almost a billion Web pages on the Internet, the search is on for unique- ness among sites. If everybody used FrontPage 2000 and did not bother learning HTML code, all Web pages would look somewhat alike. Not that FrontPage 2000 lacks rich features that enable you to design smashing Web pages. But it simply does not contain an unlimited feature set. Practical limits placed on development tools mean that if you truly want to fine-tune your Web sites so they sing, you must master HTML. The Web sites that look amateurish are almost all designed by HTML programmers who used development tools but either didn't take the time to

Done!

hone the site's design by working over the automatically-created HTML code, or didn't know enough HTML to do more than the standard cookie-cutter Web site.

Want proof? Spend the next 29 hours or so learning how you can use HTML to make your Web sites rock.

REVIEW

- HTML programming requires knowledge of Web page design, creation, and maintenance.
- Users return again and again to Web sites that maintain fresh content.
- HTML plays a vital role in Web page design.
- HTML contains command tags that format Web pages.
- Web page designing programs, such as FrontPage, are powerful but still require knowledge of HTML for proper Web page design.

QUIZ YOURSELF

1. Why does the HTML programmer's job require more than just the creation of new Web sites? (See "Become an HTML Programmer!")
2. What does the abbreviation for HTML stand for? (See "What Exactly is HTML?")
3. HTML code contains the graphics and formatted text that comprise Web pages. True or False? (See "HTML Tags Format Data.")
4. Why is Notepad still in use by some HTML programmers? (See "Text Editors and Other Programs.")
5. How can a Web page development system, such as FrontPage 2000, help and hinder authors of the Web? (See "Text Editors and Other Programs.")

HTML for Web Page Creation

Session Checklist

✔ Create your first Web page

✔ Learn the minimum HTML code to produce a Web page

✔ Understand basic HTML formatting command tags

✔ Understand that browsers do not support the same HTML code

**30 Min.
To Go**

You begin this session by creating your very first Web page from scratch (actually, from HTML!) using an editor such as the Windows 98 Notepad editor. Although the page will be extremely simple, the experience will teach you much more about the nature of HTML programming than several chapters of text could do. HTML defines the styles of your Web pages. You'll begin the example in this session by exploring the simplest job of HTML, text formatting, and you'll learn the bare-bones HTML code required by Web pages.

Creating a Web Page

As you learned in the first session, HTML is a language that defines how your Web page will look. In one sense, HTML is a text-formatting language. Although HTML does more than format text, when the first version of HTML appeared, text formatting was its primary job, second only to providing hyperlinks as cross-references to other HTML documents.

When you first learn HTML, perhaps the best place to begin is by formatting some simple text. Therefore, consider the following poem:

Roses are red,

The Web is sure growing.

You use HTML,

To keep your page flowing.

If you want to put this poem on a Web page, completely unformatted, you could not do so without using some HTML. In other words, every Web page requires a minimum amount of HTML code. Without the minimum HTML tags, the file would be no different from an ordinary text file, such as a text file that might end with the txt filename extension. Given that HTML is a language comprised of command tags, as you learned in the previous session, you must insert more advanced formatting tags around this poem before the poem can ever appear formatted on a Web page.

Minimum HTML

This section teaches you the minimal HTML code needed to produce a Web page and how the code should be set up. Keep in mind that the minimum code lets you create only an unformatted Web page. Formatting command tags will be covered later in this session.

Filename Extension

A Web page, defined in an HTML file, always has the filename extension html (or htm if you want to be compatible with Windows 3x users, although fewer and fewer of them exist). The html extension separates the file type from ordinary, unformatted text files whose extensions might be txt.

Many browsers, such as Internet Explorer, will refuse to open your file with an extension such as txt, except by starting another program such as Notepad and loading the text file into that secondary program for your viewing and editing work. Some browsers will open a file whose name does not end with the html extension, but will refuse to interpret any HTML command tags. In such a case, the file will appear inside the browser window displaying the nitty-gritty command tags themselves instead of performing the formatting actions that the command tags request.

Beginning and Ending <html> and </html>Tags

Every Web page should begin with the following HTML start tag:

```
<html>
```

Every Web page should end with the following HTML end tag:

```
</html>
```

The poem, therefore, looks like this with those two enclosing tags:

```
<html>
Roses are red,
The Web is sure growing.
You can use HTML,
To keep your page flowing.
</html>
```

More is needed to make this an appealing Web page.

All HTML tags are enclosed between angled brackets. Often, related tags appear in pairs with one beginning the formatting process and the other terminating that format. The `<html>` **and** `</html>` **tags indicate the very beginning and ending of a Web page. The** *end tag* **contains the same command name as the start tag except it begins with a forward slash to distinguish where the tag pair begins and ends.**

The start and end tags may or may not be on the same line. For example, take the following section of HTML code:

```
<b>
This is boldface text
</b>
```

This example is identical to the following example in the way a browser handles it:

```
<b>This is boldface text</b>
```

It is common to nest tag pairs inside other tag pairs. By doing so, you can boldface words inside a Web page's italicized body of text. Therefore, don't be surprised to see many command tags begin before you see the first end tag.

Lowercase Versus Uppercase in Tags

It is common to use lowercase for all HTML tags. Most browsers and computers do not care if the tag is uppercase, as you saw in the previous session's example. Uppercase tags can help you keep the tags more easily separated from the surrounding text that the tags format. Nevertheless, a move is underway to standardize using lowercase tags because some computers, most notably UNIX-based machines, often distinguish too literally between uppercase and lowercase in command names. To be safe, develop a good habit and write lowercase tags.

Spaces in Code

You may not use spaces between a tag's opening angle bracket, its forward slash (if it is an end tag), or before the command itself. Many commands, however, include spaces both in the command as well as in the command's *attribute,* which is an optional value that some tags support. For example, here is a valid `<a>` command tag with a space that separates the tag name from its attribute:

```
<a href="http://www.abc.org/image.jpg">
```

The following is illegal in many browsers because of the location of the first space:

```
< a href="http://www.abc.org/image.jpg">
```

The reason the spacing around the command tag's angled brackets and the command itself is so critical is that you do not want your browser mistaking normal text for a tag. If angled brackets appear in your Web page's text that is to be displayed, those angled brackets will not be interpreted as possible HTML command tags unless they follow an exact format required by HTML. Also, many times you will see quotation marks around attributes, as shown in the previous example. The quotes are often optional.

Viewing your page

If you want to view the Web page with the poem, do the following:

1. Start Notepad.
2. Type the poem in the previous section with the `<html>` and `</html>` tags.
3. Save your text file with the html extension so your Internet browser can display the file properly.

You can even use a word processor to create your HTML code, but be sure that you save the file in text format and use the html filename extension.

4. Start your Web browser. From a browser, you can open files on your own computer just as you open Web pages on other computers over the Internet.

5. Select File ⇨ Open and type the full path and filename or browse your files for the file you saved earlier. Then click OK.

When you click OK, the poem is displayed along the top of the browser window, as shown in Figure 2-1.

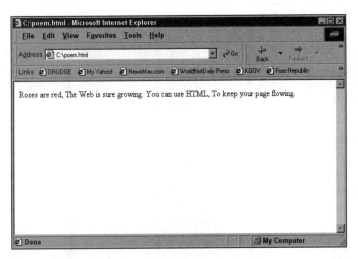

Figure 2-1
Your HTML file appears in your browser's window.

As you can see, the poem all rests on a single line, even though the poem spans four lines of your HTML file. Web browsers do not, and should not, make assumptions about line and paragraph spacing. You will learn how to separate the poem onto different lines with the formatting commands, which are discussed in the next section. Keep in mind that if you do not issue formatting commands, the browser will perform no formatting on the data you send to the browser.

You can use a general text editor or one designed specifically for HTML coding. One of the nice things about a text editor designed for HTML, as opposed to a straight text editor such as vi or Notepad, is that many of today's HTML editors color-code tags to help you keep your code accurate. For example, BBEdit and FrontPage 2000's HTML editing windows color all commands one color, command options (such as Title values) in another color, and certain punctuation and auxiliary HTML tags in another color. Once you familiarize yourself with these color schemes, you will be able to glance through your HTML code on the screen and more quickly locate lines and commands that you want to edit.

Adding Formatting Command Tags

**20 Min.
To Go**

Congratulations, you have created your first Web page. Obviously, you have a ways to go before you create the next dot.com Web-based company, but you've taken your first step. You can see that a simple Web page requires little more than typing text surrounded by `<html>` and `</html>` command tags.

Head and title tags

One optional but crucial item you must add to every Web page that you create from this point forward is a title for the browser window in which your Web page appears. You are probably used to seeing the title at the top of almost every Web site you visit. The title defines the page and sometimes displays needed information such as a filename reference.

Never let the Web browser pick a window title for you. By default, the HTML filename appears in the title bar, if you don't assign a title name. For example, the title shown in Figure 2-1 is the same as the HTML filename displayed to the left of the browser name. You owe it to your Web audience to describe as much as you can about the page they are viewing. Users who view multiple Web sites on their screens at the same time can read the tiled windows' titles to determine what each window contains.

The title command tag must appear inside a special section of your Web page called the *header section*. Before adding the title's tags, you must first create the header section with the <head> and </head> command tags. Start these tags immediately after the opening <html> tag, like this:

```
<html>
<head>
</head>
Roses are red,
The Web is sure growing.
You can use HTML,
To keep your page flowing.
</html>
```

Add ample spacing to make your HTML files readable and to make the command tags and HTML sections pronounced. Subsequent HTML examples in this weekend course include plenty of this *whitespace* to make the file readable and easy to maintain.

As in word processing, the header section of a Web page contains information about the Web page that often does not change from page to page on the site. Most Web sites contain multiple pages, and the header section defines the title and other heading information for each page on the site. The most important element you can include is the browser window title tag, <title>, and its corresponding end tag, </title>.

The value that you type between the title tags becomes the actual title you want the Web browser to display in the browser window's title bar.

```
<html>

<head>
<title>Poem to make you feel good</title>
</head>

Roses are red,
The Web is sure growing.
You can use HTML,
To keep your page flowing.

</html>
```

Figure 2-2 shows the resulting browser window. The browser window displays the poem's title, "Poem to make you feel good."

The window's title

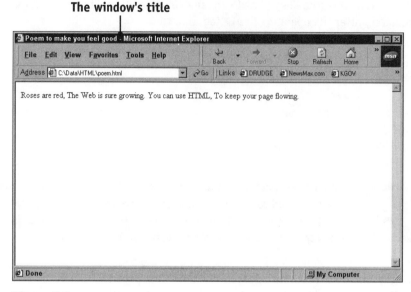

Figure 2-2
The title describes the file to your Web audience.

Finally, most HTML programmers place the body of the Web page in its own section, the *body section*. As you see from the successful display of the Web page in Figure 2-2, a body section is not required for simple Web pages such as the one being created so far. Nevertheless, the body section helps you organize more advanced Web pages, and most HTML programmers agree that a bare-bones Web page should include the <body> and </body> command tags. The body section is the page's meat-and-potatoes section that contains the bulk of information on that page.

The body section follows the header. The sample HTML-based poem now looks like this:

```
<html>

<head>
<title>Poem to make you feel good</title>
</head>

<body>
Roses are red,
```

```
The Web is sure growing.
You can use HTML,
To keep your page flowing.
</body>
</html>
```

Break tags

As mentioned in the previous section, the poem should appear with each line on a separate physical screen line. As you may now assume, a new command tag is required.

Use the *break tag* to break lines. The format of the tag is as follows:

```
<br>Text that appears on its own line
```

The <br> tag is special because, unlike so many other command tags, <br> has no corresponding end tag. The <br> tag is a stand-alone tag because it requests that the browser move down to the next line on the screen before displaying the text that follows.

Adding <br> to the beginning of each line in the poem produces a four-line poem. Here is the complete HTML file:

```
<html>

<head>
<title>Poem to make you feel good</title>
</head>

<body>
<br>Roses are red,
<br>The Web is sure growing.
<br>You can use HTML,
<br>To keep your page flowing.
</body>
</html>
```

Figure 2-3 shows the final Web page creation. The poem is now formatted and includes a title and a body.

\<body\>

\<title\>

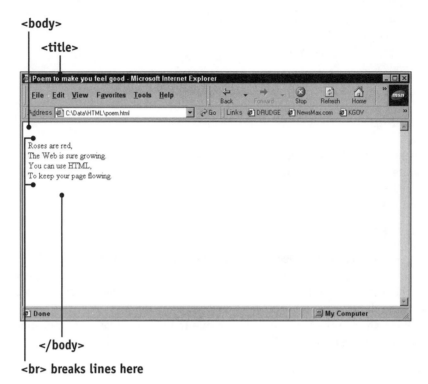

\</body\>

\<br\> breaks lines here

Figure 2-3
You've now seen the complete creation of a simple Web page.

The \<br\> **tag creates a line break at each location in which it is placed. The first line of the poem would appear one line higher without the** \<br\> **tag in front of it. You can put the** \<br\> **tag at the end of a line to force a line break for subsequent text.**

10 Min.
To Go

A more complete example

To help initiate you into HTML, Listing 2-1 contains the code for a more complete HTML example with a graphic image. Although the example is not extremely complex or advanced, by studying the code and the corresponding Web page in Figure 2-4 you will gain insight into what's ahead in the late Friday evening and early Saturday sessions of this course. Think of this example as whetting your appetite for more advanced HTML commands.

Listing 2-1
HTML code with text

```
<html>

<head>
<title>My First HTML Poem</title>
</head>

<body>

<h1 align="center">An HTML Poem</h1>
<hr>
<p align="center">Roses are <font color="#FF0000">red
</font>,<br>
The Web is sure <font size="4">growing</font>.<br>
You can use <u> HTML,</u><br>
To keep your page <i>flowing</i>.</p>

</body>

</html>
```

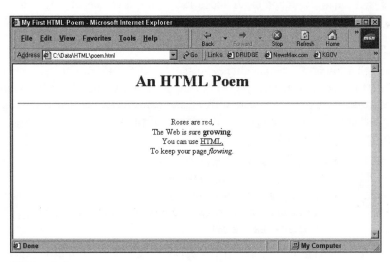

Figure 2-4
A more complete formatted Web page with text and a graphic image.

Some HTML tags, such as <h1> and <hr>, appear in Listing 2-1, and you haven't mastered them yet. You will learn all about Listing 2-1's HTML tags and many more as you progress through this weekend course. Most are extremely simple; for example, <hr> tells the browser to draw a horizontal line across the browser window.

The only potential problem you may have in understanding Listing 2-1 is the strange value in the following tag: <font color="#FF0000">. **The value** #FF0000 **is an internal representation for the color red. As you'll learn in Saturday morning's sessions, you can represent specific color values numerically.**

The Browser Determines the Language

Whereas programmers use HTML to format text, as shown in the previous example, the <title> tag demonstrates that HTML is not simply used for that purpose. The <title> tag does not format text or even the Web page; instead, it determines the title that appears in the browser window's title bar.

The browser used by your Web page's user determines exactly the way that your page appears. Many browsers do not support the same HTML code that others support. Although newer browsers often provide support for the latest HTML command tags, the HTML language is evolving, as you learned in the previous session. One of the ways that a new command tag is added is by a browser company. For example, when Internet Explorer arrived on the scene, Microsoft enabled that browser to read HTML instructions that had never been written before because no browser was designed to support these new commands.

Unlike other kinds of programming languages, such as C++, no central committee determines the next command tag to add to the next version of HTML. Although a Web consortium does exist to maintain HTML standards, most new command tags come from Microsoft and Netscape, the developers of the two most widely used browsers on the market today.

The *World Wide Web Consortium,* **found at** http://www.w3.org/, **contains the latest information related to new and upcoming additions you can expect to see in HTML. These additions often appear because of a browser company adding command tags to its browser's feature set.**

The result of the above facts is that the appearance of your Web page can vary when viewed on different computers. Throughout this weekend course, design issues become extremely important when using HTML, and an understanding of how different browsers support different levels of HTML also becomes critical. I pay

Done!

particular attention in the next session to maintaining proper design issues that enable you to create Web pages that look good on *any* browser that you may use to display your page. You will not have to write to the lowest-common dominating HTML code to produce extremely fresh and attention-grabbing Web pages.

Most of the figures in this book are shot using Internet Explorer because that's my primary Internet browser, but when major HTML differences exist between browsers, you'll be the first to know as you progress through the weekend.

REVIEW

- Command tags often appear in pairs, such as <html> and </html>.
- All HTML code requires the minimum command tags <html> and </html>.
- Command tags can be uppercase or lowercase, but a move is under way to standardize with lowercase.
- Use a <title> and </title> command tag pair to specify a title in your Web page's browser window.
- Specify exactly where you want your Web page's lines to begin and end; the browser will not break lines automatically.
- Many HTML codes format your Web pages to look good.
- New HTML commands often come about when a new browser supports them.

QUIZ YOURSELF

1. What are the two filename extensions all HTML files must use? (See "Minimum HTML.")
2. Which pair of command tags must enclose all Web pages? (See "Minimum HTML.")
3. Which command tags enclose your Web page's header section? (See "Adding Formatting Command Tags.")
4. Which command tags enclose your Web page's body? (See "Adding Formatting Command Tags.")
5. Why does the <br> tag not need a matching end tag? (See "Break Tags.")
6. What is one of the ways that a new HTML command tag gets created? (See "The Browser Determines the Language.")

Web Page Design

Session Checklist

✔ Learn how your users' environments may differ

✔ Create Web sites with all users in mind

✔ Utilize HTML validating programs to optimize your Web site

✔ Answer initial design questions

✔ Publish your Web site

✔ Learn about the available free hosting services

**30 Min.
To Go**

In this session, Web page design takes precedence over HTML code because your HTML code will suffer if you do not design your site properly. This book's goal is to teach you HTML in a weekend, and to do that, not a lot of time can be spent on design. Other texts exist that do a superior job of teaching Web page design. Nevertheless, you must understand early how your site is viewed by different users on different kinds of computers, and you must understand some of the trade-offs associated with proper Web site design. At the end of this session, you will learn the procedures required to publish your Web site on the World Wide Web and the available Web sites that provide free hosting services.

Considering Your Environment

As you learned in the previous session, your Web page looks different on different computers. You must understand the technical design issues that await you as an HTML programmer. Even among the same kinds of computers, different users have varying screen sizes. To make things even worse, if that's possible, users with the same computers and the very same monitors might set their monitors to different resolutions! Figure 3-1, for example, shows a Web page displayed at 800×600 pixels of resolution. Figure 3-2 shows the same Web page displayed at 640×480. Notice how much less of the Web page the lower resolution displays.

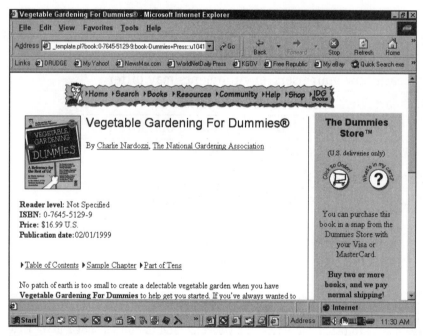

Figure 3-1
At 800×600, the Web page looks complete.

Actually, the resolutions 800×600 and 640×480 are misleading because the user's browsers consume much of the screen because of the menu, toolbars, and status bar. A more realistic design area, if you want to hit virtually every Web user in the world, is only 580×315 on a Mac and 635×314 on a PC.

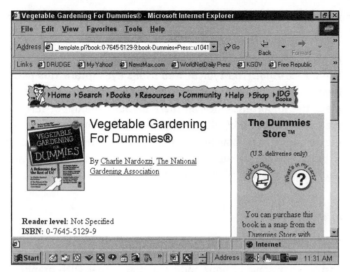

Figure 3-2
At 640×480, the Web page is missing some content.

What's an HTML programmer to do?

The problem of your varying Web audience is not insurmountable. Nevertheless, you must keep the majority of your users in mind when you design a page. Given that you've stepped up to the challenge of becoming an HTML programmer, you may have a more powerful computer than many of your Web page's users. In addition, your computer may be faster. For example, if you have a DSL connection, you get spoiled and perhaps forget about those golden days of 28.8 modem access. Many people live in areas without the benefit of DSL, this author being one of them. Therefore, you must consider not only the resolution of your target audience, but also the speed at which the Web pages you create will load.

Never overestimate the patience of your Web audience. The longer your Web page takes to load, with high-resolution graphics and active content, the less likely someone is to wait for the loading to finish. Instead of waiting, they will go to another site.

Web sites are not single pages; they are multi-paged. Once your users click downward into your site, you can more freely offer Web pages that require scrolling. Once you grab the user, subsequent pages might contain higher-resolution images and more text. At some point, your users will be willing to wait or scroll because they have delved into your Web site to find content. The first page, called the *home page,* is where you should most consciously consider the general-purpose Web user's screen size and page-loading time.

As you design your HTML pages, keep thinking *top-to-bottom* and *left-to-right*. The typical Web user's eyes follow this pattern. Design primarily for the upper-left hand portion of the screen, and place the important material there because the upper-left is the area seen first and by all users of your page. Loading time and resolution determine how much of the rest of your page the user sees without having to scroll. The more scrolling a user has to do to see your page, the less likely that user is to stay on your page.

A world without images

In addition to keeping your audience's resolution and page-loading speed in mind, you must also consider that some of your audience views pages with graphics turned completely off. Figure 3-3 shows a screen that should contain several graphic images, but graphic placeholders are in their place. Web browsers offer the option to turn off the display of images (unless the user clicks on an image to trigger that image's download and display), and the slower the connection, the more likely a user is to turn off images so the pages load quickly. As you design your Web page, keep in mind that you should display text around images to label clearly the image's purpose so text-only users will understand what your page contains.

A constant trade-off exists between speed, resolution, and content, and you'll make trade-offs as you design every single element of your Web page. For example, you may design a super graphic image that you want placed in the background of your HTML page. Before placing that image, however, you'll have to adjust the image's resolution to be as low as possible, while still maintaining as much of the image's quality as you can. The trade-off can be painful, because great-looking images at high resolution do not always translate well to a lower resolution. If you don't mind losing some of your audience, you may choose to display images at the higher resolution. The important thing is not setting the resolution but being aware of the trade-offs and that some users will give up on your page before the page has had a chance to load completely.

More and more Web sites now make available several versions of the same site. On the site's home page, hyperlinks may be available that take viewers to a text-only page or a higher-resolution, graphics-oriented page for users with faster connections.

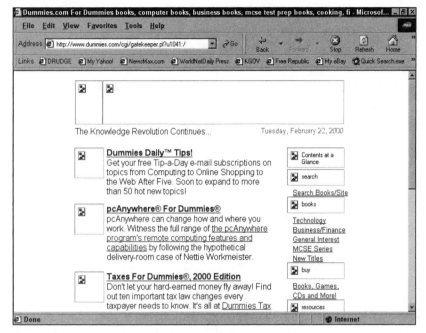

Figure 3-3
Graphic placeholders on the Web page indicate that the display of Web page images is turned off.

Validating Your Page

**20 Min.
To Go**

All Web designers feel the trade-offs discussed in the previous session. Fortunately, tools exist that help you hone your HTML code so that your site produces the maximum benefit given the aforementioned constraints. Your site will load quickly because you've taken the time to make your site technically efficient. One of the many such tools available is called an *HTML Validator* (see http://www.html validator.com/), a product you can purchase that offers suggestions on improving your site's efficiency. AI Internet Solutions provides the HTML Validator on their HTML Validator Web site that provides the best-known site advice products in the industry. Many Web designing programs, such as Dreamweaver, currently offer similar advice for your Web page.

The current versions of programs you might use to accent your HTML creation, such as the Adobe PhotoShop and Microsoft PhotoDraw graphics programs, offer advice for creating images that work well for the majority of users who may see your site.

Once you finish designing your Web page, the validating routines found in these programs perform actions such as:

- Checking your HTML code and informing you which browsers will have trouble displaying the code
- Informing you which graphic images will take too long to load
- Determining which colors on your Web site are nonstandard
- Locating mismatched start and end command tags
- Advising you on alternative fonts that might display more effectively

As you progress through the rest of this weekend course, you'll learn how to design around many common problems in HTML coding. (For example, Saturday's morning sessions will discuss which colors are considered *Web safe,* that is, displayable on the majority of the browsers.) As you write more and more HTML code, you'll begin to spot trouble areas on your own and work around them, but you'll still find that these HTML validating programs are extremely useful for catching small problems you might miss. Although you may use a simple text editor to create the bulk of your Web page, an HTML validation program such as HTML Validator helps maximize your design to the largest possible audience.

Initial Design Considerations

Before setting out to create your Web page, consider the following:

- Who is your audience?
- What is your message?

Surely, these design questions are so obvious they can go without being asked, right? Actually, not only do they need to be asked, they also need to be asked before, during, and after a Web site is developed.

Consider the technical design issues discussed in the previous sections. Suppose you are designing a Web page that provides support for iMac users. You would not want to limit yourself by making your Web page efficient for both Mac and PC users. The colors available to the Mac user typically are more numerous than the colors available to the PC user. You would be freer to use these additional colors since your site is geared specifically to the Mac.

Session 8 describes proper color selection.

In addition to the technical design issues that you'll master more fully as you progress through this weekend, your site's makeup of pages and how those pages connect determine the feel that you want your site to convey.

Although they are rare, some Web sites are completely comprised of a single page. Many personal home pages that keep friends and family updated on the latest information of a family consist of a single page or two that effectively convey all the information needed. On the other hand, corporate Web sites that include product information, ordering, and contact information might consist of a hundred or more Web pages.

Many Web sites have a central theme or primary topic that conveys a message. If you cannot narrow your site to a central theme, consider rethinking your site and possibly dividing the site into two separate sites.

Constantly match your fonts and graphic images with your topic as well. For example, if you want to portray a friendly, noncorporate feel, use fonts that convey less of a formal, business feeling and that add more of a fun flair to your site.

Once you've decided on your primary topic, keep focused on that topic. Once you've created some Web pages, test whether or not your pages fit your topic by asking others to view the pages and see how close they can come to determining your primary topic and the overall goal of the site.

Web structures

HTML programmers structure Web sites differently because the goals of Web sites differ greatly. As you've seen in this session, the audience and the primary topic determines the look and feel of the site.

Generally, Web sites fall into one of these three categories:

- *Sequential* or *Linear:* Each page in the site is just a continuation of the preceding page. The home page or start page is simply the first page in the sequential link of pages. Sites that are based on the sequential structure often are reading sites that tell a specific story or that need to teach the user a subject in a specific order.

- *Hierarchical:* The home page is considered to be the top of the Web site, with subsequent pages branching out from the home page. The hierarchical site is the most common site, often being used for both corporate and personal pages, with the home page being the launch pad for the rest of the site's areas.

- *Web:* Pages are linked as needed, but no single page, including the home page, has priority over the other pages. When a site contains data that does not fall in a specific preset order, the Web structure is used to give the user several avenues of branching among the pages. An inventory system designed for a corporate intranet would make a good candidate for this structure.

Figure 3-4 shows the three structures that Web designers use to determine the logical order for users to navigate a site. Some Web sites provide areas that contain more than one structure. Your site's message determines the site's structure.

The Web page design walkthrough

No text on Web page creation would be complete without the typical steps an HTML coder takes to design the page. That list follows, but unlike many tasks in computer programming, Web page design is not a procedural task. A Web page is never finished. The elements on your Web page today probably will change tomorrow and will be completely different in a month of two. Following are the steps you follow when you first design your site, but you'll be returning to them, in a different order, as your site evolves.

To design your Web page, you will:

1. Determine your site's theme and primary topic or task.
2. Determine the structure that best suits the site.
3. Sketch your site's home page to begin working on the tone of the entire site; your home page sets the standard format for the rest of the site.
4. Collect the text and graphic images that will appear on the site.
5. Create the initial page and block out the areas consumed by the headings, sidebars, menus, footers, and body of the page.
6. Enter the text and add the images to their appropriate locations.
7. Add hyperlinks to and from other pages you will be creating, as well as to other resources on the Internet you want to link to.
8. Publish your Web page.

Sequential Page Structure

Home Page

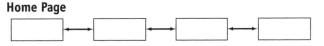

Hierarchical Page Structure

Home Page

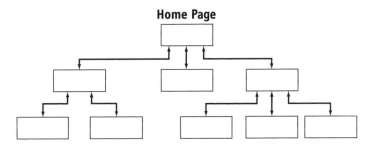

Web Page Structure

Home

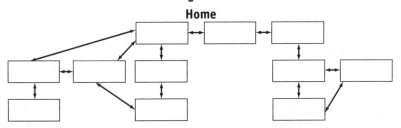

Figure 3-4
The three common Web site structures determine how users navigate Web sites.

In addition to being an ongoing process versus a straight, sequential order of steps, several of the Web page creation steps require a surprising amount of work. For example, collecting graphic images entails locating images you can use, creating your own images from a source such as a scanner, digital camera, or drawing program, and working those images so that their colors and resolution work well in the majority of browser windows that will display your site.

 Saturday morning's sessions on graphics will explain more about optimum colors and image resolution.

Once you begin to create Web pages, you will find yourself critiquing other Web sites. Such critique is good. You learn by watching how others create Web sites. Most Web browsers enable you to view the HTML source code used to create that site. (You can do this by selecting View ⇨ Source or a similar option that usually appears on Web browser menus.)

You will learn many Web design techniques by studying HTML code for the sites that you like. Don't steal the code, however, but learn what the HTML coder used to produce the site and experiment with your own styles that you gleam from other sites along the way.

Publishing Web Pages

10 Min. To Go

Knowing HTML does not get your Web site published, only created. You must have an avenue to get your Web page on the official Internet set of pages, and that means getting a Web address (called a *URL* for *Uniform Resource Locator*) assigned to your site.

Once you create your site, you need to do the following to publish your Web pages:

1. Determine a *domain name,* the portion of the Web address that appears before the .com, such as myNewPage in http://www.myNewPage.com; that domain name must be unused by anyone else.

2. Register your domain name. By registering, you find out if your domain name exists, and, if not, you pay to own that domain name for a specific period of time. The cost typically runs from $100 to $150 for a three-year registration.

3. Locate and register with a *Web host,* a company that uses its computers to serve up your Web pages 24 hours a day to the Internet. Many Web hosts also verify whether or not your domain name is already in use, and if not, will register the domain for you so that you can use a Web host at the same location. Although you can use your own computer as a server to the Internet, you're typically better off hiring the services of a host because a host can provide backup services, generally has equipment required for high-capacity Web page visits, and utilizes redundant storage technology to ensure that the site stays up. Free Web hosting services are also available. These are discussed in the next section.

4. Publish your Web pages by uploading your HTML code and images to the host's site. Generally, the host will tell you exactly how to go about publishing on that specific host machine. You might use a program called *FTP* (for *File Transfer Protocol*) to transfer the site from your computer to the host, but many hosts have their own special requirements.

5. Test your site by traversing all pages and hyperlinks, making sure that the site performs to your satisfaction.

Available Free Hosts

Many Web sites, most notably the portals such as Yahoo! and Geocities, offer Web hosting services for free. You can register at these sites for Web hosting space and upload your images and HTML code directly to their servers for instant (and free) Web pages.

Many of the free Web hosting services display banners and pop-up window advertisements on top of your Web page when users visit your home page. In addition, you are limited to the domain name that you can use. Generally, your site's name will be prefaced with the Web host site's name, such as http://www.geocities.com/mysite.html. **In this URL,** geocities **represents the Geocities Web site.**

These sites are perfect for experimenting and learning HTML, as well as for designing your early Web pages. Instead of paying for professional Web hosting services, you can place your initial Web page designs on these free Web hosts and make sure the pages perform as you expect.

Some of the free Web hosts are:

Done!

- Geocities (http://www.geocities.com/)
- Yahoo! (http://www.yahoo.com/)
- Microsoft Network (http://www.msn.com/)
- America Online (http://www.aol.com/)

REVIEW

- Design Web pages so that your users can see the most information possible.
- The speed of your user's connection and their screen resolutions affect the loading and display of your Web page.
- The faster your pages load, the more likely users are to stay at your Web site.
- An HTML Validator will inform you of trouble spots on your Web pages.
- Design and maintain your Web site with your audience and target topic in mind.
- A Web host will register your Web site's domain name and act as a server for your Web site.

QUIZ YOURSELF

1. Which resolution displays the most information: 640×480 or 800×600? (See "Considering Your Environment.")
2. Which corner of the screen should hold the most important links and site information? (See "What's an HTML Programmer To Do?")
3. How do some Web users eliminate the slow loading speed of images? (See "A World without Images.")
4. True or False: You cannot view other Web sites' HTML source code because the code is secured with passwords. (See "The Web Page Design Walkthrough.")
5. What is the job of the Web host? (See "Publishing Web Pages.")

Maintaining and Improving Your Web Site

Session Checklist

✔ Properly maintain your Web site

✔ Optimize the organization of your computer's files and folders

✔ Test and maintain your Web site on your own local Web server

✔ Allow your Web site to reflect the ever-changing HTML

✔ Learn about Web programming tools to accent your HTML code

**30 Min.
To Go**

O ne of the primary jobs of the HTML programmer that you should learn is proper site management. The choices you make when you first design a Web site, such as choosing proper folders on your own computer in which you store the site's files, can help or hamper your job later as your site grows.

In addition to managing a site properly, you need to stay abreast of the tools and new technologies available to help you improve your Web site. This session explores some of the HTML tools and other Web page languages that have become available that you can implement along with your HTML pages.

Success Means Constant Web Site Maintenance

Keep your Web site fresh if you want users to return. When someone begins to create a Web site, they have little understanding as to how involved and time-consuming even simple Web sites become. Even small changes to a single Web page often require that you perform these steps:

- Download the Web page to edit to your computer.
- Make the change.
- Upload the changed page.
- Test and review the page to ensure that the change works.

The final step, testing, may require that you work on the page more than once. Often, when you make a change, other parts of your site are affected. Perhaps a hyperlink to an object on your page changes, or perhaps you replace a figure that is still referenced from another page on your site. Although HTML validating programs may help you locate these missing links, other unexpected problems can arise. You should view your site in as many browsers and on as many different kinds of computers as possible to ensure that your site looks good in various configurations. The bottom line is that you should consider Web maintenance to be a job that always takes longer than you expect but is required for a site to be successful.

Think of the Web sites that you often visit. Those sites not only provide information you need, but they also stay fresh and keep your interest piqued.

 If you work from a modem or an integrated services digital network (ISDN) connection, this process is even more time-consuming considering the slow speed at which you must upload and download the pages you are editing.

The testing stage needs to include the same proofreading as printed documents require. Read your changes carefully to make sure the grammar and spelling are correct. Sloppy HTML programmers use sloppy spelling and poor grammar.

The Best Way to Organize Your Files and Folders

Not only must your Web site appear organized to your users, but also you must organize your own computer's files that contain a working copy of your Web site. Create a new folder for each Web site you want to produce. The folder that you create is the

Web site's primary folder. Next, inside each Web site's primary folder, create a sub-folder named *images* where you place every image for that site. By doing so, you head off problems that may arise. If you use an image more than once, for example, the user's browser will only need to load the image one time if you place that image in your images folder and reference that folder in your HTML page. In addition, you will not have to deal with extended paths to images when they all reside in the same folder. If you change an image in the folder, all hyperlink references to that image will not have to change.

Never put multiple versions of your Web page in the same primary folder. For example, if you have four separate versions of your Web page for four foreign languages, keep each of those versions in their own primary folder with their own images folder. Although doing so means that you might be maintaining four separate versions of the same images, you eventually save time with simpler hyperlinks throughout your sites.

Despite seeming as though you're stuck in the Dark Ages, try to limit yourself to the old DOS standard of 8.3 filenames, using htm as the filename extension unless your HTML editor supports the html filename extension. Most of today's computers recognize more characters, but you'll ensure that problems won't arise with legacy browsers and Web hosting software that you may still run into. In the world of computers, good documentation is vital, and 8.3-character filenames certainly do not allow extended self-documentation of filenames. However, for a few more years, such filenames are probably the safest to use.

Should You Turn Your Computer into a Local Web Server?

If you work from home, or from a small business that does not provide for a 24-hour Web server, you have the option of turning your computer into a local server. The drawbacks are that you must keep the server active at all times, day and night, connected to the outside world somehow. If you are linked to the Internet with a modem or ISDN line, you do not have the power to serve up multiple Web pages at once, if your site receives traffic that warrants the serving of more than one page simultaneously.

Despite its drawbacks, however, there is one benefit from turning your computer into a server: With your own local server, you can accurately test your site because you can create, edit, and maintain your entire Web site on your local server. You won't waste time uploading your changes only to find that you must make additional corrections to fix a broken link or other error before uploading the pages once again. Instead, you'll perform all testing and editing on your own server, correcting mistakes there. Then, once the site is exactly the way you want it, you can upload the site to a more powerful, full-time server on your Web host's system.

Most PC operating systems, including Windows 98, allow users to create their own local Web server.

20 Min. To Go

The Ever-Changing HTML

Your job of learning HTML will cease only if something replaces HTML on the Web. As discussed in Session 2, new command tags are introduced with virtually every new browser that appears. In addition, new techniques for using current HTML commands continue to evolve to help you maintain and create elegant, fast, attention-grabbing Web sites.

Stay abreast of new browser features when they are released by visiting the manufacturer's Web site to learn the new commands. You can incorporate these changes as you update your Web site. Many Web sites exist that act as resources for you, the HTML programmer. The following Web sites are useful because they not only contain design tips, but they also contain HTML code samples and tutorials that keep you up-to-date on the latest HTML versions:

- WebMonkey (http://hotwired.lycos.com/webmonkey/): Provides expert HTML and design tips
- HTML Reference Page (http://hotwired.lycos.com/webmonkey/reference/html_cheatsheet/index.html): Provides an HTML cheat sheet
- Experts Exchange (http://www.experts-exchange.com/): Answers to problems you might be having with your HTML code
- iSyndicate (http://www.isyndicate.com/): Provides content you can use on your site
- CAIM Web Style Guide (http://info.med.yale.edu/caim/manual/index.html/): Provides standard guidelines to help you create an acceptable Web site with all the common elements

Take a few moments out of your weekend crash course to look at these sites now so you'll understand the kinds of resources that you and other HTML programmers can rely on to bring the latest Web creation help to your screen. Sites such as

WebMonkey provide expert advice and columns that they update regularly to keep you informed. As you create and edit your site, you will enjoy the invaluable help these support sites can provide.

**10 Min.
To Go**

HTML and Company

As you work with HTML, you will think of elements (for example, text, graphics, applets, objects, and Excel spreadsheets) you want to add to your Web site that HTML simply cannot handle. HTML is only the first tool in the HTML programmer's bag of tricks. Although you have chosen this weekend to learn HTML, you need to know what else is in store for you once you master HTML because if you do not, you'll be frustrated over HTML's seeming lack of features. The reality is, HTML is extremely powerful and does its job above and beyond the call of duty. Nevertheless, you need to understand the tools that interact with your HTML code so that you will better understand how active Web pages work and you'll know what you will be able to use later to improve and maintain your sites.

DHTML

DHTML is known as *Dynamic HTML*. DHTML actually doesn't exist as its own language, but it describes a set of tools that browsers might support that activate sites by enabling those sites to respond to actions performed by the users. DHTML includes support for the following items with which you should begin to familiarize yourself:

- *CSS*, or *cascading style sheets:* With CSS, you can design your own formatting command tags to facilitate easier and more consistent Web site formatting than with HTML alone. Several versions of CSS have been released. Most notably, *CSS Level 1* (CSS 1) allows you to define new formats for your Web pages much like Microsoft Word style sheets do, and *CSS-P,* or *cascading style sheets-positioning (also known as CSS 2),* enables you to specify exact positions for text, graphics, and other HTML Web page elements.

- *JavaScript:* This is an interactive programming language, much like the C++ programming language, which enables you to embed small programs called *applets* into your HTML code.

Internet Explorer 3.0 was the first browser to introduce the DHTML concept by offering CSS Level 1 command tags, and other browsers promptly followed. Currently, all releases of all major browsers support CSS, CSS-P, and JavaScript, but when you design your sites, you must keep in mind that not all Web users have the latest browsers. If your page contains DHTML but someone views your page with an older browser, many of the active elements on your page may not work properly.

Beginning in Session 19, you will begin learning some of these DHTML concepts in detail. You don't have to be an advanced JavaScript programmer to take advantage of JavaScript and other DHTML elements in your Web sites. For example, you can produce *rollover effects,* shown in Figure 4-1, which change buttons on your Web page into other items (such as different colors that appear as the user points to buttons with the mouse, or perhaps buttons that turn into drop-down menus) as the user moves the mouse pointer over those buttons. You can do this by adding some cut-and-paste JavaScript code that you'll find in later sessions to your HTML pages.

The rollover effect

Figure 4-1
JavaScript enables the buttons on your Web page to change as the mouse pointer is moved over them.

XML

XML means *extensible Markup Language* and provides a sort of extension, or superset language, to HTML and DHTML. XML goes beyond HTML to describe any kind of data file and provides database support. Programs that support XML, such as Microsoft Word, can interpret XML command tags that look and act a lot like HTML tags. Browsers that do not support XML will ignore the XML tags.

Generally, browsers are programmed to ignore tags that they do not recognize as opposed to displaying an error message. Therefore, the browser you obtain today will run tomorrow's Web pages with HTML, XML, and just about any other tag-based language even though the browser may not execute the commands requested inside those unknown tags.

XML supports CSS and all of the DHTML commands. Actually, XML is a superset of DHTML. The *extensible* in XML, however, goes far beyond HTML or DHTML. With XML, you literally can create your own markup language. The language can closely match your site's design. For example, if your site sells bread, you can create an XML tag that is called `BreadSpecial` that you use for the special of the day.

The weekend is not nearly long enough to tackle HTML, DHTML, and XML. Fortunately, if your goal is to develop exciting Web pages, XML is not a language you will need to worry about for some time unless you need to embed external data such as a Microsoft Excel spreadsheet inside your Web pages. (Excel saves its Web-based spreadsheets in the XML format.) Even then, Excel will handle all the XML, and your job is only to locate a browser that can display XML in addition to HTML. XML's benefits come in handy once you've mastered HTML and envision extending HTML to match your site's goals more closely using XML.

ActiveX controls

Microsoft's version of Java, ActiveX, offers a way to embed programmable objects, such as input fields. These special controls respond to the user's events when using the control, such as clicking the control's panel. One of the drawbacks of ActiveX controls is that when you design the control, you must compile the control on every type of computer that will use the control. The advantage of ActiveX, however, is its cross-platform abilities across various company tools. A Visual Basic programmer can create an ActiveX control, and an HTML programmer can embed that control on the server's site for distribution along with Web pages.

CGI

Many commercial Web sites contain *CGI,* or *Common Gateway Interface,* code. CGI is not a language but a scripting service by which the server of the Web page contains code written in a procedural Web language, such as *Perl.* The server executes the code when the user of the Web page triggers the code, as might happen when the user clicks a button to place an online order. The CGI code does not appear in the HTML code and is not visible to the user.

ASP

ASP stands for *Active Server Pages* and represents *server-side programming,* a fancy term for the programs that run on the Web host's machine as opposed to programs that run on the user's computer. To utilize ASP, your Web host must utilize Microsoft Web server extensions. Not unlike CGI and other scripting languages, ASP runs on the server's computer, but the results appear on the user's Web page. ASP uses the *DLL,* or *Dynamic Link Library,* concept so that only one copy of an executable routine has to be in memory at one time, saving on resources.

Done!

Not every language and scripting service available to the HTML programmer is discussed here because of time limitations of the weekend. For example, VBScript and Java are languages that an HTML programmer can use to accent a Web page.

REVIEW

- A constant maintenance of your site, although necessary, is a time-consuming job that tends to take longer than expected.
- Proofread your Web site to keep a professional appearance and to ensure that the site works well.
- Store your Web site in its own folder for simple access to your files.
- Consider running a Web server from your own computer if you want maximum control over your site.
- If you want to activate your Web site, use DHTML.
- HTML programmers can use several scripting languages to add custom and secure features, such as electronic commerce, to a Web site.

QUIZ YOURSELF

1. What problems can occur when you make changes to your site? (See "Success Means Constant Web Site Maintenance.")

2. Which folder should hold your site's images? (See "The Best Way to Organize Your Files and Folders.")

3. What are some drawbacks to using your own personal Web server? (See "Should You Turn Your Computer into a Local Web Server?")

4. True or False: Windows 98 users cannot turn their computers into Web servers. (See "Should You Turn Your Computer into a Local Web Server?")

5. What do cascading style sheets accomplish? (See "DHTML.")

PART

I

Friday Evening
Part Review

1. What does HTML stand for?
2. Why is Web page maintenance important?
3. What are command tags?
4. Which symbols enclose command tags?
5. What happens if a browser is too old to recognize a command tag that you embed in your HTML code?
6. True or False: A multipage Web site can contain a different header for each Web page?
7. How do Web browsers display text lines of text that are not preceded or followed by the <br> tag?
8. What impact does a user's screen resolution have on your site?
9. Which portion of the screen are all users going to see first?
10. How are placeholders used to display parts of Web pages?
11. Why might you want to offer several versions of your Web site?
12. How can tools such as HTML validators improve your site?
13. What are the three primary Web structures?
14. What is the job of a Web host?
15. What advantages does an images folder provide?
16. What naming convention works best for filenames?
17. What are the advantages to running your own Web server?

18. What are the primary components of DHTML?

19. True or False: Scripts, such as CGI, do not appear inside the HTML source code on a user's site?

20. Describe rollover effects.

☑ **Friday**

☑ **Saturday**

☐ Sunday

PART

II

Saturday Morning

Text on Your HTML Page

Session Checklist

✔ Make text the centerpiece of your site

✔ Create a template for your Web pages

✔ Master font selection and learn new tips for adding them

✔ Learn the common text-formatting command tags

**30 Min.
To Go**

This morning you will begin to learn specific mechanics of HTML coding. The cornerstone of any Web page is the text. Although your graphics accent the text message you want to convey, the text contains the detailed information your users want to know about.

With HTML, your Web page can contain more text-formatting command tags than ever before. Most browsers in use today support all of the text tags that you'll learn in this session.

Text Is the Foundation

The text that you put on your Web site speaks to the world. As mentioned in Session 4 of last night's sessions, you'll want to proofread your Web page to ensure that you've used proper grammar and correct spelling. The text that you display is a reflection on you, the author of the Web page.

If your site contains written articles and columns, consider writing them using a word processor with a grammar and spelling checker. Then save the article as a text file, with a txt filename extension, and import it into your HTML code from within the text editor. Save the file with the htm or html extension if your word processor saves directly in the HTML format. If, instead, you type the text directly in your HTML editing program as you write the HTML, the command tags will get in the way and you won't have the benefit of spelling and grammar checking.

Never forget your goal: the Web page's information, not the HTML code that you write to produce that information. Concentrate on accuracy and well-flowing text. The text must work on its own before it works inside your HTML code.

Depending on your Web site's goals, you will need to decide the optimum amount of text to display at any one time. Generally, you'll want to keep your home page short on text (as well as graphics that will consume loading time). Consider the IDG home page shown in Figure 5-1.

By keeping the text short and placing the opening text snippets on the home page, the user can glance at the overall Web site and select the exact information desired.

Your Web Page General Layout Template

Figure 5-2 shows a general model for the layout of all HTML code. Web pages often contain the following sections:

- Header
- Title
- Body
- Footer

Clicking here displays more text

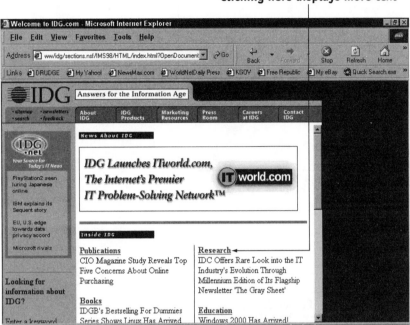

Figure 5-1
Keep text to a minimum on your Web site's home page.

In Session 2 of last night's sessions, you learned some of the command tags that produce these Web page sections. The footer section is new to you, but as you can guess, the footer appears at the bottom of your Web page just as the header section starts your Web page. Footers often contain contact information and perhaps a navigational bar that links the Web page user to other pages on the site. No formal footer tags exist; nevertheless, most Web pages have an obvious footer section that helps terminate the information on the page.

One of the ways to ensure that your Web pages contain all the important elements is to create a *template* that contains a Web page's bare-bones layout to help you structure the text on your Web page. Listing 5-1 shows one such template. You can store this template on your hard disk, perhaps under the name Template.html, and then load the template and save it under a new filename when you create subsequent Web pages.

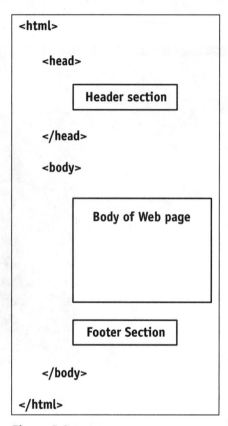

Figure 5-2
Virtually all Web pages follow this general layout.

Listing 5-1
A template to help you lay out your Web page

```
<html>
<head>

   <title>Window title goes here</title>

</head>

<body>
```

```
<p>
The body of the Web page, text and graphics, appears here
</p>

</body>

</html>
```

The `<p>` and `</p>` tags begin and end paragraphs. Actually, the end tag, `</p>`, is optional, but future HTML versions may require the paragraph's end tag, so get in the good habit now of using `</p>`. The paragraph tag forces a blank line on the screen that shows the beginning of paragraphs — in effect, inserting a double-carriage return for each `<p>`.

The other tags in Listing 5-1 are explained in Session 2.

If you create your initial Web page with a Web page designing tool, such as Dreamweaver or FrontPage, the program will handle writing the basic tags in your template as you build the page. Once you have the basic page designed, you can then edit the HTML code to make the page look exactly the way you desire.

The Yale C/AIM Web Style Guide site (htttp://info.med. yale.edu/caim/manual/index.html/**) outlines a Web style guideline that ensures that your site follows an acceptable, standard layout. Of course, the Web's beauty is that your site *doesn't* have to conform to all the others. Nevertheless, general design principles span all Web pages, and as a newcomer to HTML, you will gain design and layout insights as you scan this site.**

20 Min. To Go

Dealing with Specific Font Limitations

As you already learned, all text that appears between the `<body>` and `</body>` tags appears on the browser's screen. Without line or paragraph breaks, the text does not appear on separate lines, and without text-formatting tags that might italicize or boldface words and phrases, the text appears in the browser's default font.

The most commonly used font for the Mac is Helvetica. The most commonly used font for PC-based systems is Arial. Both fonts are *sans serif* fonts (*sans* means *without* in Latin); that is, they contain straight lines and circles without any extra bubbles, lines, or curves to the characters.

Sans serif fonts require less resolution than serif-based fonts and, as a result, are more readable on Web screens. The extra resolution necessary to display serif fonts generally is not available to ordinary text on the Web browser's screen because the resolution for each character is too narrow. Figure 5-3 demonstrates this. The more readable letter *a* (on the left side of the figure) is in a sans serif font; the letter *a* on the right is a serif-based font, Times New Roman (which is the same as the Mac's Times font).

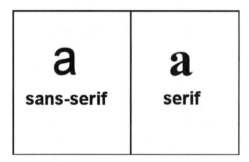

Figure 5-3
Sans serif fonts, like the one on the left, are more readable on Web screens.

In addition, you will not be able to determine which fonts are available on your Web page's user's computer. For example, although you may have the latest version of a font called *HumorousGothic,* chances are that users viewing your Web pages won't have HumorousGothic. Generally, you'll need to keep your fonts simple and attempt to use fonts available to all Web page users.

Specifying a font

If you want to specify a font, use the `<font>` and `</font>` command tag pair. The attribute `face=` determines the font (technically, the *typeface*) that you request for your Web page's text. The format is as follows:

```
<font face=One or more fonts go here>
```

You can control the font used for individual characters, words, sentences, paragraphs, or complete Web pages depending on what falls between the start and ending `<font>` tags. (A few methods for controlling the font with the `<font>` tags are discussed in the following sections.) Again, you must remember that your users work on different systems and that special, unusual fonts are risky. If the target browser does not support the font you specify in the `<font face=>` tag, the browser will substitute a different font and the resulting font will not always be close to what you requested.

Alternating Between Fonts

Alternating fonts in your code can help you determine which fonts are easier to read by the browser. The following HTML code alternates between Arial and Times New Roman fonts on each line displayed:

```
<p><font face=Arial>Italy ice cream,</font></p>
<p><font face=Times New Roman>called gelato,</font></p>
<p><font face=Arial>is the richest, creamiest ice cream in the
world.</font></p>
<p><font face=Times New Roman>Buon Apitito!</font></p>
```

Figure 5-4 shows these code lines inside the browser. The Times New Roman font, a serif font, is smaller and more difficult to read on computer screens than the Arial font.

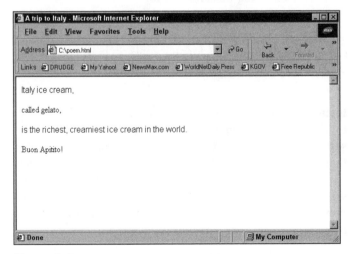

Figure 5-4
Alternating fonts demonstrate which styles are easier to read on the monitor.

Specifying Multiple Font Names

Notice that the `<font face=>` tag accepts one or more font names. If you specify multiple fonts, separated by commas, enclose the list between quotation marks. The target browser begins at the leftmost font in the list and attempts to display the subsequent text in that font. If the font is unavailable, the browser picks the next font in the list and goes down the line until the browser can match a font or has to use one of the default fonts. The following tag requests that the subsequent text appear in the Century font if available, then in the Schoolbook font if Century doesn't exist on the browser's computer, and finally, Antique. If none of the three is available, the user's browser selects the default font.

```
<font face="Century, Schoolbook, Antique">
```

Never enclose each font in the list inside its own pair of quotes. Always include the entire font list inside a single pair of quotation marks, as shown in the previous example.

Specifying Sans Serif and Serif Fonts

To ensure that you get a sans serif font on all systems, PCs, and Macs, you could use the following `<font face=>` tag for sans serif fonts:

```
<font face="Arial, Helvetica">
```

The following `<font face=>` tag works for serif fonts on both PCs and Macs:

```
<font face="Times New Roman, Times">
```

Instead of specifying an exact font name, and risking the target computer substituting a different font, you can specify serif, sans serif, or monospace for the font name. The target browser will then use the default font that fits that description. Monospaced fonts display each character, from the narrowest to the widest, using the same column width so that all the screen's characters line up together. The `<tt>` and `</tt>` *typewriter* command tag pair also displays text in monospaced format.

The next session describes some ways you can make new fonts available to every system that views your Web page.

Graphic fonts

One of the best ways around the lack of fonts on target browsers is to use whatever font you prefer, no matter how rare or new that font is, and save the text as a graphics image in a program such as PhotoShop. The image will appear on your Web page exactly as you intend. Such textual images are great for banners and headlines whose font styles help to portray a certain image, such as flying serifs for an airline's name. In addition, you can accurately control spacing between characters (called *kerning*) or between lines (called *leading*), which you cannot do in HTML.

The drawback to using a graphic image over using text is that the image will take much longer to load than the text equivalent takes. In addition, your users won't be able to highlight the text on the screen and cut and paste the text as they can regular text. (The user can, however, save the Web page image to disk as a graphic image.) The rules for creating graphics in general apply also to font image files.

 Sessions 6 and 7 cover the use of images in your pages.

**10 Min.
To Go**

Formatting Your Text with Command Tags

Given the limitations of available fonts, you should concentrate more on making the standard available fonts look good. You can effectively use text in your Web pages by controlling the size and style of your text. You can do this with the common text-formatting command tags.

Presentable headlines

A headline often appears before a body of text and is larger than the body to make it stand out. Users can glance through the headlines, as shown in Figure 5-1, and select the articles that they want to view in more detail.

HTML supports a standard headline command formatting tag that virtually every Web page uses. The format for the headline tag is as follows:

```
<hn>
```

In this example, *n* ranges from 1 to 6, with 1 being the largest and 6 being the smallest font. A corresponding `</hn>` end tag terminates the headline size.

Figure 5-5 shows the result of the following code that demonstrates the six decrementally smaller headline tags:

```
<h1>This is headline 1's size</h1>
<h2>This is headline 2's size</h2>
<h3>This is headline 3's size</h3>
<h4>This is headline 4's size</h4>
<h5>This is headline 5's size</h5>
<h6>This is headline 6's size</h6>
```

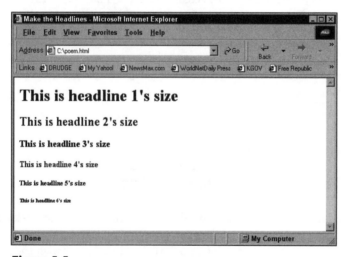

Figure 5-5
The headline tag gives you six decrementally smaller headline sizes.

The headline tags enable you to organize your headlines in an outline format so that your top headline can be the largest, and then as you use subheadlines, you can adjust the size down. Of course, HTML programmers rarely nest headlines more than three deep and virtually never use `<h4>`, `<h5>`, or `<h6>`. Notice that the headline tags automatically issue a line break at the end of the headline, so you do not have to use `<br>` or `<p>` tags. By default, browsers left-align and boldface headlines. In the next session, you will learn how to align headlines and other text in the center or in the Web page's right margin.

PCs display headlines slightly larger than the same sized headlines on Macs because of the different resolution used on the two systems. Generally, the difference does not destroy the effects on your Web page, but to be sure, you may want to test your pages on both systems if the size of your headlines will negatively affect your Web page layout.

Never use a headline tag just because you want to boldface and enlarge body text. Although headline text is boldfaced by default, you'll learn later in this session how to apply boldfacing to specific text.

Font size

You can format normal text in a variety of sizes like your headlines. The `<font>`'s `size=` attribute controls the size of text. The format is as follows:

```
<font size=n>
```

In this example, *n* ranges from 1 to 7. Unlike the headline tag, however, the lower the number the *smaller* the font size. This discrepancy is one of those issues that has been with HTML since the first version, and will remain until the last. As with many attributes, the number may or may not appear inside quotation marks; the quotes are optional.

Figure 5-6 shows the result of the following code that demonstrates the seven incrementally larger font size tags:

```
<font size=1>This is font size 1</font> <br>
<font size=2>This is font size 2</font> <br>
<font size=3>This is font size 3</font> <br>
<font size=4>This is font size 4</font> <br>
<font size=5>This is font size 5</font> <br>
<font size=6>This is font size 6</font> <br>
<font size=7>This is font size 7</font> <br>
```

The `<basefont>` tag with the `size=n` attribute specifies the size of all text in your document that is not specified by a `<font>` tag. In addition to size, the `<basefont>` tag can specify color and several other attributes.

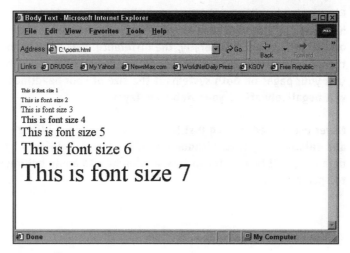

Figure 5-6
The font size tag gives you seven incrementally larger font sizes.

Session 20 teaches you how to write CSS, cascading style sheets, which make many of the individual text-formatting tags discussed here obsolete. Familiarize yourself with these text-formatting tags because tons of Web pages still use them. Often, the individual tags are used to format specific areas of a page and a CSS is not defined. In addition, CSS is easier once you understand the individual formatting tags.

Character formatting

All the standard formatting styles are available to you when writing HTML code. You can italicize, boldface, underline text, and more.

HTML programmers cringe when they see underlined text on a Web page. Generally, hypertext links appear on the screen as underlined text, and when underlining is used on nonhyperlinked text, users waste browsing time attempting to click the hyperlink that does not exist. Good design dictates that you use italics and typefaces to emphasize text.

Use the <b> and </b> tag pair to indicate boldfaced text. The following HTML statement produces a boldfaced word in the middle of a sentence:

```
This sentence contains one <b>boldfaced</b> word.
```

Session 5—Text on Your HTML Page   69

Notice that you must include a space around the tags, just as you would do if the <b> and </b> tags did not exist. The formatting tags add no spacing to your text.

Use the <i> and </i> tag pair to indicate italicized text. The following HTML statement produces an italicized word in the middle of a sentence:

```
This sentence contains one <i>italicized</i> word.
```

If you must underline text, use the <u> and </u> command tag pair, as done here:

```
This sentence contains one <u>underlined</u> word.
```

Use the <strike> and </strike> tag pair to create text with a *strikethrough* effect; for example, you might use strikethrough to cross out items no longer offered for sale. The following line strikes through two words:

```
This sentence contains <strike>two words</strike> that use the
strikethrough effect.
```

Mathematical equations often require *subscript text* (text that falls below the normal text baseline) and *superscript text* (text that appears above the normal text baseline). Use the and tag pairs to add subscript and superscript text to your site, as shown in the following formula:

```
The value is equal to this equation: a<sub>1</sub> + b<sup>2</sup>
```

Done!

Figure 5-7 shows the result of putting all of this section's sample lines together to display formatted HTML-based text.

Figure 5-7
Examples of formatted characters in HTML-based text.

Part II—Saturday Morning
Session 5

REVIEW

- You can create articles in a word processor to help ensure grammar and spelling accuracy.
- The articles that you create in a word processor can be saved as a text file with the html (or htm) filename extension.
- You can create a template that works as a starting point for subsequent HTML Web pages.
- Specify multiple fonts so your font requests are followed when possible.
- The text-formatting command tag pairs `<b>` and `</b>`; `<i>` and `</i>`; and `<strike>` and `</strike>` indicate boldfaced, italicized, and strikethrough text, respectively.

QUIZ YOURSELF

1. Why keep your home page text to a minimum? (See "Text is the Foundation.")
2. What does a template help you do? (See "Your Web Page General Layout Template.")
3. Why does some Web text appear differently on different computers? (See "Dealing with Specific Font Limitations.")
4. What is the difference between serif, sans serif, and monospaced fonts? (See "Dealing with Specific Font Limitations.")
5. Which font tag determines the font size used for your entire Web page unless overridden for specific text? (See "Font Size.")

6

Improving the Look of Your Web Page's Text

Session Checklist

✔ Align text, add line breaks, and use proper spacing

✔ Add horizontal rules to separate headlines and articles

✔ Increase and decrease the font size of your text

✔ Understand font selection considerations

✔ Use lists in your text to display detailed information

**30 Min.
To Go**

I n this session, you learn how to spruce up the appearance of your Web site's text. As with printed documents, you can control the alignment, spacing, and size of your text. You can also add horizontal lines to separate bodies of text from headlines and to produce sections on your Web page. In addition, HTML supports several kinds of list formats that you can add to your text to help organize the presented data.

Text Alignment and Spacing

As with word-processed text, you can control the alignment and spacing of the text on your Web page. For example, for detailed technical material that you make available on your site, you may want few separating blank lines. For lighter material, the more whitespace you provide, the better the appearance.

Better paragraph spacing

As you learned in Session 5, the <p> tag defines a new paragraph by inserting a double carriage return at the point of the <p> so that subsequent text appears as a new paragraph from the previous text. The <p> tag displays somewhat strangely in some browsers by adding too much or not enough spacing between paragraphs. To overcome this potential problem, some HTML programmers prefer to use two <br> tags in place of the <p> to ensure that exactly two carriage returns appear between paragraphs. Two carriage returns between two paragraphs, in effect, produce one blank line between them.

Many of the newer browsers, such as Internet Explorer 5, have an HTML interpreter that properly decodes a single <p> tag as two <br> tags, and other browsers are quickly becoming more consistent. In the meantime, you may want to retain the de facto standard of using two <br> tags when you want exactly one blank line to appear between paragraphs.

Session 9 describes how you can use a 1-bit pixel graphic image, an extremely small image, to space text and graphics precisely.

Paragraph alignment

The <p> tag with the align= attribute determines the left, right, or centered alignment of the paragraphs in your Web page. The format of the <p align=> tag follows:

```
<p align=right|left|center>
```

No end tag appears because <p align> works in place of the <p> and begins a new paragraph by skipping one blank line (in modern browsers) and beginning a new paragraph. In fact, <p align> *is* the <p> tag with the optional align attribute. Without the align attribute, the paragraph will always align to the left margin.

The <center> **and** </center> **command tag pair also centers paragraphs to the middle of the screen's margins, and** <center> **offers the additional benefit of centering graphic images.**

Never attempt to fully justify paragraphs. Beginning in HTML 4, a <p align="justify"> **tag attribute exists, but many browsers offer little or no support for this relatively new tag that attempts to make both the left and right edges of a paragraph straight, as would appear in most newspaper columns.**

Figure 6-1 shows the resulting three paragraph alignments produced by the following code:

```
<font size=3>
<p align=left>This paragraph will appear left-justified on the
screen. The left edge of the paragraph will be straight while the
right edge will be ragged. By the way, the ending paragraph tag is
optional but good HTML programming style dictates that you include
a closing paragraph tag with each start tag you put on your site.
</p>

<br><br>

<p align=center>This paragraph will appear centered in the middle
of the screen. Both the left and right edges of each line will fit
perfectly in the center of the screen. Notice that the HTML tags
do not force the browser to align both the left and right edges.
Both edges remain ragged when you center a paragraph.</p>

<br><br>

<p align=right>This paragraph will appear right-justified on the
screen. The right edge of the paragraph will be straight while the
left edge will be ragged. Sometimes, a graphic image on the left
side of the text makes the right-alignment a good option.</p>
```

You can apply the alignment tag to headlines as well as to body text.

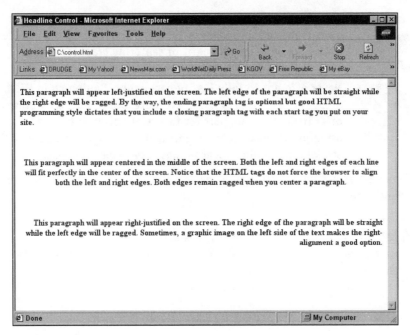

Figure 6-1
The <p align> tag controls the alignment of your paragraphs.

Line breaks and spacing

When your Web page users look at your pages, they might have their browsers set to full-screen mode or the browser windows might be smaller than the maximized window allows. Fortunately, the browser wraps your HTML text to whatever window size the user displays.

The automatic wrapping feature is the primary reason why browsers do not automatically add line breaks when your HTML code includes text returns on multiple lines. Consider the following HTML:

```
<p>This is line one.
This is line two.
This is line three.
```

In the browser window, this code produces one continuous line that reads:

```
This is line one.This is line two.This is line three.
```

If the browser added line breaks at the end of every line of text and, in addition, the browser wrapped lines automatically when the user resized the browser window, your text could end up looking very strange indeed. That's why you decide when you want the line breaks.

Not only do browsers ignore returns in your text, but also they do not recognize the tab character or multiple spaces that you might embed in text while working in your text editor. Tabs, multiple spaces, and returns all collapse into a single space when viewed in the browser window. To add indentions at the beginning of your Web page paragraphs, several options are available, few of which are extremely elegant. For example, a <spacer> tag exists that enables you to provide exact horizontal and vertical adjustment of text, but not all browsers support <spacer>. Perhaps that's why few paragraphs of text ever appear on Web pages with the first line indented.

You can also pre-format your HTML text; that is, you can request that the browser respect the same text spacing that you used when you entered the text. One way is to use the <pre> and </pre> tags. Any text that you enclose between <pre> and </pre> retains the spacing you used, such as an indent in the first line of your paragraph.

The following HTML code ensures that the paragraph's first line is indented and that each line spans a separate line in the browser's window:

```
<pre>
     HTML is the abbreviation for HyperText Markup Language.
HTML simplifies Web page formatting. In addition to text
formatting, HTML formats the placement of graphic images on your
page.</pre>
```

Quoting long passages

The <blockquote> and </blockquote> tags are useful for quoting long passages of text. These tags format the text that they enclose by indenting the left and right margins of the text — shrinking and setting apart the text from the surrounding paragraphs. No additional <p> or <br> tags are required.

Figure 6-2 shows the result of the following HTML code, which formats a long quote:

```
<h1 align=center><font size=6 face="Arial">Philosophical
Thought</font></h1>
```

```
<p><font face="Arial" size=4>The line from Plato to St. Augustine
to John Calvin links the thoughts of each. Calvin's theology is
rooted deeply in Greek philosophy and today's Calvinists thank
Plato for their beliefs. As Dr. Hill states,</font></p>

<blockquote><font face="Arial" size=4>"First we must see the
origin. Immutability means unchanging. This is the basis for many
of the tenets of Calvinistic doctrine. But, where did the idea of
immutability come from? The answer is Plato. "
</blockquote>
```

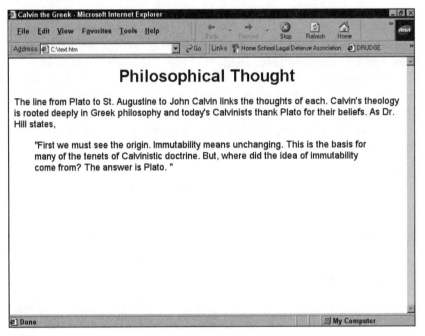

Figure 6-2
Long quotes look good when formatted with the <blockquote> tag.

**20 Min.
To Go**

Separating Text with Horizontal Rules

One of the best ways to separate blocks of text, even headlines from the body text within articles, is to add a horizontal, separating line between the blocks. In HTML terminology, such a line is called a *horizontal rule*.

Horizontal rules enable you to underline complete lines of text or headlines without resorting to a true underline that is more easily confused with a hyperlink. In addition, a horizontal rule does not preclude the possibility of making your headline a hyperlink; in other words, a headline can be a hyperlink as well as sit atop a horizontal rule.

The <hr> tag produces a horizontal rule. The rule is gray and has a 3-D effect.

The following code repeats a headline and the beginning of the article twice, once with a single rule and once with two horizontal rules. By adding multiple horizontal rules, you can add an artistic effect to your articles.

```
<h1 align="center"><font size="6" face="Arial">Philosophical
Thought</font></h1>
<hr>
<p><font face="Arial" size="4">The line from Plato to St.
Augustine to John Calvin links the thoughts of each. Calvin's
theology is rooted deeply in Greek philosophy and today's
Calvinists thank Plato for their beliefs. As Dr. Hill
states...</font></p>

<br><br>

<h1 align="center"><font size="6" face="Arial">Philosophical
Thought</font></h1>
<hr><hr>
<p><font face="Arial" size="4">The line from Plato to St.
Augustine to John Calvin links the thoughts of each. Calvin's
theology is rooted deeply in Greek philosophy and today's
Calvinists thank Plato for their beliefs. As Dr. Hill
states...</font></p>
```

Figure 6-3 shows the resulting Web page that contains the three horizontal rules.

The gray rule is somewhat boring, but effective. You can use graphic images to create more colorful rules if you prefer, as Session 9 shows.

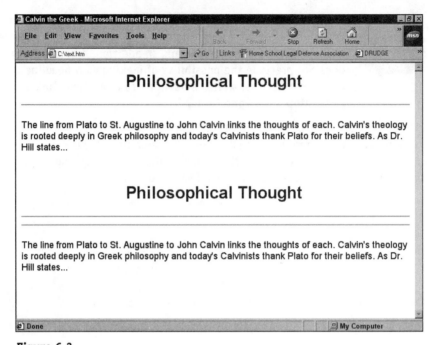

Figure 6-3
Horizontal rules help separate headlines from articles.

The <hr> tag supports several attributes with which you can change the way the rule appears on your Web page. You can add a size= attribute to control the number of pixels used in the line. The following tags display horizontal rules at different widths:

```
<hr size=5>
<hr size=10>
<hr size=20>
```

In addition to specifying the width in pixels, you can align the rule to the left, center, or right edge of the browser window with the align attribute, like this:

```
<hr align=center>
```

Of course, alignment seems to make no sense, because the rules you've seen so far all span the entire browser window width. But you can specify an optional width attribute that controls the width of the rule. Specify the width attribute as a percentage of the browser window. The following tag displays a 3-bit pixel horizontal rule that spans 25 percent of the browser window and is aligned against the right edge of the window. (The start of the rule begins 75 percent to the right of the window.)

```
<hr size=3 align=right width=25>
```

Bigger and Smaller Font Sizes

Although usually frowned upon by HTML programmers, you'll see the tags `<big>`, `</big>`, `<small>`, and `</small>` throughout the Web pages that you visit, and you might even find yourself resorting to them in a pinch. These tags increase and decrease the font size on your Web page. CSS, as you'll learn in Session 20, is reducing and, in many instances, eliminating the need for many text-formatting tags such as these.

The `<big>` and `<small>` tags base themselves on the size of the document's font, set by a `<basefont>` tag earlier in the document. Every time the browser comes upon a `<big>` tag, the browser increases the text size for subsequent text until a corresponding `</big>` tag appears. For example, if you place two `<big>` tags before a `</big>` end tag, the browser displays the enclosed text two sizes larger than the `<basefont>` size, and so on. The `<small>` and `</small>` tags work in the opposite manner, by making the text smaller than the current `<basefont>` size with each occurrence of `<small>`.

The words in the following example become larger and smaller according to the command tags:

```
<basefont size=1>
These <big>words <big>grow <big>larger <big>and
<big>larger.</big></big></big></big></big>.

<basefont size=7>
These <small>words <small>get <small>smaller <small>and
<small>smaller.</small></small></small></small></small>
```

Figure 6-4 shows the result of this code in a Web page.

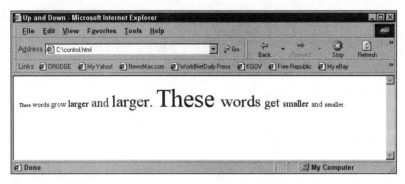

Figure 6-4
The <big> and <small> tags increase and decrease font size.

Additional Font Selection Considerations

Most computer screens display 72 pixels per inch, so a 12-point character appears on the screen in a one-sixth inch of height. A 12-point character offers little room for the serifs that come on many fonts, especially the more elegant fonts such as Gothic and slanted script fonts.

Technically, different font names specify different *typefaces*. A typeface such as Schoolbook differs from the typeface of *Times New Roman*. Often, programmers use the more general term *font* to refer to the different font names, and that loose usage will continue here.

Don't give in to the need to make gigantic headlines. Check out the popular sites on the Web, such as Microsoft (http://www.microsoft.com/) and Yahoo! (http://www.yahoo.com/), and you'll see that they do not make use of overly large headlines. Instead, they are able to fit more information on the page that would otherwise be wasted on ugly, large type.

Never mix too many fonts on a page. If you find yourself using four or more fonts on the same Web page, you are probably using too many and your page will seem more like a ransom note than a calm, readable, and uniform page. Try to keep similar fonts on similar elements; that is, use the same font for all headlines, the same font for all titles, and the same font for all hyperlinks that appear on the same page.

Today's browsers do a fairly good job at font substitution. For example, if you specify a sans serif font that is unavailable on the user's system, the browser can often recognize that the font is a sans serif font and substitute another. If, however, you use less common fonts that you buy from third-party font dealers, the chances are less likely that the browser will be aware of that font's name. No matter how good your special fonts make a Web page appear, sticking with the simple ones will make your pages more uniform on more systems. If you truly need to utilize a special font, create the text in a graphics program such as Illustrator and save the file as an image. The same image, therefore, will appear in every Web browser.

Keep your eyes on new browser technologies that appear in the future. A move is under way to provide the downloading of fonts from a Web server to the user's system. Once downloading of fonts is available, you can use any font available on your own computer for Web design, and that font will be sent to the user's computer if the user doesn't have that font (assuming the user okays the font download, presumably). No font downloading standards have been universally approved, although Microsoft has designed the *OpenType* font-downloading system and Netscape has its *Dynamic Fonts* system in place. Keep checking the W3 Web consortium (`http://www.w3.org/`) for news on which downloading standard becomes the accepted norm. Although the downloading of fonts will add time to the site's arrival on the user's system, Internet speeds are always increasing. In addition, once the fonts proliferate, downloading will become less frequent as users accept more and more fonts arriving with their associated Web pages.

**10 Min.
To Go**

Putting Lists in Your Text

Given that the Web is used to disseminate information, often that information presents well in a list format. HTML makes presenting your data in list form easy by supporting several list tags. With HTML, you can add the following kinds of lists to your Web pages:

- *Ordered lists* that present information in an order, such as the steps needed to bake a recipe

- *Unordered lists* that present information that does not fall in a given order, such as a list of products that you sell on your Web site

- *Definition lists* that present terms and definitions where the definitions are indented and appear below the terms

Ordered lists

The <ol> tag begins an ordered list on your Web page. Within the list, you need to precede each item with the <li> tag (no end </li> tag exists) so the browser knows where each item in the list begins. At the end of the list, the </ol> tag ends the ordered list.

The following code describes how to start a car:

```
<ol>
<li>Put the key in the ignition.
<li>Turn the key.
<li>When the engine turns over, release the key.
</ol>
```

When your Web page contains this code, the browser automatically numbers the list, beginning with 1. The nice thing about the browser's automatic numbering, as opposed to you numbering the list yourself, is that you can add items, remove items, and rearrange items in the list without having to renumber the list yourself. The browser will always renumber the list before each display. Figure 6-5 shows how the list appears in the browser window.

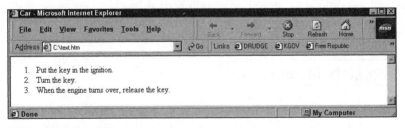

Figure 6-5
The browser automatically numbers ordered lists.

Unordered lists

Unordered lists are easier to create than ordered lists because no starting value exists. By default, the browser displays a *bullet,* a shaded circle, at the beginning of each item in the list.

The following code creates an unordered list:

```
<ul>
<li>CPU
```

```
<li>Hard disk
<li>CD-ROM
</ul>
```

Figure 6-6 shows how the list appears in the browser window.

Figure 6-6
Each item in an unordered list begins with a bullet.

You can override the bullet style with the type attribute. The type attribute must appear inside quotation marks and can be one of the values from Table 6-2.

Table 6-2
Unordered Type Attributes

Type name	Bullet's appearance
circle	Circle with clear center
disc	Circle with filled, dark center
square	Square with filled, dark center

Definition lists

Use the <dl> tag to begin a definition list. Each term in the definition list must begin with the <dt> tag, and each detailed line of the definition list must begin with the <dd> tag.

Although definition lists may sound more complicated than the previous list styles, definition lists are easy to understand once you see one produced. The following code produces a definition list that might appear as part of a self-defense site:

```
<dl>
<dt>caliber
```

```
<dd>The internal diameter of the barrel of a gun or of a bullet
casing.
<dt>centerfire
<dd>A gun that fires ammo by striking the center pin in the
cartridge.
<dt>recoil
<dd>The kick that you experience when a firearm presses back
against you during firing.
</dl>
```

Figure 6-7 shows how the definition list appears in the browser window.

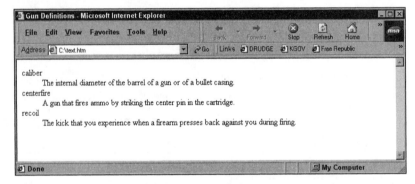

Figure 6-7
The definition is indented from the term in a definition list.

Done!

Definition lists aren't just for definitions. You can use definition lists to describe other Web site links, using the Web site name or URL as the term and formatting the site's description as the definition. Name and address lists also work well in definition list format.

REVIEW

- Be careful when using <p> because of the inconsistency that some browsers provide with handling spaces between paragraphs.
- By aligning your text with the left edge of the browser window, the center of the window, or the right edge of the window, you create a better page layout for your text.

- Keep your text from wrapping when the user resizes the browser window.
- The `<blockquote>` tag sets off long passages of text, such as a quotation.
- You'll see the `<big>` and `<small>` tags still in use, but a move is under way to stop using them because of the increased usage of style sheets.
- HTML makes adding lists to your Web sites easy with the `<ol>`, `<ul>`, and `<dl>` tags.

QUIZ YOURSELF

1. What can you use as a substitute for the `<p>` tag to ensure that your paragraphs break with a single blank line between them? (See "Better Paragraph Spacing.")

2. Which tag substitutes for `<p align=center>` and enables you to center graphic images as well as paragraphs? (See "Paragraph Alignment.")

3. What is the primary reason why browsers do not automatically add line breaks when your HTML code includes text returns on multiple lines? (See "Line Breaks and Spacing.")

4. What are the tags still in use that make text larger or smaller than the base size? (See "Bigger and Smaller Font Sizes.")

5. What is the difference between the three list styles? (See "Putting Lists in Your Text.")

HTML Graphics

Session Checklist

✔ Add graphics to your Web page and master the two primary
graphic file types

✔ Use the `<img>` tag to work with images on your Web pages

✔ Specify the width and height of your images

✔ Deal with users who turn off their image display

✔ Distinguish between interlaced and noninterlaced images

✔ Adjust your images' gamma value

**30 Min.
To Go**

I n this session, you'll learn the mechanics of placing graphic images on your
Web pages. You'll also learn what attributes to use to speed up the loading
of graphics and to get around users who turn off their image display. Much
of what you learn this weekend about Web page graphics centers not only on the
actual HTML tags needed to display the images, but also on the graphic theory
required to use graphics effectively.

Kinds of Graphics and File Types

The term *picture* actually doesn't describe all the kinds of images a Web page can display. Your Web page can display pictures, line drawings, computer-generated artwork, scanned images, images brought into the machine from an electronic drawing tablet, images for free and for sale on the Internet, clip art that comes with drawing programs, and even mouse-drawn images created in paint programs. If your computer can create or load it, a Web page can display it.

The more graphics-intensive your site is, the more visually appealing that it may be. However, it is less likely that users will wait on the site to load before giving up and going elsewhere. Obviously, if your site is a graphics-oriented site, as would be the case for an art gallery's preview site, users know what to expect and are willing to wait longer than a potential customer who simply wants to know what time your customer service personnel begin working. And, as you already know from Friday evening's sessions, you should keep your home page free of intensive graphics no matter what service your site provides and bury the intensive graphics deeper in the site where your users will stick with you more.

Many different graphic images exist. You can locate graphic files stored with many filename extensions, but you should use only two image types when placing images on your Web page, and they are as follows:

- *GIF* (pronounced *"jiff"*) files, also known as *graphic interchange format* files, were originally developed for the CompuServe online service. GIF files can display up to 256 colors and work well for images with pure colors such as logos and paint-produced programs.

- *JPEG* or *JPG* or *JPE* (pronounced *"j-peg"*) files, created for the *Joint Photographic Experts Group,* can display millions of colors and are great for high-resolution images such as photos.

 Never embed an image with another file extension on your site, because a browser does not support other graphics file formats. Most graphics programs will convert your image to GIF or JPG format with the File ⇨ Save As command.

Generally, you'll use the JPEG format for photographic images and GIF for all other kinds of graphics you place on your Web pages. JPEG's high availability of colors makes JPEG a good standard for photos. Small text on top of a JPEG image does not always display well because the edges can look rough and grainy. That's why GIF works well for logos and other images that typically include text as well as a graphic.

GIF images also provide exceptional support for a concept called *transparency*. You can specify a color on a GIF image that will be transparent to its background.

Session 15 describes more about creating and placing transparent images on your pages.

When preparing your images, remember that most computer monitors have 72 pixels per inch (usually referred to as *dpi* or *dots per inch*) resolution. If you offer images with a high resolution, you are wasting page-loading time. The one exception is when your users want to print your site's images. Printer resolutions are higher than monitor resolutions, with some reaching 1200 dpi. Instead of providing these kinds of graphics on your primary Web pages, however, you may want to offer a Web page with special printer versions of images that your users may need to print.

20 Min. To Go

Working with Graphics

Working with images on your Web page takes little effort. The `<img>` (for *image*) tag does all the work for you. The `<img>` tag supports several attributes, but the `src=` (for *source*) attribute is the one that specifies the name and location of the image.

Placing an image

Here is the format of the `<img>` tag that collects the graphic image and displays the image on the Web page:

```
<img src="location of image">
```

No end tag is necessary. The *location of image* generally is the images folder you've stored in the same location as your site's HTML files. You also can add a link to an image located on another Web site. If you first copy that image to your own site's images folder and refer to that copy, assuming you have permission to copy and use the image, your Web site link will remain good even if the other site changes.

The following tag tells the browser to locate and display the image named ourhouse.gif:

```
<img src="images/ourhouse.gif">
```

If you combine this tag with other tags, the image appears inline with surrounding text. In such a case, the text and the image take different places on the screen. The following code produces the image shown on the browser screen in Figure 7-1.

```
<h1><font face=Arial>Welcome to our new home</font></h1>

<font size=4 face=Arial size=4>Although we are snowed in, we love
it here in the country.</font>

<p><img src="/images/ourhouse.gif"></p>

<p><font size=4 face=Arial>(At least the gravel road doesn't stir
up much dust in the winter!)</p>
```

Figure 7-1
The <img src> tag lets you display images on your page.

Framing an image

You can add a border around your images by using the border= (for *border*) attribute inside the <img> tag. If you specify a border value higher than 0, the browser will place a border around the image. The following command tag draws a border ten pixels wide around the image:

```
<img src="/images/ourhouse.gif" border=10>
```

Keep in mind that many formatting command tags, including these graphic tags, are also supported by CSS, the cascading style sheets that you'll learn about in Session 20. In addition, you can learn CSS rapidly after you've seen how the individual tags work to format pages.

Aligning an image

As with paragraphs, you can align graphic images to the left edge, center, or right edge of the browser window. The align=left (for *align left*) and align=right (for *align right*) <img> attributes handle the left and right alignment. Insert either align=left or align=right in the <img> tag when you want to align the image against the window edge. The following tag places the image against the window's right edge and adds a 10-pixel border, as shown in Figure 7-2:

```
<img src="/images/ourhouse.gif" align=right border=10>
```

To center an image, enclose the image between the <center> and </center> tags like this:

```
<center>
<img src="/images/ourhouse.gif">
</center>
```

The align attribute overrides a <center> tag that may still be in effect. In other words, if an image appears inside a <center> and </center> pair of tags, and that image contains an align=right attribute, the image will be right-aligned and not centered in the browser's window.

Border

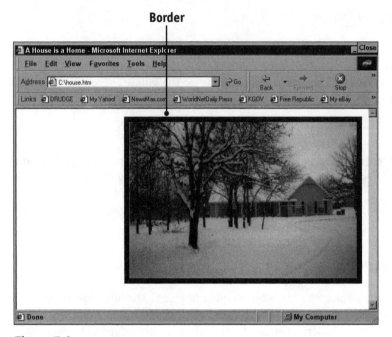

Figure 7-2
The image is right-aligned against the window edge with a framed border.

Specifying the Image Size

**10 Min.
To Go**

When a browser loads a Web page that contains one or more images, the browser must calculate the size of each image to make room for the graphics and to format the other text and images. You can speed the loading of the pages you create with HTML by specifying image sizes inside the <img> tag. You can specify the number of pixels, high and wide, that the image requires.

Most of today's graphics programs can determine the exact pixel size of any image and display the size. You can often locate the image size in the menu option labeled Properties.

Use the width= (for *width*) attribute to specify the image's pixel width, and use the height= (for *height*) attribute to specify the image's pixel height. The following line displays an image on the Web page at an exact width of 600 pixels and a height of 400 pixels:

```
<img src="/images/ourhouse.gif" width=600 height=400>
```

You can combine all of the `<img>` **attributes you've seen in this session in a single** `<img>` **tag.**

When you specify the incoming graphic's size, you not only save loading time, but you also can resize the image to grow or shrink in the receiving Web page. If you specify a width and height attribute value that is smaller than the image's actual size, the Web page will shrink the image. If you specify a width and height attribute value that is larger than the image's actual size, the Web page will expand the image.

The actual width and height attributes only shrink or grow the image's size on the Web page but do not speed up or slow down the loading of the image. In other words, the full image loads with the Web page, and the width and height attributes only determine the size at which the Web page will display the image in the browser window.

Never change an image's height or width value by itself unless you want the image to appear out of proportion. In other words, if you want to shrink the width of an image by 25 percent, be sure to specify a height attribute value that is also 25 percent smaller than the image's original size.

Figure 7-3 shows the same image with three different sizes. The first image is displayed without height and width attributes in the `<img>` tag, so the image comes in at its actual size. The second image is smaller because of smaller height and width attributes, and the third image is larger because of larger height and width attributes.

Keep in mind that an image does not actually grow or shrink when you change the height and width attributes. The image's original size determines what the browser receives, and the `<img>` tag determines how the browser displays the image. If, for example, you attempt to display a larger image that runs far past its original width and height size, the image will appear grainy because there is not enough of the image to expand well past a given point.

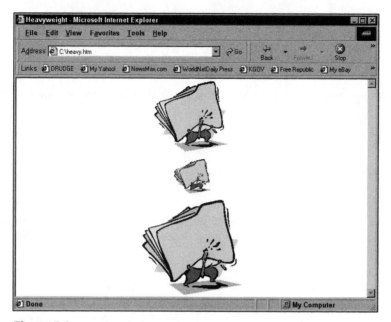

Figure 7-3
The same image appears on this Web page in three different sizes.

If you want to take an image and expand its size dramatically, and the expansion causes the image to appear grainy on receiving Web pages, consider loading that image into a graphics program such as PaintShop Pro and enlarging the actual image. The graphics program can help correct color and resolution problems that might arise when you grow the image too large in HTML. Of course, increasing the size of the image in the graphics program also increases the loading time when that larger image loads in the Web page. Loading time versus resolution is one of the trade-off issues that you'll constantly balance as you develop Web pages.

 Some graphics programs will remove header information that comes embedded in many GIF images. You can reduce the size of a GIF image by 10 percent and speed loading time by removing the image's header information.

 Many HTML programmers attempt to keep their home pages 35K or less, meaning that the total size of the home page, including all text and graphics, comes to no more than 35K. Even this size can be too slow, so attempt to make the size as compact as possible. A 35K Web page takes about 25 seconds to download using a low-end 14.4 Kbps modem, and 12 to 15 seconds using a 28.8

Kbps modem, which is too long for some users to wait. Many Web
pages are far greater than 35K, and such a limit can be extremely
frustrating. The good news is that the entire Internet speed, its
bandwidth, should be moving faster as technologies improve.

When Users Turn Off the Image Display

As noted in Session 3, some users turn off the loading of graphic images.
Therefore, you must constantly keep those users in mind when designing your Web
page. Obviously, if your Web page's mission is to display pictures or show artwork,
you can consciously cater to the users who have high-speed Internet connections
or to users who don't mind waiting on the images to load.

The <img> tag supports the optional alt= (for *alternative image*) attribute that
lets you display text in place of an image whenever the user turns off the display
of graphics in the browser. The text that follows the alt= tag, enclosed in quotation marks, appears in the user's browser window when graphics are turned off.
The user, therefore, knows what the image is supposed to be and can either decide
to view that particular graphic image by clicking it or ignore the image and concentrate on the text.

Generally, you should add alternate text to your <img> tags whenever you place
images on your page. The following line displays the message, Jayne's Picture,
instead of the actual picture if the user's images are turned off:

```
<img src="images/jayne.jpg", alt="Jayne's Picture">
```

Figure 7-4 shows a Web page with the graphic images turned off but with alternative text descriptors that describe what the user does not see.

Even if the user's graphics are turned on, the alt= **attribute
provides an additional benefit. When the user hovers the mouse
pointer over the image, the text pops up in a small box next to
the mouse pointer. Therefore, the user might point to an image
to read what your alternative attribute says about the image.
Therefore, make your** alt= **attribute values descriptive.**

If you place borders around images that are decorative on your Web page, you
should specify the alt= attribute for those images, too, so that text can be displayed instead of the actual border. Use a blank attribute value on such images,
as done here:

```
<img src="images/borderpaisley.jpg", alt="">
```

Alternate image tags

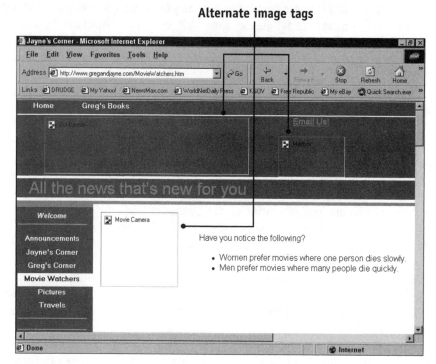

Figure 7-4
The alternative text gives the text-only browser information about the pictures.

As an added bonus for users who display pages with images turned off, if you specify the size of each image using the height= and width= attributes, the browser pads the space where the image would normally go instead of displaying an unpadded, small icon. The difference is that the browser respects your page layout and does not change the location and spacing of headlines and other elements that might appear on your page. In Figure 7-5, the browser properly formats the page layout, even though graphics are not present, because of the width= and height= attributes on each of the graphic's tags. Figure 7-6, on the other hand, shows a jumble of icons; the browser does not lay out the page properly because it cannot make guesses as to how wide and high the images are supposed to be without the proper attributes.

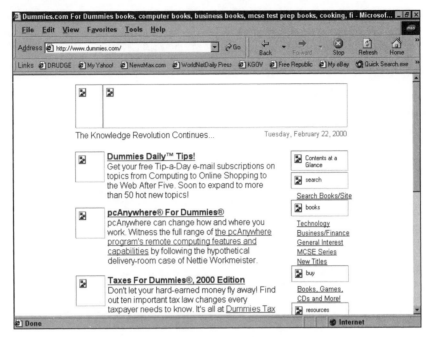

Figure 7-5
With the width and height measurements, room is allocated for the actual images.

Interlaced versus Noninterlaced Images

An *interlaced image* is a GIF image that appears blurry at first and then slowly gets crisper as the page loads. A noninterlaced image will not appear in the user's browser window until the browser gets the entire image. However, an interlaced image will appear although seemingly out of focus. The browser gets the image a layer at a time, with each layer making the image crisper and clearer. Nevertheless, even the blurred first or second version of the image that appears as the page loads is often enough for the user to see what the image holds and make a decision to wait based on the first impression.

Interlaced JPEG images, called *progressive JPEGs*, are now available but few browsers support them.

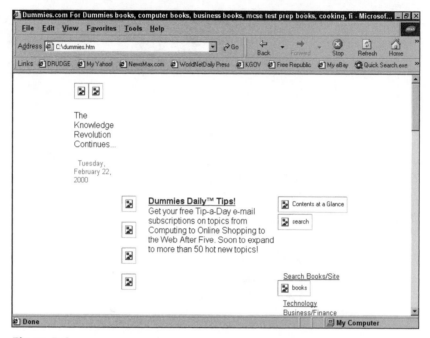

Figure 7-6
Without width and height measurements, the page layout is harmed.

The user might want to see the image in its final form, or the user might opt to traverse to a different Web site before the image clears up. Either way, the user has the choice to decide sooner than would be possible if the image were a noninterlaced image.

The decision to use interlacing is not done at HTML coding time. Instead, you determine whether or not an image is interlaced when you save it in a graphics program. As an HTML programmer, you should care about interlaced images because they affect how you want to design your site. If you want your images to be hidden until the entire image arrives on the user's page, don't use interlaced images. You will save some loading time because noninterlaced images load faster although the user won't see any of the image until the entire image arrives in the browser.

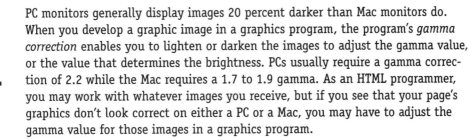

Gamma Correction

Done!

PC monitors generally display images 20 percent darker than Mac monitors do. When you develop a graphic image in a graphics program, the program's *gamma correction* enables you to lighten or darken the images to adjust the gamma value, or the value that determines the brightness. PCs usually require a gamma correction of 2.2 while the Mac requires a 1.7 to 1.9 gamma. As an HTML programmer, you may work with whatever images you receive, but if you see that your page's graphics don't look correct on either a PC or a Mac, you may have to adjust the gamma value for those images in a graphics program.

REVIEW

- Graphics add flair to your Web site.
- JPEG images are generally used for photos, and GIF images are generally used for all other artwork.
- Keep in mind the trade-off of loading speed versus graphic resolution.
- The `<img>` tag with the `align=left` and `align=right` attributes lets you left- and right-align your images properly in the Web page window.
- The `border=` attribute inside the `<img>` tag lets you add borders around the images you want framed on your Web page.
- The `<img>` tag supports the optional `alt=` attribute that lets you display text in place of your graphic images.

QUIZ YOURSELF

1. Which graphics type is best for logos? (See "Graphic File Types.")
2. What is the screen resolution of most monitors? (See "Graphic File Types.")
3. How can you center an image in the window? (See "Aligning an Image.")
4. True or False: When you decrease the display size of an image by specifying small `width=` and `height=` attributes, you increase the page-loading speed. (See "Specifying the Image Size.")
5. Why would you ever use a blank `alt=` attribute for an image on your Web site? (See "When Users Turn Off the Image Display.")

Working with Color in Text and Graphics

Session Checklist

✔ Determine your Web page's color strategies

✔ Use color codes to specify exact colors

✔ Utilize browser-safe colors to make your Web site universal

✔ Add color to text and your Web page background

**30 Min.
To Go**

Be forewarned — this session contains some color theory and less hands-on HTML coding than any session so far. If you are not an artist, you may have little interest in learning about colors and color palettes. However, understanding colors as they apply to the Web is far different from understanding colors that an artist must master. Here, you learn how to use Web colors so that they display properly as opposed to the millions of colors that will mislead you into thinking that your Web page looks like what you intended when it does not.

Color Strategies: Codes and Safe Colors

Although there might be *someone somewhere* using a monochrome monitor to browse the Web, you can ignore this lonely user and assume that your Web page users are going to be seeing your pages in glowing colors. In addition, you can assume that your users will view your Web pages in more than 200 rich colors. 200 or more colors ought to be enough to satisfy any Web designer, right?

It turns out that 200 or so colors provide an extremely limited *palette* (the color collection) of colors from which you can use on your pages. A photograph contains millions of colors, with many colors shading and radiating into other colors and moving to many different hues and tints. You'll recall from the previous session that JPEG files can contain millions of colors. Such files immediately and considerably downgrade in quality when viewed with little more than 200 total available colors.

 If you have JPEG images that you want to display on your Web page, and you use a paint program to decrease the number of colors in that image, you may actually *increase* the file size and the time it takes to download an image! JPEG images are optimized to display a wide range of colors as efficiently as possible. You are usually better off just letting the JPEG image load into the reduced color palette. Decreasing colors of your GIF files, on the other hand, can reduce both the file size as well as the image's loading time.

Color codes and palettes

The three colors red, green, and blue combine differently to reproduce every color in nature. Actually, the human eye interprets combinations of these colors as other colors. When the human eye sees red and green, a yellow tint forms from that combination. Perhaps you've heard the terms *RGB inputs* or *RGB monitors*. The *RGB* simply stands for *red, green,* and *blue* and describes inputs or monitors that combine these three colors to produce all other colors that people see on such devices.

Therefore, every color you see on a computer screen is comprised of a combination of red, green, and blue. To see the pure red color, for example, your monitor forms a combination of full red, no green, and no blue. Thought of another way, your monitor uses 100 percent of red, 0 percent of green, and 0 percent of blue to produce the red color. To produce the color cyan (had anyone really heard of the color cyan before the first PC color graphics card used something called *cyan* as one of its 16 colors?), which is an aqua blue, your monitor uses 0 percent red, 100 percent green, and 100 percent blue to produce this blue-green color.

Given the digital format of computer data, a single byte or memory location can represent the value 0 through 255 (for a total of 256 numbers). Therefore, to represent different colors, a three-number color code is used to represent different combinations of colors. Gray requires an equal amount of light red, light green, and light blue. Instead of using the percentage scheme of 50 percent red, 50 percent green, and 50 percent blue, the computer uses the numeric range from 0 to 255 to represent colors. Therefore, gray would be 128-128-128.

Many Windows programs offer a color palette, such as the one in Word 2000 shown in Figure 8-1, to show a color range from which you can select. Notice the color values, red, green, and blue, with the values 0 through 255 next to each color to specify the color-code combination. You can usually click on a color, and the program automatically determines the three-color number combination needed to represent the chosen color. In addition, you can enter the three numbers next to Red, Green, and Blue, and the selection tool moves to that color in the vast color array.

These three numbers produce an individual color

Figure 8-1
A color palette automatically displays color codes and produces colors.

By providing these palette selection tools, programs somewhat hide the three-number combination that goes on under the computer's hood to produce the colors that you see. In other words, if you want to select a custom color for a word processing document, you only have to display the palette and click on the color without worrying about the three-number combination that represents that color internally.

If you code in HTML (for a total of 256 numbers), however, the problem is that you do not have such a palette in a text editor. Even though some text editors now support color palette selections (you can click a color, and the editor automatically places the numeric combination in your code), you must understand colors and how the computer displays them in more detail than you would if you programmed with something other than HTML. The bottom line is that you often must specify colors in your Web page using the numeric color codes.

Browser-safe colors

If you multiply 256 times 256 times 256 (with each 256 representing one of three-number color codes), you get a large product — 16,777,216 combinations to be exact. Although nature contains an infinite amount of colors in the analog color spectrum, 16 million colors is an ample supply of colors for your site. Nevertheless, a problem exists with a vast number of your users' systems in that they use 8-bit color cards and, consequently, even though they can display more than 16 million colors, they can display only 256 of those colors at any one time. Therefore, your Web sites should contain no more than 256 colors on the page at one time.

8-bit color cards allow for the display of only 256 colors at once because 0 through 255 is the range that can be represented in 8 bits of *binary* (the base-2 numbering system used inside your computer).

To make matters worse, Windows-based computers suffer further because Windows reserves 20 colors for its own use. That leaves only 236 colors that you can be sure will be available to you. Although the Mac doesn't limit these 20 colors, even Mac browsers that can display 256 colors don't offer a lot more color options than a PC browser can offer.

Can things get more limited? They can. To be as standard as possible and to utilize the three-number color-coding scheme efficiently, Web browser designers came up with a palette of 216 colors that you, as a Web page creator, can use safely. That is, with these 216 *browser-safe colors,* sometimes called *Web-safe colors,* you can be assured that all Web browsers in the world will display these colors properly without relying on distorting trickery that washes out the effect of other colors.

Specifying Browser-Safe Colors

The browser-safe colors chosen by browser makers are an even sampling of colors from each of the three red, green, and blue RGB colors. The browser-safe colors span the entire 16-million color range, taking the sampling of 216 colors, evenly spaced all along the 16-million color spectrum. The browser-safe color values appear in Table 8-1.

Table 8-1
Browser-Safe Colors

Decimal	Hexadecimal Equivalents
0	00
51	33
102	66
153	99
204	CC
255	FF

Ignoring the second column for a moment, if you keep the three numeric color codes matched up with the values in Table 8-1, your colors will always be browser-safe. In addition, the colors that you see on your own browser will *always* match the colors that every user will see when he or she looks at your Web page. Therefore, if you specify a green color of 0-153-0, that color appears on everybody's Web page in the same color intensity, hue, and tone. (Keep in mind the RGB order in which the first value always determines how much red is in the color, the second determines how much green is in the color, and the third value determines how much blue is in the color.) In other words, 0-153-0 is a safe color to use on your site, as well as for text and the graphics you create, because that same color will reproduce accurately in all other browser windows.

Remember that the color intensities increase as the values increase. In other words, a red value of 102-0-0 will appear much darker than a red value of 255-0-0. A red value of 204-0-0 will be 20 percent less intense (that is, 20 percent darker) than the red that 255-0-0 produces.

Most graphics programs these days provide you with a browser-safe color palette from which you can choose when creating GIF images, borders, and other graphic elements you might create for your Web pages. Instead of knowing the color codes, you can just point-and-click on the browser-safe colors provided.

The second column in Table 8-1 lists *hexadecimal* equivalents for the decimal numbers. A hexadecimal number (also called a *hex* number) is a number based on the base-16 numbering system as opposed to the usual base-10, or decimal number system, that everybody learns as a child. Hexadecimal numbers range from 0 to F because, after the number 9, the numbering system continues A, B, C, D, E, and F (lowercase equivalents are okay).

The bottom line is that every decimal number has a hex number equivalent that must be used in your HTML code. From Table 8-1, you can see that 204 is the same as the CC hex value. Therefore, if you represent the color code of 204-51-153, you can also specify the number using hex values such as CC-33-99. From the CC, you know that a hex number is being used, but if the numeric value does not include any hex values that use letters, you won't know if the value is supposed to be hex or decimal. Therefore, a shortcut exists in HTML that lets you specify hex values without any redundancy or confusion to the decimal equivalents.

Begin all hex values with a pound sign (#) and do not use the embedded dashes. Therefore, #CC3399 (or #cc3399) is the same hex value for the color code CC-33-99 (which is the same as 204-51-153 decimal).

What does all this mean? When you choose colors from a graphics program, you will probably be able to point to the color you want or enter decimal values for the red, green, and blue combinations. But when coding HTML, you'll enter the hexadecimal value to represent your Web page's colors.

Never use nonbrowser-safe colors. Actually, you can use any color you want from the 16-million color palette, but be warned that your page may look entirely different from what you expect because of the color substitutions that browsers will surely make. To be safe, stick to the browser-safe colors.

The big 16 colors

If you limit yourself to only 16 colors, and that is truly limiting, HTML has assigned names to the 16 most common colors of the PC platform. (The PC was chosen as a least-common-denominating system.) Although I cannot show you the actual 16 colors on the pages of this book, Table 8-2 lists the HTML names for these 16 colors, along with their hex equivalents.

Table 8-2
16 Common Colors You Can Reference by Name

HTML Color Name	Hexadecimal Value	HTML Color Name	Hexadecimal Value
Aqua	#00FFFF	Navy	#000080
Black	#000000	Olive	#808000
Blue	#0000FF	Purple	#800080
Fuchsia	#FF00FF	Red	#FF0000
Gray	#808080	Silver	#C0C0C0
Green	#008000	Teal	#008080
Lime	#00FF00	White	#FFFFFF
Maroon	#800000	Yellow	#FFFF00

To use one of the 16 colors, you can specify the name in any tag that accepts a hexadecimal color value instead of using the hex value. The following tag changes the background to teal:

```
<body bgcolor=teal>
```

If you misspell a color in the tag, the browser will substitute a color of its own choosing.

What about those nonbrowser-safe colors?

Although you've displayed images with far more than 216 colors and things seemed okay, when more than the browser-safe colors appear, your browser sometimes plays a trick on you to make you think that you are seeing more colors than are actually possible. The browser *dithers* the color by combining two or more browser-safe colors. If you magnify the screen, you see that the colors are actually combination pixels. At normal viewing levels, you do not see that the colors form simply because two different colors are side-by-side.

So, you may wonder why you simply don't let the browsers dither whatever colors you upload. One problem is that dithering produces impure colors. That deep-ocean, squid-ink purple color is not really the color you sent; instead, it is a bunch of tiny color combinations. The image with the dithered colors will never look as good as it would look if the browser displayed the actual, real color sent to it.

Even though dithering often goes unnoticed, and clear photos appear on your Web page in spite of it, you need to stick with the browser-safe colors when *you* control the colors you pick for text, logos, and GIF images. The more dithering that takes place on your Web page, the more grainy the page appears. Even if the user doesn't notice it, a Web page with dithering shown next to the same nondithered Web page is less appealing. Therefore, when you choose colors for your site, on the items that *you* create and add to your page, you should use only the 216 browser-safe colors.

Browsers rarely dither background colors. A background image can consume the entire background of a Web site. Sometimes, a background may only be a single solid color. Dithering would be apparent on such a large colored image; therefore, most browsers substitute a close browser-safe color for the nonbrowser-safe color that you select.

Adding Color to Text and Backgrounds

**10 Min.
To Go**

All that theory is worthless if you don't see the practical use of color codes. Actually, applying the color codes is simple using HTML code. You can color text, backgrounds, and other Web page elements using the hex codes. The only problem is locating the hex value of the color you want, but again, most graphics programs display browser-safe color palettes now with the hex equivalents.

Suppose you want to make the text in your entire Web page the highest intensive, or brightest, green possible. You can add the text= attribute to the <body> tag as follows:

```
<body text=#00FF00>
```

As with many attributes, you'll often see the hex value enclosed within optional quotation marks.

The text= attribute changes all the text on the Web page. To change only specific text, use the color= attribute inside a <font> tag. The following code displays the middle word (which is red) in red:

```
<p>This text has a <font color=#FF0000>red</font> word inside it.</p>
```

The <font color=> tag overrides any <body text=> tag in effect.

If you want to change the background color of your Web page, use the bgcolor= attribute inside the <body> tag. To create a blue background for your Web page, on top of which all subsequent text will appear, you code the <body> tag as follows:

```
<body bgcolor=#0000ff>
```

Done!

Tip

Generally, light backgrounds with darker text are more readable than dark backgrounds with lighter text. When in doubt, hardly anything works better than the standard white Web page background.

REVIEW

- Only a limited number of colors are available to all Web users.
- All Web colors are formed by combining red, green, and blue.
- Color codes represent the 16 million colors possible on today's computers.
- Graphics programs often eliminate the need for you to locate a color code, but you still must specify the hex number when you write HTML code, with 16 exceptions.

QUIZ YOURSELF

1. What does *RGB* stand for? (See "Color Codes and Palettes.")
2. How many colors can an 8-bit graphics card display at one time? (See "Browser-Safe Colors.")
3. What is the hexadecimal equivalent to the following decimal code: 204-0-51? (See "Specifying Browser-Safe Colors.")
4. True or False: You can specify the 216 browser-safe colors by name inside command tags. (See "The Big 16 Colors.")
5. What does the browser do when it receives a nonbrowser-safe color (assuming the user's graphics card is an 8-bit card and 256 colors already appear on the screen)? (See "What About Those Nonbrowser-Safe Colors?")

Text and Graphics Organization

Session Checklist

✔ Align an image's surrounding text horizontally and vertically on the Web page

✔ Add spacing around images and create your own horizontal rules

✔ Use graphics in headlines and place your own images on the background of your Web pages

30 Min. To Go

I n the past few sessions, you've seen how to place text and you've seen how to place graphics on your Web pages. This session shows you how to combine text and graphics on a Web page to produce effective presentations of your Web content.

Aligning Images and Text

Consider the following HTML code. The Web page that contains this HTML code displays text, a graphic image next, and then more text. The image, obviously, must appear somewhere in the middle of the text. The question is how will the text surround the image? Will the text wrap around the image or will the three areas — the two text areas and the image area — comprise three distinct bands on the Web page?

```
<p><font size=6>When a Web page combines text and graphics, the
placement and alignment of the image determines where the image
falls in relation to the surrounding text.</p>

<p><img border=0 src="images/man.gif" width=190 height=176>

The image can fall any number of places in relation to the text.
You have full control, through HTML, on the alignment of the
image and text.</font></p>
```

Figure 9-1 shows the Web page that results from this HTML code. As you can see, by default, the page contains three distinct bands: the first text, the image, and the final text. Only a small portion of the text resides on the same line as the figure.

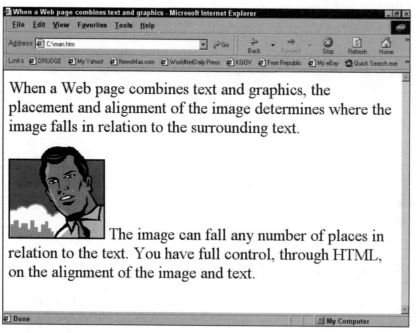

Figure 9-1
By default, your images and text consume different areas of the Web page.

The three separate areas appear because of the paragraph tags. If you remove the paragraph tags, things can get messy depending on the browser. Without the paragraph tags separating the figure from the surrounding text, the figure goes inline with the text and falls in the middle of the text without any proper line breaks.

Horizontal image alignment

The `<img>` tag supports the `align=` attribute that you learned about in Session 7. The `align=left` and `align=right` attributes align the graphic image on the page. In addition, `align=left` and `align=right` affect how the image adjusts to surrounding text. That is, if you use the `align=left` or `align=right` attribute in the `<img>` tag, subsequent text appears to the left or right of the image.

Remember that the `align=left` **and** `align=right` **attributes determine how** *subsequent* **text appears, not text already displayed. Therefore, all previous text that appears in your HTML code displays on the page in its normal fashion. When the** `<img>` **tag appears with an** `align=left` **or** `align=right` **attribute, any remaining text on that page begins next to the image.**

The following code is identical to what you have seen in the previous example except that the `<img>` tag includes the `align=right` attribute. This means that the image, not the text, aligns horizontally to the right side of the window and the text appears to the left of that image, as Figure 9-2 shows. The text that follows the `<img>` tag appears to the left of the image; this text is not extremely lengthy, but as you can see from the figure, it appears on the same horizontal area as the image and does not wait to appear after the image downloads. If you include the `align=left` attribute, the image will appear on the window's left side.

```
<p><font size=6>When a Web page combines text and graphics, the
placement and alignment of the image determine where the image
falls in relation to the surrounding text.</p>

<p><img border=0 src="images/man.gif" width=190 height=176
align=right>

The image can fall any number of places in relation to the text.
You have full control, through HTML, on the alignment of the
image and text.</font></p>
```

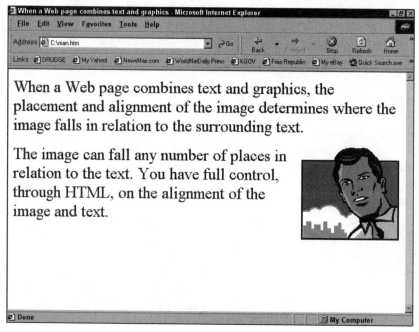

Figure 9-2
The align= attribute can determine on which side of the image the text appears.

Vertical image alignment

The text that appears to the left and right of the image in Figure 9-2 looks somewhat strange because of a few reasons: The text is not long enough to fill the area next to the image, and the text aligns at the top of the image and does not rest on the image's baseline, nor is it centered to the image's vertical area.

The <img> tag supports three vertical alignment attributes with which you can better align the image to the text. You can specify align=top (the default), align=middle, or align=bottom to determine how the image aligns with the base of the text.

Figure 9-3 shows the result of all three vertical alignment attributes by showing an image aligned to the top of the text's baseline, the middle, and the bottom of the text's baseline, according to the following HTML code:

```
<p><font size=6>Aligns with the align=top attribute.
<img border="0" src="images/girl.gif" width=190 height=157
align=top></p>
```

```
<p>Aligns with the align=middle attribute.
<img border="0" src="images/girl.gif" width=190 height=157
align=middle></p>

<p>Aligns with the align=bottom attribute.</font>
<img border=0 src="images/girl.gif" width=190 height=157
align=bottom></p>
```

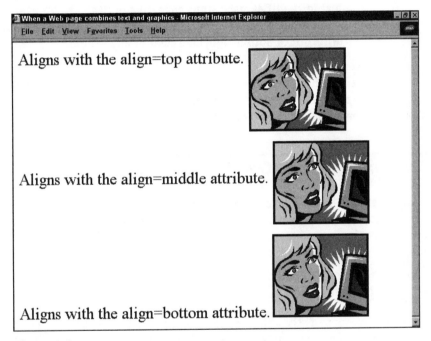

Figure 9-3
The image is aligned with the text's vertical baseline in three different ways.

Never mix an `align=left` **or** `align=right` **attribute with one of the vertical alignment attributes. HTML goes by only the final** `align=` **attribute that you specify in an** `<img>` **tag list. If you want the image to align on the left or right side of the text when you use one of the vertical alignment attributes, enter the text before the** `<img>` **tag. Enter the text after the** `<img>` **tag if you want the image to appear to the left of the text. The text precedes the image placement, hence the text appears to the right of the image.**

**20 Min.
To Go**

The `<br>` **tag supports** `clear=left, clear=right,` **and** `clear=all` **attributes that enable you to stop or change the alignment of an image from that point forward in the text. In other words, if you left-align an image so that the subsequent text appears to the right of the image, place the** `<br clear=left>` **at the point where you want the text to stop appearing next to the image. The text will stop appearing until the entire left margin is clear of the image. If you specify** `<br clear=right>`, **the subsequent text in the HTML page stops appearing until the right margin is free of the image. The** `<br clear=all>` **tag resumes the display of text once both margins are clear of any images.**

A special vertical alignment attribute, `align=absmiddle`, aligns an image in the very center of a horizontal line of other graphics and text. If you want an image to appear in the center of its surrounding images and text, instead of aligning the image only to text alone, use `align=absmiddle`.

Spacing Images and Creating Horizontal Rules

Several methods enable you to control exact spacing between images, and the next section explains one of the easiest ways. In addition, you can create your own images that become horizontal rules to eliminate the boring gray horizontal rule that appears as a result of the `<hr>` tag that you learned about in Session 6.

Increasing image space

The `<img>` tag supports the `hspace=` attribute that determines how much blank space, in pixels, an image contains on its left and right sides. The `vspace=` attribute controls blank space at the top and bottom of an image.

The best way to learn these spacing attributes is to see them in action. Figure 9-4 shows the same image displayed three times with text appearing to the right of the image in each case.

Listing 9-1 contains the code necessary to produce Figure 9-4. The first image shows the text as it appears with no added spacing specified around the image. The second image appears with horizontal space added to the image. The final image appears with vertical space at the top and bottom of the image.

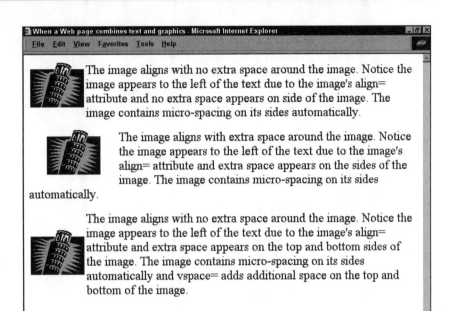

Figure 9-4
The effect of adding extra horizontal and vertical space around an image

---

Listing 9-1
Increasing the blank pixel area on an image's sides

```
<img border="0" src="images/italy.gif" width=105 height=85
align=left>
<font size=5>The image aligns with no extra space around the
image. Notice the image appears to the left of the text due to
the image's align= attribute and no extra space appears on the
side of the image. The image contains micro-spacing on its
sides automatically.


<p>



<img border="0" src="images/italy.gif" width=105 height=85
align=left hspace=35>
```

Continued

Listing 9-1   *Continued*

```
The image aligns with extra space around the image. Notice the image
appears to the left of the text due to the image's align= attribute
and extra space appears on the sides of the image.
The image contains micro-spacing on its sides automatically.
</p>
<p>

<img border=0 src="images/italy.gif" width=105 height=85
align=left vspace=35>
The image aligns with no extra space around the image. Notice
the image appears to the left of the text due to the image's
align= attribute and extra space appears on the top and bottom
sides of the image. The image contains micro-spacing on its
sides automatically and vspace= adds additional space on the
top and bottom of the image.</font>
</p>
```

Creating your own horizontal rules

If you want to spruce up the gray horizontal rules that appear as a result of the
`<hr>` tag, you can create your own. Feel free to create all the horizontal rules you
want. The horizontal rule files should be GIF images.

The only thing you need to remember when using GIF files as horizontal rules
is that you should perform an `align=center` command before using your own
rule images so that text does not flow oddly around a graphic horizontal rule
that's supposed to be separating text sections.

 **Use graphic horizontal rules that repeat a simple pattern to
create separating rules that do not distract from the text and,
more importantly, the images on your Web page.**

Just about any graphics program will create fancy horizontal rules with little
effort on your part. Sometimes, a simple colored line, three or four pixels wide,
makes the perfect horizontal rule for a page. Although the standard horizontal
rule that appears because of the `<hr>` tag works well for just about any page
of any design, unique rules can help distinguish your Web page.

**10 Min.
To Go**

Using Headline and Background Images

Two additional uses of graphics are their placement in headlines (which are covered in Session 5), such as banner ads, and as background images produced from an enlarged version of a graphic image. The next two sections discuss these two additional uses.

Headline graphics

When you use an image in a headline, as you might do when placing a banner advertisement at the top of your Web page, be sure to enclose the image inside the page's `<hn>` tag.

Consider the following code:

```
<h1 align=center>
<img src="images\myad.gif" border=4 alt="Site's Income">
</h1>
```

A headline image can appear between any of the headline tags, `<h1>` through `<h6>`. The headline tags are explained in Session 5.

Figure 9-5 shows the result of placing an image inside headline tags. Although the headline tags are not required for the image to appear before the text, since you can easily use an `<img>` tag inside the Web page body to display an image before text begins, the headlines enable you to easily maintain the headline placement later. You can add additional headline levels or change the headline level of the image without having to restructure the body of your page.

Background images

As you learned in Session 5, the `bgcolor=` attribute of the `<body>` tag colorizes your Web page background. You are not limited to single colors that the tag provides. You can place your own image on the background of your Web pages. Use the `background=` attribute inside the `<body>` tag using this format:

```
<body background="image.jpg">
```

Figure 9-5
Images work well inside headlines.

Not every image works well as a background for your Web page. Keep the following in mind:

- Do not make your background image stronger than your Web page. If the background includes rich colors and crisp lines, the text and graphics that you intend to place over the image will be less noticeable. The background is exactly that: a background.

- A light background is almost always preferable to a dark background. Several exceptions to this exist, however. Black actually makes a good background for some text. You will have to experiment.

- You can create your own background images. All you need to do, if you create a background that continually repeats a pattern, is create only the small, single instance of the pattern, and the browser will repeat that image until the Web page background is full.

- Even though the image repeats, the browser only has to load the image one time. Therefore, a background takes only as long to load as the single pattern image takes to load.

- When you create your background's pattern, make sure that the pattern has no border.

- Your background image patterns can be large, but make sure the pattern fits well within a small browser. Then, when the image repeats, even inside the small browser, at least two full images will appear in the browser background.

Done!

Figure 9-6 shows an effective background image that is rather different from the typical repeated pattern image. The image repeats only once, but the double image encloses the rest of the page fairly effectively. (On large monitors powered by high-resolution graphic adapters, the image repeats three or more times.)

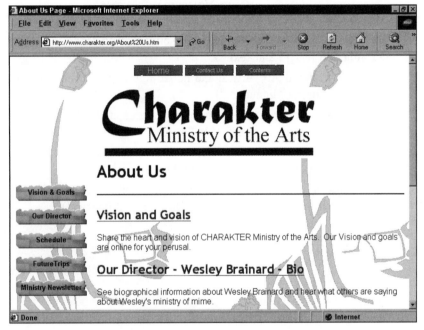

Figure 9-6
When a background image repeats, the load time takes only as long as the single image takes to load.

REVIEW

- You can align your images properly with text and with other images on your Web page.
- Extra space around some graphics often set apart the image from other elements on your Web page.
- You can create your own horizontal rule images with just about any graphics program when the normal gray horizontal rules are not enough.

- Headline graphics, such as banner ads, can be enclosed inside <hn> tags.
- A background image repeats until your entire Web page background is filled.

QUIZ YOURSELF

1. Which attributes align graphics with text on your Web page? (See "Aligning Images and Text.")

2. What happens if you mix vertical and horizontal alignment attributes? (See "Vertical Image Alignment.")

3. How can you vertically center an image on an area of the Web page that contains other images and text? (See "Vertical Image Alignment.")

4. Which attributes increase the horizontal and vertical spacing of blanks around your Web page? (See "Increasing Image Space.")

5. True or False: A light background typically, but not always, works best with light text in the foreground. (See "Background Images.")

Hyperlinks Connect the Web

Session Checklist

✔ Master URL basics

✔ Specify hyperlinks to other Web pages

✔ Insert thumbnail pictures in hyperlinks

✔ Specify hyperlinks within your own Web pages with bookmarks

✔ Distinguish between base URLs and relative URLs

**30 Min.
To Go**

In this session, you learn how to create the links, also called hyperlinks, which enable your Web page users to jump to and from your page to other pages of information on the Web. You also learn how to create bookmarks that allow users to jump to and from areas of interest on the same Web page. It is the hyperlink that made HTML such a required format for Web pages. Hyperlinks are simple because of the anchor tag, <a>, that makes the links possible.

URL Basics

As you know, a URL (Uniform Resource Locator) is the Web address of a specific document. URLs not only point to Web pages, they also might point to other items such as graphic images. Therefore, if a Web page contains a JPEG, and you know the name of that JPEG, you can type the URL for that page followed by /item.jpeg/ and your browser will display that figure inside your browser window.

Never leave a space between the <img> **tag and the closing** </a> **anchor tag. Otherwise, a small blank space, called a** *tick,* **might appear on your Web page between the image and the next item on the page.**

The standard format of URLs is:

```
protocol://site address/directory/filename
```

Most Web pages contain a home page, named index.html, which appears by default when a browser points to that address. Therefore, in most cases, the following URLs are equivalent:

```
http://www.goodsite.com/index.html/
http://www.goodsite.com/
```

The protocol is often http that represents a Web page, but the protocol can also be any of the protocols listed in Table 10-1.

Table 10-1
Protocol Values

Protocol	Description
file	A file on the local computer
ftp	File transfer protocol for file downloads
http	Transfer protocol for Web pages
mailto	A Simple Mail Transfer Protocol (also known as SMTP) window for sending e-mail
nntp	A specific newsgroup article
news	A newsgroup

By far, the most common protocol used is the http protocol that represents other Web pages. Many of the protocols require special handling.

In the next session, you learn how to use the `mailto` protocol to embed mail links inside your page.

Never use the `file` protocol to link to a file on your own computer unless you use a reliable and fast server that is up *24/7* (24 hours a day, 7 days a week). If, for example, you link to a file on your home computer, you cannot ensure that your computer will be logged onto the Internet all the time, and several users at once will slow the system and protocol to a halt.

Specifying Hyperlink Tags

The primary method for representing a hyperlink is to use the `<a>` tag with the `href=` attribute. The `<a>` tag includes the URL for the hyperlinked Web page. The *a* in the `<a>` tag means *anchor*. A hyperlink's end points are known as anchors, hence the tag.

The `<a>` tag also requires an end tag, `</a>`. Here is the basic format of the `<a>` tag:

```
<a href = "URL">hot spot text</a>
```

The reference inside the `<a>` tag represents the hyperlink, also known as the *hot spot* (or the anchor), that the browser jumps to when the user clicks on the hot spot (or hyperlink) text. The format's *hot spot text* represents the text that appears in your Web page that the user clicks on to move to that new anchor.

The following `<a>` command directs the user to Microsoft's home page:

```
<a href="http://www.microsoft.com">Check for a new Windows
release</a>
```

When the browser gets to this code, the browser displays the text, `Check for a new Windows release`, and the browser turns that text into a hyperlink by typically underlining that text. When the user points to that hyperlink, the user's mouse pointer often turns into a pointing hand to indicate that the text represents a link and is not simply regular underlined text.

Never underline regular, nonhyperlinked text because users get confused when some underlined text indicates a hyperlink and other underlined text does not.

Browsers differ in how they display hyperlinks. In addition, the user might turn off the underlining of hyperlinks. For example, in Windows 9x running Internet Explorer 4 and higher, users can, at the operating system level, display hyperlinks that appear in a new color but not underlined until the user points to the hyperlink, at which time Windows underlines the link. Using style sheets (see Session 20) enables you to turn off the default underlining beneath links completely.

The location of the <a> tag inside surrounding text determines exactly where the hyperlink falls. In other words, only the text indicated as the hot spot text is the actual hyperlink. Figure 10-1 shows how each of the following three similar hot spots differ:

```
<br><br>
Your version of Windows determines whether or not you have
Internet Connection Sharing.
<br>
<a href="http://www.microsoft.com">Check for a new Windows
release</a>

<hr>
<br><br>
Your version of Windows determines whether or not you have
Internet Connection Sharing.
<br>
Check for a new <a href="http://www.microsoft.com">Windows</a>
release.

<hr>
<br><br>
Your version of Windows determines whether or not you have
Internet Connection Sharing.
<br>
Check for a new <a href="http://www.microsoft.com">Windows
release.</a>
```

In the first section in Figure 10-1, the hyperlink is "Check for a new Windows release" because this phrase is indicated as the hot spot text in the first example above. The second hyperlink is "Windows," and the third hyperlink is "Windows release," since these paragraphs serve as the hot spots in the second and third examples above.

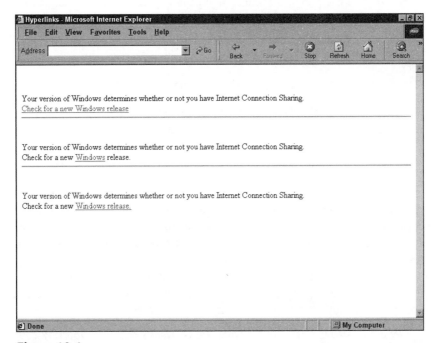

Figure 10-1
The hot spot text determines what the user clicks.

 Many browsers display an unclicked link (called an *unvisited link*) in one color, a clicked link (called a *visited link*) in another, and a link-in-progress (a link you've clicked but for which the page has not opened yet, called an *active link*) in a third color. These colors inform the user of which links have been visited.

Text is not the only item you can place inside the anchor tags. You can also place graphic images. The section on thumbnail pictures discusses the use of images as hyperlinks.

 Never omit the closing </a> tag even though some HTML programmers do. Talk is under way between some browser makers to require the end tag, although to do so will make many existing Web pages that don't specify the </a> tag work improperly.

**20 Min.
To Go**

Controlling hyperlink colors

As mentioned in the previous section, Web page hyperlinks change colors to indicate whether or not the user has selected those links yet. You have the option of leaving the choice of link colors up to the user's browser or specifying the hyperlink colors yourself. (The colors that change as the user visits links are called *link renderings*.)

The following attributes specify colors for the anchor's links:

link=   Determines the color of the unvisited hyperlink

alink=   Determines the color of the active link, the link that the user has clicked but whose page has not yet opened

vlink=   Determines the color of the visited link, a link that the current user has visited

Suppose your user visits your Web site for the first time. All the hyperlinks will be one color, the link= attribute's color. When the user clicks a link, that link changes to the alink= attribute's color until the link loads. Then, when the user returns to your page, the link appears in the vlink= attribute's color. If you have not specified one or more of the colors, the user's browser will determine the links' colors. The color you specify can be a hexadecimal color code or one of the 16 color values supported by name as explained in Session 8.

Never stray too far from the browser's default hyperlink color scheme or you will confuse the users. Some Web sites that have extremely different themes, such as a science fiction-based Web site, might work well with a new set of hyperlink colors, but generally, the browser's default colors are the ones that you should stick with.

Specifying hyperlink titles

Use the title= (or title) attribute with the <a> and </a> tags when you want a pop-up description, called a *tool tip,* to appear when the user points the mouse to the hyperlink. Without a title, the tool tip will be the URL that the link references. Here is an example of the title= attribute:

```
<a href="http://www.company.com/info.html" title="Address
Information">To mail letters</a>
```

Figure 10-2 shows such a title at a hyperlink. After a moment, the hovering mouse cursor produces the title text.

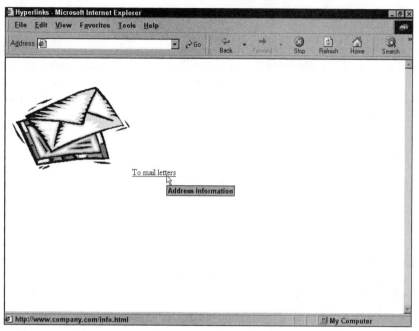

Figure 10-2
The address information tool tip appears when the mouse points to the hyperlink.

Opening a new window

When the user clicks on the hyperlinks you've seen so far in this session, the user's browser window changes to the page of the new link. If, instead, you want to open a new window when the user clicks your hyperlink's anchor tag, use the `target="_blank"` attribute. The original window, such as your home page, will remain open, and the new, second window will contain the hyperlinked Web page. The following line opens the image in a new window:

```
<a href="happyFace.jpg" target="_blank">
```

Normally, the `target=` attribute supports the use of frames that you'll learn about in Session 18, but the `target="_blank"` attribute works with or without frames and provides a way for you to open a new window to display the target of the hyperlink. The new window pops up on top of the user's window so that both contain information.

Specifying the tab order of hyperlinks

The anchor tag supports the tabindex= attribute, which determines the *tab order* of the links on the Web page. Suppose a Web page contains 20 hyperlinks. The user can press the Tab key to highlight each link in succession and press Enter when the link that the user wants to see is highlighted. This way, the user can view links with only a keyboard instead of using the mouse. The value that follows the tabindex= attribute must be a positive number, beginning at 1, that determines the order of the links highlighted as the user presses Enter. No two numbers can be the same throughout a page's links. The following statement ensures that the link is the first thing the user tabs to:

```
<a href="http://www.mySite.com/" tabindex=1>
```

WebTV Internet users often use keyboard commands instead of mouse-based commands. In addition, when you add the keyword selected **to one of your page's links, that link will be the default link when the WebTV user first views your Web page.**

The problem with the tabindex= attribute is that tabindex= is not supported by all browsers. The tabindex= attribute is a new feature of HTML 4.01. No problem occurs if the user's browser fails to recognize the tabindex= attribute. If the browser does not recognize the attribute, the user's tab order will be the default tab order generated by the browser.

Thumbnail Pictures

As noted earlier, you can place graphic images inside you anchor tags. When you enclose an image instead of text between the <a> and </a> tags, the image becomes the hot spot that produces the hyperlink when the user clicks the image. Typically, the only hint that the image is a hyperlink is the context of the image on the page (such as a pointing finger that indicates a continued thought) and the cursor that changes to the pointing hand shape when the user hovers the mouse pointer over the image.

If the hyperlink image has a border set to a value greater than one pixel, the border color will be the same color as the link= **attribute color in other hyperlinks. Such a border adds another clue that the image acts as a hyperlink.**

A thumbnail image is a small, fast-loading version of a larger picture. You can place a thumbnail image on a Web page with any image tab and then make the thumbnail a link to the larger version. The following code turns a small thumbnail image into a link to a larger image:

```
<a href="images/ourLarge.gif">
<img border=2 src="images/ourSmall.gif"
  alt="ourhouse.gif (171805 bytes)" width=100
  height=66>
</a>
```

Figure 10-3 shows what happens when the user clicks a thumbnail image on a Web page that uses the `target="_blank"` attribute: The hyperlink produces the full-sized image in a new window. By opening the larger image in a separate window, the user can go ahead and visit other links while the image loads in its own window.

Figure 10-3
The thumbnail gives the user a preview of the larger image.

Always specify the file size if a hyperlink is going to load an extremely large graphic image or Web page. You might want to add a tool tip or include text below the image that specifies the file size, such as `Beautiful car (140K)`.

**10 Min.
To Go**

Inserting Bookmarks to Links on the Same Page

Bookmarks, also known as *markers* or *fragments,* are hyperlinks to areas on the same page instead of a different Web page. One of the most useful places to insert a bookmark is at the bottom of a long Web page. With the bookmark at the bottom of the page, the *source* would, when clicked, return the user to the top of the page (the *source*). Bookmarks, unlike regular links, never send the user to a different page, only to a destination on the current Web page. The bookmarks eliminate the need for scrolling back to the top of a long Web page. You might include a bookmark that reads, `Go to Top of Page`, and when the user clicks this bookmark, the browser jumps to the top of the page, eliminating the user's need to scroll up a lengthy page.

You must use two anchor tags to create a bookmark link — the bookmark's source `<a>` tag and the bookmark's destination `<a>` tag. The destination tag uses the `name=` attribute to determine the hyperlink's destination. In such a tag, you completely replace the `href=` attribute with the `name=` attribute, as in the following example that names the current spot, the top of the Web page, *top:*

```
<a name="top"></a>
```

Later, one or more regular `<a>` links, the destination links, might appear so that when the user clicks the link, the browser scrolls back to the top of the page.

If you type text between a bookmark's destination anchor tag, the text appears on the screen but will not be underlined or colored as it would be if the tag indicated a hyperlink. Therefore, the following creates a destination bookmark named PeachPit and displays the text `Peaches` on the screen:

```
<a name="peachPit">Peaches</a>
```

The reason that the bookmark is not indicated by coloring or underlining is that the bookmark is simply a tag that defines the location of a bookmarked link. This location, `peachPit`, is where the browser will jump to when the user clicks a bookmark source link that sends the browser to this destination.

Although you can combine `name=` and `href=` in the same tag, doing so can confuse you later when you maintain the page. You can more easily maintain two separate tags for the two different kinds of links.

Throughout your Web page, one or more anchor tags, the destination tags, can reference that source bookmark. When the user clicks one of these references, the Web browser jumps to the bookmark specified. To set up a link that directs the browser to the bookmark, create an anchor tag using the normal `href=` attribute but insert a pound sign (#) before the bookmark's name.

The following line creates a pointer to the bookmark named top:

```
<a href="#top">Go to top of page</a>
```

Although this destination link looks like a regular hyperlink, with the appropriate color and link underline, the user's screen will not load a new Web page; instead, it will jump to the top of the current page where you've specified a bookmark such as the following:

```
<a name="top"></a>
```

Never begin a hyperlink's text with the phrase, "Click here," as in "Click here to see a picture." Such links are considered redundant at best and show a lack of professionalism in a site's creation. You can assume that your users understand simple Web operations, such as hyperlinks. Maintain more professional links, such as "Mary's photo," instead of wordy ones, such as "Click here to see Mary's photo."

Absolute URLs versus Relative URLs

Not every hyperlink requires a complete Web address. HTML supports both *base URLs* (also called *absolute URLs,* those URLs with the complete pathname, such as `http://www.myWeb.com/photos.html/`) and *relative URLs* (such as `photos.html`). The difference is that you can specify a relative URL as long as the link resides in the same directory as the current Web page.

Suppose your Web page resides at `http://www.myWeb.com/` and is named `index.html`, which implies that the full path to your Web page is this:

```
http://www.myWeb.com/index.html/
```

As long as `photos.html` also resides in the same directory as `index.html`, the following references are exactly the same:

```
http://www.myWeb.com/photos.html
```

and

```
photos.html
```

Relative links really do not load any quicker than absolute links, but relative links do offer the advantage of being easier to move. If your base directory changes, you won't have to change any link that is relative based on your directory. You'll only need to change the absolute URLs that refer to the old path.

Done!

All the standard directly traversal codes work in relative URLs, such as the single dot that means current directory and the double dot that means the parent directory. The following `<a>` tag contains a relative URL that begins two directories higher than the current one:

```
<a href="./../address.html">
```

REVIEW

- URLs include an item's protocol, which is often `http`.
- The `<a>` and `</a>` end tags specify the anchor point of a hyperlink.
- Only rarely will you want to change a hyperlink's color scheme. It's better to stick with the browser's default colors.
- Your page's hyperlinks can replace the current browser window with a new page or open a new window with the linked page, depending on the presence of the `target=_blank` attribute.
- Thumbnail images are good uses of hyperlinks that link to larger images.
- Although you can specify the tab order of the links on a Web page, many browsers do not support the tab order that you request.
- Relative URLs are quicker to code than full, absolute URLs, as well as being easier to maintain.

Quiz Yourself

1. Which <a> attribute specifies the hyperlink's URL? (See "Specifying Hyperlink Tags.")

2. Why is it better not to use underlines when specifying nonhyperlink text? (See "Specifying Hyperlink Tags.")

3. What is the difference between a Web page's unvisited hyperlink, an active hyperlink, and a visited hyperlink? (See "Controlling Hyperlink Colors.")

4. What is the difference between a bookmark and a hyperlink? (See "Inserting Bookmarks to Links on the Same Page.")

5. What directory does a relative URL use for its base directory? (See "Absolute URLs versus Relative URLs.")

PART

II

Saturday Morning
Part Review

1. In which section does the `<title>` tag reside?
2. Why is it best to specify HTML tags in lowercase letters?
3. What happens when a browser's computer does not contain the fonts necessary to render the fonts in your HTML page?
4. How do you specify the largest headline font?
5. True or False: The `<p>` tag is equivalent to two `<br>` tags.
6. How can you align a paragraph of text against the right side of the browser window?
7. Which tag centers both text and graphics?
8. How can you set off long passages of quoted text from surrounding text?
9. What is a horizontal rule and which tag creates one?
10. What is the difference between an ordered list and an unordered list?
11. Name another use for a definition list besides a definition of a term.
12. What is the safest number of colors to use on Web page if you want your page to be uniform across all browsers?
13. What is a hexadecimal color code?
14. What does *RGB* stand for?
15. What happens if you increase an image's size too much?
16. True or False: You can specify a background image but not a background color.

17. What is a hot spot?

18. Describe what an active link is.

19. How do you open a link in a new window?

20. True or False: Bookmarks generally do not include text that appears on the Web page.

PART

III

Saturday
Afternoon

E-mail Links, Comments, and Special Characters

Session Checklist

✔ Make it easy for users to send you e-mail with e-mail hyperlinks

✔ Add ample comments throughout your HTML code

✔ Use character codes when you want to display special characters on your Web page

**30 Min.
To Go**

In the previous session, you learned how to set up hyperlinks that jump from page to page and between bookmarks of a current page. One of the protocols you read about was the mailto protocol. In this session, you learn how to use the mailto protocol to set up e-mail links in your Web page, enabling users to send e-mail to you easily. This session then branches off into two new topics. It shows you how to add as many comments as is reasonable to your HTML code to make maintenance easier, as well as how to use character codes to display special characters on your Web page.

Creating E-mail Links

When you offer your users a chance to give you feedback, you can supply them with
a link that opens their default mail system's new e-mail message window. If you
choose not to provide such a simple link, your users probably won't go through the
trouble of contacting you.

Consider the Web pages you visit. Are you more likely to send e-mail to someone who supplies only their e-mail address or send e-mail to someone who adds
an e-mail link right on the page you are visiting? Without the link, you must
type the e-mail address (assuming it appears on the page) or, at best, copy and
paste the address into your e-mail program that you must start yourself. An e-mail
link both starts the user's default e-mail program and opens a new message window to make completing and sending the e-mail quick and easy.

Uses for e-mail links

E-mail links on your site are useful for many reasons, including:

- Getting feedback about your site's usefulness
- Receiving requests for different information on the site
- Contacting a customer service department
- Providing an online employee directory

Specifying e-mail links

To specify an e-mail link, simply use the mailto protocol in place of the typical
http protocol. The following line adds an e-mail link to a Web page:

```
<a href="mailto:abc@company.com">Customer Service</a>
```

The e-mail anchor looks and acts just like other kinds of hyperlinks. The link
appears underlined and in the browser's default link color. (You can override the
colors using the link color attributes you learned in the previous session.) When
the user clicks the e-mail link, a mail window, such as the one in Figure 11-1,
opens. The user can type a subject, a message, and then click Send to get the
message to the address you specified in the link.

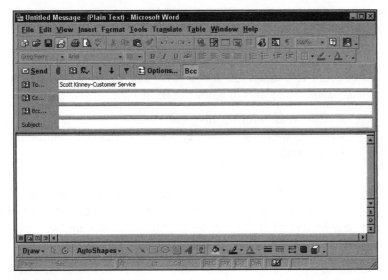

Figure 11-1
The opening of a mail window with a click makes it easy for Web users to send you e-mail.

Other `mailto` **protocol attributes are sometimes available, such as** `subject=` **that fills in the subject for you, but most browsers do not support these options because no industry standard has been agreed upon. Some day, extra** `mailto` **attributes might become standard, but it will take a while for the majority of users to update their browsers. It is better to let your users fill in the subject and message body than to attempt to use some of these unusual** `mailto` **protocol attributes.**

Problems rarely, but might, occur if the user does not have an e-mail program set up within the browser's options. If no e-mail program is set up, the selected `mailto` hyperlink will produce an error message within the user's browser as a result of the Web page link. Such an error happens so rarely that you can safely ignore the potential problem; most users have e-mail accounts readily set up for use.

Part III—Saturday Afternoon
Session 11

**20 Min.
To Go**

Adding Comments to HTML Code

As you write more HTML code, your Web pages will become larger, making the maintenance of your HTML complicated. One of the best favors you can do for yourself is to add ample comments as you write HTML code.

Another reason for learning how to code comments is that more advanced Web page elements, such as JavaScript, require the use of comments.

A comment is a note that you include inside your HTML code. The browser completely ignores comments! Your comment can span 30 lines of HTML code, and the browser gracefully ignores all of the comment's text. Comments are not browser commands. They are notes for the programmer that explain the HTML code.

Some uses for comments are:

- Displaying a list of changes made to the Web page since its original publication to the site, along with the HTML programmers who made those changes.

- Explaining sections of HTML code; when some code or a graphic image name seems to be cryptic, a well-placed comment can explain what the HTML programmer had in mind.

- Executing JavaScript code that can activate your site and make your Web page interactive.

- Reminding you to add certain features that you may have omitted from the early versions of the site.

- Explaining why you used a certain tag when another, more recent tag, may be more acceptable. For example, you may want to explain why you used individual tags and no style sheets if you know your audience generally uses older browsers.

- Commenting out a section of HTML code that you want to hide from the browser, perhaps to test another area of the Web page or to eliminate a new feature for a specified period, at which time you remove the comment.

- Inserting a comment to inform your clients where certain data goes when the client is ready, if you create Web pages for others to use. For example, a comment can inform a client where a new price goes when the price becomes available.

If you've ever written computer programs in a non-HTML programming language, you've seen comments before.

Comments, like tags, are enclosed by <!-- and ‡ start and end tags. Here is the format of an HTML comment:

```
<!-- Comment text goes here -->
```

The space after <!-- is required. The comment's text can take one line or span many lines. The comment ends at the closing comment tag, -->. The HTML code continues immediately after the comment.

Consider the following code:

```
<br>Announcement: Our new automobile cleaner is here!<br><br>
<!-- Photograph of the cleaner being used appears below -->
<img src="X331.JPG" width=400 height=300 border=3>
```

Often, the names of graphic files are cryptic, but the comment can help clarify the image's purpose. Doing so at the comment, so close to the image, will keep the HTML programmer from having to maintain a table of image descriptions and filenames displayed on the page.

Comments make great holding areas for contact information. The following comment at the top of the HTML code tells subsequent HTML coders where to locate the original page authors:

```
<!-- Original HTML design and code: August 26, 2001
     Programmer: Terry Kirk
     Designer: Kim Lu
     Production Company:
        Design Webbers
        101 E. Oak
        St. Louis, MO  60699
        (888) 555-1234
-->
```

All versions of HTML, since version 1, recognize the comment tags.

Inserting Special Characters on Web Pages

When you must display special characters, your browser might interpret those characters as HTML code instead of displayable characters. In addition, some special characters don't appear on your keyboard. To display special characters, you must use character codes that represent these symbols.

For example, suppose you create a Web site that explains how to write HTML code. On such a site, it would be reasonable to assume that the following text may need to appear on the site:

```
Use the paragraph tag, <p>, to insert a blank line between
paragraphs.
```

The problem with such text is that if you embed this inside HTML code, you'll get results that look something like that in Figure 11-2. The <p>, a special character, does not show up because the browser thinks the <p> is a tag. The browser, therefore, performs the tag's purpose instead of simply displaying the tag.

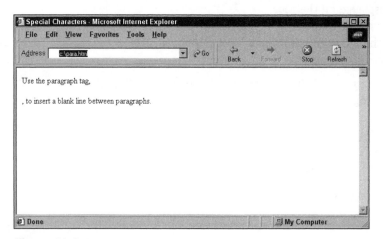

Figure 11-2
The browser thought that a tag was embedded in the text.

Not only might you want to display tags themselves on your Web page, but you also may want to display special characters that do not appear on the typical computer keyboard, such as the copyright or foreign currency symbols.

HTML supports numerous codes that you can use to represent special characters on your Web page. Table 11-1 lists several of the special characters and the corresponding codes. Although the table is lengthy, spend the rest of this session looking through the characters so you know what is available for you to use. To produce the line that included the paragraph tag in the previous example, you could use the greater-than and less-than character codes on the screen like this:

```
Use the paragraph tag, &#60;p&#62;, to add a blank line between
paragraphs.
```

Many of the character codes have an equivalent *character entity* (also shown in Table 11-1) that enables you to use a more memorable mnemonic for some of the codes. For example, you can specify è or è when you want to display the small *e* with a grave accent, è.

Table 11-1
Special Character Codes

Character	Code	Character Entity
"	&#34;	&quot;
#	&#35;	
$	&#36;	
%	&#37;	
&	&#38;	
'	&#39;	
&	&#38;	&amp;
<	&#60;	&lt;
>	&#62;	&gt;
¡	&#161;	&iexcl;
¢	&#162;	&cent;
£	&#163;	&pound;
	&#164;	&curren;
¥	&#165;	&yen;
¦	&#166;	&brkbar;

Continued

Table 11-1 *Continued*

Character	Code	Character Entity
§	&#167;	&sect;
¨	&#168;	&uml;
©	&#169;	&copy;
ª	&#170;	&ordf;
«	&#171;	&laquo;
¬	&#172;	&not;
®	&#174;	&reg
¯	&#175;	&hibar;
°	&#176;	&deg;
±	&#177;	&plusmn;
²	&#178;	&sup2;
³	&$179;	&sup3;
´	&#180;	&acute;
>	&#181;	&micro;
¶	&#182;	&para;
·	&#183;	&midot;
¸	&#184;	&cedil;
¹	&#185;	&sup1;
º	&#186;	&ordm;
»	&#187;	&raquo;
¼	&#188;	&frac14;
½	&#189;	&frac12;
¾	&#190;	&frac34;
¿	&#191;	&iquest;

Character	Code	Character Entity
À	À	À
Á	Á	Á
Â	Â	Â
Ã	Ã	Ã
Ä	Ä	Ä
Å	Å	Å
Æ	Æ	Æ
Ç	Ç	Ç
È	È	È
É	É	É
Ê	Ê	Ê
Ë	Ë	Ë
Ì	Ì	Ì
Í	Í	Í
Î	Î	Î
Ï	Ï	Ï
F	Ð	Ð
Ñ	Ñ	Ñ
Ò	Ò	Ò
Ó	Ó	Ó
Ô	Ô	Ô
Õ	Õ	Õ
Ö	Ö	Ö
×	×	
Ø	Ø	Ø

Continued

Table 11-1 *Continued*

Character	Code	Character Entity
Ù	&#217;	&Ugrave;
Ú	&#218;	&Uacute;
Û	&#219;	&Ucirc;
Ü	&#220;	&Uuml;
Ý	&#221;	&Yacute;
Þ	&#222;	&THORN;
ß	&#223;	&szlig;
à	&#224;	&agrave;
á	&#225;	&aacute;
â	&#226;	&acirc;
ã	&#227;	&atilde;
ä	&#228;	&aauml;
å	&#229;	&aring;
æ	&#230;	&aelig;
ç	&#231;	&ccedil;
è	&#232;	&egrave;
é	&#233;	&iacute;
ê	&#234;	&icirc;
ë	&#235;	&emul;
ì	&#236;	&igrave;
í	&#237;	&iacute;
î	&#238;	&icirc;
ï	&#239;	&iuml;
Ð	&#240;	&eth;

Character	Code	Character Entity
ñ	&#241;	&ntilde;
ò	&#242;	&ograve;
ó	&#243;	&oacute;
ô	&#244;	&ocirc;
õ	&#245;	&otilde;
ö	&#246;	&ouml;
÷	&#247;	
ø	&#248;	&oslash;
ù	&#249;	&ugrave;
ú	&#250;	&uacute;
û	&#251;	&ucirc;
ü	&#252;	&uuml;
ý	&#253;	&yacute;
þ	&#254;	&thorn;
ÿ	&#255;	&yuml;

One code not included in the table is   that creates a nonbreaking space. If you embed   between two words, for example, the browser will not break a line between them but will keep the two words together.

Most browsers provide support for most of the characters in Table 11-1. If you use the special characters, test your page in several of the more popular browsers to make sure that the codes work as you expect. (Such advice is true of all pages; always view your Web pages in as many browsers and in as many different resolution levels as possible to ensure that your Web page retains the look you prefer.)

Done!

When you use one of the special characters, a comment is necessary to inform other HTML coders, as well as yourself, exactly what the character code represents. Also, some, but not all, of the special characters follow the same character-code pattern as the ASCII table.

REVIEW

- When clicked, e-mail links open up a mail window in your Web site that enables users to write to you easily.

- An e-mail hyperlink includes the standard underlining and hyperlink colors.

- Comments in your HTML code, such as a note to remind yourself to add a feature later on, make Web site maintenance much simpler.

- Use character codes when you cannot produce special characters from your keyboard or when a special character, such as the less-than sign, might be interpreted as a command tag.

QUIZ YOURSELF

1. Name three reasons to provide an e-mail hyperlink on your site. (See "Uses for E-mail Links.")

2. What is the protocol value that opens the user's default e-mail's new message window? (See "Creating E-mail Links.")

3. Why does the browser ignore comments? (See "Adding Comments to HTML Code.")

4. Why should you put contact information in your HTML code comments? (See "Adding Comments to HTML Code.")

5. Why must you use special character codes to display special characters on your Web page? (See "Inserting Special Characters on Web Pages.")

Tables Organize Data

Session Checklist

✔ Learn the ways that tables can help you organize data on your Web site

✔ Learn how to prepare a spreadsheet-like table that you can use as a basis for complex tables

✔ Improve the look of your tables by adding borders, aligning data, and spanning cells across columns and rows

✔ Use some advanced page layout tricks to make more powerful tables

**30 Min.
To Go**

Some of the most interesting Web sites work well because they are built on tables. Most HTML tutorials begin teaching HTML tables by making spreadsheet analogies. The spreadsheet makeup of cells and rows is so familiar that such an analogy makes a good place to start. Nevertheless, tables don't stop with tabular data. Tables can hold any kind of data, not just text. Unfortunately, a weekend crash course does not provide enough time to make you an official Table Guru, but you will, before this session ends, hold many table tips in your bag of tricks that you will hone as your use of tables grows.

How Tables Help You Organize Data

Tables help you organize data on your Web site. Some of the ways you can use tables are to:

- Present newsletter information in columns, as shown in Figure 12-1.
- Display tabular information, in a spreadsheet-like manner, such as price lists and inventories.
- Add borders around text and graphic images in a uniform manner.
- Format your entire Web page layout, including the placement of graphics, text, banners, sidebars, headers, and footers.

Figure 12-1
Tables help organize the data in newsletter Web sites.

As you can see, tables are not limited to simple spreadsheet-like formatting, even though the best place to begin learning about tables is to see them in use with such data. The rest of this session develops such a spreadsheet-like table so you can learn the fundamentals. You then can apply those fundamentals to other kinds of tables.

Preparing Columnar Data Tables

Tables consist of rows and columns. A useful table might contain only one row and three columns. The purpose of the table determines how elaborate the table must become. Tables can be nested, which means that they can reside inside other tables. Therefore, a single cell might contain an entire table, and one of the inside table cells might hold yet another table.

Never embed more than two levels of tables if your Web page loads slowly. A single table, even one with many rows and columns, loads much faster than a table that contains other tables. The power of these nested tables, however, makes them so useful that your application should determine whether or not you nest tables instead of simply considering load time. In addition, some browsers, most notably Netscape 4, do not display nested tables properly unless the user has upgraded to a more recent version.

Tables require several different kinds of table-related command tags. You cannot type table text directly into HTML as rows and columns of information because browsers ignore all extra spaces and tabs in your HTML source.

Creating tables

All tables begin with the `<table>` command tag and terminate with a subsequent `</table>` command tag. Within the table, you'll specify rows with the `<tr>` (for *table row*) tag and columns with the `<td>` (for *table detail*) tag. In addition to cells that hold data, you may also create header cells that hold titles for the data in the columns.

When you design and create tables, keep the following order in mind at all times: top-to-bottom and left-to-right. You'll create all tables one row at a time from the top to the bottom of the table, and you'll add individual cells, or columns, one at a time in those rows from the left to the right.

One of the best ways to begin a table that contains simple columnar data is to type the data directly into your HTML code. Remembering that HTML completely ignores extra spaces and tabs that you use, you can more easily plan your table by using your text editor to create the initial layout.

Don't just type the data in rows and columns, however, because you must remember the top-to-bottom, left-to-right nature of HTML tables. For example, type data in each row (top to bottom), beginning with the first row. Before you type data in the next row, enter the columnar data (left to right) for each row, one cell at a time. Consider the following code that presents a bookseller's inventory:

```
<table>
Title
Quantity
Price

Laughing Kids
24
$19.95

I Stood Still
13
$7.95

Make Money Now
52
$22.95
</table>
```

The first three items (Title, Quantity, and Price) are the table's column titles, called *header cells* in HTML terminology. (How to set up the column heads is covered in the section that immediately follows this one.) The remaining rows fall below the header cells.

The code, as it now stands, does not make much of a table. The <table> tag does no formatting but serves only to tell the browser where the table might begin and end. Therefore, all the text in this code will appear in one line across the browser screen. The text does comprise a table given the <table> tag, however. You must divide the text into rows and columns to make the table look like a table.

Specifying the header cells

The <th> tags specify which cells are header cells. Once you've typed the data, put <th> tags before each header cell value. At the end of each header cell, include a </th> end tag. The code from the previous section now looks like this:

```
<table>
   <th>Title</th>
```

```
   <th>Quantity</th>
   <th>Price</th>

   Laughing Kids
   24
   $19.95

   I Stood Still
   13
   $7.95

   Make Money Now
   52
   $22.95
</table>
```

`Title` will appear at the top of the table's first column; `Quantity` will appear at the top of the table's second column; `Price` will appear at the top of the third column.

Specifying the rows

When you use the <tr> tags, your table begins to look like a real table. Insert <tr> before the data value that begins each row and </tr> at the end of each row. The code looks like the following:

```
<table>
<tr>
   <th>Title</th>
   <th>Quantity</th>
   <th>Price</th>
</tr>
<tr>
   Laughing Kids
   24
   $19.95
</tr>
<tr>
   I Stood Still
   13
   $7.95
```

```
</tr>
<tr>
   Make Money Now
   52
   $22.95
</tr>
</table>
```

At this time, the table is shaping up in rows, as shown here:

```
     Title        Quantity    Price
Laughing Kids 24 $19.95
I Stood Still 13 $7.95
Make Money Now 52 $22.95
```

 The `<th>` tag automatically boldfaces the header cells to help separate them from the data cells. You can always format the header and data further with the available formatting tags.

Obviously, the table needs work. The data does not properly align in columns, but that should not be a surprise considering no `<td>` tags appear yet to separate the data into columns.

Specifying the columns

Use the `<td>` tag before each cell value, followed by the `</td>` end tag to specify columns. This will complete the standard table. Here is the code to do just that:

```
<tr>
   <th>Title</th>
   <th>Quantity</th>
   <th>Price</th>
</tr>
<tr>
   <td>Laughing Kids</td>
   <td>24</td>
   <td>$19.95</td>
</tr>
<tr>
```

```
      <td>I Stood Still</td>
      <td>13</td>
      <td>$7.95</td>
   </tr>
   <tr>
      <td>Make Money Now</td>
      <td>52</td>
      <td>$22.95</td>
   </tr>
```

The table now appears in nice rows and columns, with each column wide enough to hold either the longest cell data or the longest header. Here is the table as it now stands:

```
        Title      Quantity   Price
Laughing Kids      24         $19.95
I Stood Still      13         $7.95
Make Money Now     52         $22.95
```

Much work is left, but the basic structure is now in place. It may seem as though HTML tables are time-consuming to create. However, you'll combine many of the steps that this session has broken down individually when you create your tables. In addition, you'll begin formatting the tables more appropriately earlier in the process. The next few minutes concentrate on table formatting.

**20 Min.
To Go**

Improving the Look of Your Table

Think of all the improvements needed to make the book inventory a more useful table. The table's look would benefit from lines around and in between the table cells. Headers should consistently center or left-justify over the columns, and the cell widths need to change somewhat.

Adding borders

The <table> tag supports a border= attribute that draws borders (or lines) around and between your table's cells. The format of the tag and attribute are as follows:

```
<table border=width>
```

The *width* value is the number of pixels wide the border should consume. To create a border, therefore, you might replace the opening `<table>` tag with this:

```
<table border=8>
```

Figure 12-2 shows how a bookseller's table with a border appears in the browser window. The table looks good, actually, considering how little effort went into it.

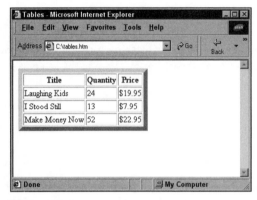

Figure 12-2
The table's shaded borders create a professional look.

Aligning data

The table tags give you complete control over your table's format, including the alignment of the header and data cells against the left or right edge of the borders as well as to other cells. You can align entire rows and columns or individual cells.

The following HTML statement aligns a table header's text so it left-justifies within the cell:

```
<th align=left>Title</th>
```

The `align=` attribute works in both header cells and data cells to align the data inside those cells to the left, center, or right side of the cells in relation to the border. Even within the same row of header cells, you may want to center some headers and left-align others.

In addition to aligning data horizontally, you can align text vertically within a row with the `valign=` attribute. The `valign=` attribute takes these three values: `valign=top`, `valign=middle`, and `valign=bottom`.

Spanning individual cells and columns across multiple rows in the table (discussed next) is when you need to vertically align data.

Spanning cells

One of the most useful aspects of HTML tables is that each cell in each row does not have to conform to the width or height of each cell in other rows. The uniqueness of the cells lends HTML tables to entire and complex Web page design.

When the cells in each row are not the same height and width, you can span individual cells and columns across multiple rows. For example, you can put the table's title in your first row and span the title across the entire table.

When using the `<caption>` tag to add a table title, in many ways, the `<caption>` tag offers little more than regular HTML text offers. The only exception is that the caption stays with the table when you move the table and is actually part of the table. The `<caption>` tag falls directly below the `<table>` tag, as follows:

```
<table border=8>
<caption>Our In-Stock Books</caption>
```

Again, the caption appears above the table. The browser does not even boldface the text as it does for column header cells. You are welcome to apply any formatting tags to the caption as long as you place those tags after the start tag, `<caption>`.

Your other option for folding a table title into the table itself is to place the title directly into the first cell of the first row and then *span,* or lengthen, that cell to consume the entire width of the table. To span across columns, you use the `<colspan=width>` tag, and to span across rows, you use the `<rowspan=width>` tag. The *width* value is the number of columns or rows that you want the cell to span.

The code in Listing 12-1 generates the table shown in Figure 12-3, with the table title appearing directly inside the table. Because of the `colspan=3` attribute, the first row spans all three columns. Without the `colspan=3` attribute, the row would consume only the first column of the table, and the rest of the table would fall beneath that.

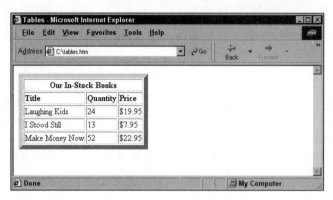

Figure 12-3
Because of the colspan= attribute, the table title now spans across the three columns.

Listing 12-1
Using the colspan= attribute to distribute a cell across several columns

```
<table border=8>
<tr>
   <th colspan=3>Our In-Stock Books</th>
</tr>
<tr>
   <th align=left>Title</th>
   <th align=left>Quantity</th>
   <th align=left>Price</th>
</tr>
<tr>
   <td>Laughing Kids</td>
   <td>24</td>
   <td>$19.95</td>
</tr>
<tr>
   <td>I Stood Still</td>
   <td>13</td>
   <td>$7.95</td>
</tr>
<tr>
```

```
        <td>Make Money Now</td>
        <td>52</td>
        <td>$22.95</td>
    </tr>
</table>
```

**10 Min.
To Go**

More Powerful Tables

Some of the formatting tricks discussed in this section can enhance the appearance of your tables. Although tables hold data effortlessly, the page layout tricks and tips you learn here make tables almost a requirement for anything more than a simple sequential, flat Web site. They lend themselves to more powerful Web page design.

Adding a background color to a table

Adding a background color to your table makes the table stand out. You can do this by adding the bgcolor= attribute inside the <table> tag to colorize all the cells in the table. As with all HTML color-related attributes, you can specify either a hexadecimal color code such as *#20CCFF* or one of the 16 named colors such as red (as discussed in Session 8).

The following statement colors the cell's background blue:

```
<td valign=top align=left bgcolor=blue>
```

Adjusting table spacing

Two attributes, cellpadding= and cellspacing=, enable you to place cells more precisely in relation to each other. You must specify the attributes in pixels with the width value as follows:

```
cellpadding=width
cellspacing=width
```

By adjusting the cellpadding= attribute, you add some room around your cell's text that is greater than the default pixel value of 1. The cellspacing= attribute increases the size of the space between the cells. The inner lines that divide the cells increase in width as you increase the cellspacing= attribute value.

Part III—Saturday Afternoon
Session 12

The `width=` attribute enables you to determine exactly how much of the Web page your table will span *no matter how wide the user's browser window is.* The default width of a table is the amount of space necessary to display that table. If, however, you specify a fixed width value, the table enlarges or contracts to respect that width. If you do not specify a width that is wide enough to display the cell contents, the browser squeezes the table and wraps the contents of the cells to respect the width that you specify.

Never specify a table width greater than 550 pixels. Users with small displays will not be able to see a wider table reliably.

Adjusting table space with percentages and multiple tables

Instead of specifying the width in pixels, you can specify the `width=` attribute in percentage terms. Therefore, you can request that a table consume 85 percent of the browser's remaining window size. Whatever the browser's window size is, the browser will adjust to 85 percent of that size. By centering the table, you can ensure that the table maintains a uniform look, in most cases, even though you cannot predict the size of the browser window that will display the table. You can also use more than one table to help accomplish appropriate spacing, among other tasks.

The example in this session will go a long way towards showing you what you can do with the knowledge of tables you now possess. Consider the partial Web page shown in Figure 12-4. The author of this page wants this information to span the user's Web page no matter how wide or how narrow the user sets the browser's window.

Although tables are simple to create and maintain, such a Web page element is *not* simple without the use of tables. The portion of the Web page you see in Figure 12-4 contains *two tables,* not just one. The tables are on top of each other, and both tables contain one row each. The top table, which forms the black band, contains one row and two columns, and the bottom table, which forms the text and the graphics, contains one row and three columns.

The reason for the two tables is so the black band across the top of the three cells can expand or contract as needed without messing up the width of the text on that band. In other words, *Today's Events* resides in the first cell to maintain its spacing, size, and height no matter how wide or narrow the Web page becomes. Yet, the rest of the cell is black and expands to fill the window no matter how wide the Web page is.

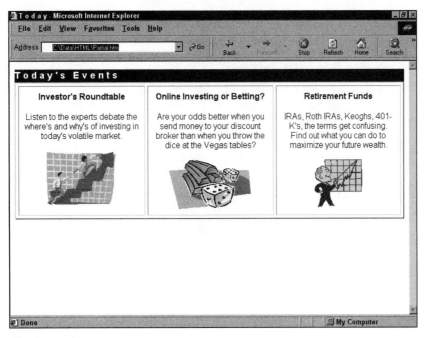

Figure 12-4
Tables make professional Web site elements possible.

Actually, the bottom table is larger but more straightforward. The Web page author created the one-row, three-column table, centered the text and graphic images inside each of the three cells, set the border size to 2 pixels, set the cellpadding to 10 pixels, and set the cellspacing to 5 pixels. (The border determines the thickness of the border lines, and the cellspacing attribute determines how wide apart the lines are that comprise the border.) In addition, the Web page author set the width= attribute in the bottom of the table to 100 percent. The table spans the user's Web browser screen no matter how wide the screen becomes.

The following code defines the bottom table:

```
<table border=2 width=100% height=177 cellspacing=5 cellpadding=10>
<tr>
  <!-- First cell of the bottom table -->
  <td width=33% height=137 valign=top align=center><font
    face="Arial" size=3>
    <b>Investor's Roundtable</b></font>
    <p><font face="Arial" size=3>Listen to the experts debate the
       where's and why's of investing in today's volatile
       market.</font></p>
    <p><img border=0 src="BD04972_.gif" width=136 height=104
       align=middle>
```

```
        </td>

        <!-- Second cell of the bottom table -->
        <td width=33% height=137 valign=top align=center><font
          face="Arial" size=3>
          <b>Online Investing or Betting?</b></font>
          <p><font face="Arial" size=3>Are your odds better when you
            send money to your discount broker than when you throw the
            dice at the Vegas tables?</font></p>
          <p><font face="Arial" size=3><img border=0 src="BD04897_.gif"
            width=160 height=94 align=center></font>
        </td>

        <!-- Third cell of the bottom table -->
        <td width=33% height=137 valign=top align=center><font
          face="Arial" size=3>
          <b>Retirement Funds</b></font>
          <p><font face="Arial" size=3>IRAs, Roth IRAs, Keoghs, 401-K's,
           the terms get confusing. Find out what you can do to maximize
           your future wealth.</font></p>
          <p><font face="Arial" size=3><img border=0 src="BS02064_.gif"
            width=94 height=91 align=middle></font>
        </td>
      </tr>
    </table>
```

Note **Notice that each cell in the lower table, defined with the `<td>` tag, consumes 33 percent of the screen width. The fact that three cells at 33 percent consume 99 percent of the screen means that the bottom table will be slightly smaller, by about a pixel or two, than the top row with the black band. However, the difference is negligible and noticeable by only the author and you.**

The top table, the black band, consists of a one-row, two-column table with no cellspacing, no border, and no cellpadding. The left cell holds the text and is fixed at 25 percent of the screen width. To fill out the right portion of the band, the second cell, also formatted with a black background color, contains a width of 75 percent and a right alignment as follows:

```
<table width=100% height=24 cellpadding=0 cellspacing=0 border=0>
<tr>
  <td valign=top align=left width=25% height=24
    bgcolor=black><font face="Arial" size=4 color=white>
    <b>T o d a y ' s   E v e n t s</b></font><br>
  </td>

  <td width=75% height=24 valign=top align=right bgcolor=black>
```

```
      </td>
    </tr>
  </table>
```

By using the width percentages, as opposed to fixed pixel widths, you can ensure that your Web pages fill out the screen as needed.

Done!

> The final part of this weekend crash course shows additional table tricks that you can use to format your site. The key is sticking with the all-important width percentages when you want your page to fill out the user's screen. Often, the right filler is nothing but an extra color band, as shown in this section. The only other option is to make your Web page stop short enough to fill the smallest of monitors and for your users with larger screens to see a white area to the right of your pages.

REVIEW

- Tables present data in ways that can be difficult without the use of tables.
- The `<table>` and `</table>` tags enclose your tables; `<tr>` and `</tr>` enclose rows; `<td>` and `</td>` enclose columns.
- Add header cells with the `<th>` and `</th>` tags for your column titles.
- Numerous methods exist for making table titles span multiple cells.
- Utilize the alignment and spanning attributes to move away from a fixed, rectangular, row-and-column look.
- Add eye-catching background colors and control spacing so that your tables maintain a professional appearance.

QUIZ YOURSELF

1. Why can't you type text in a row and column format, using tabs and extra spaces, directly into HTML? (See "Preparing Columnar Data Tables.")
2. Why might your table need header cells? (See "Specifying the Header Cells.")
3. How wide will your columns be when you use the `<td>` and `</td>` tags (assuming you use no `width=` attributes)? (See "Specifying the Columns.")

4. What is the difference between cellpadding and cellspacing? (See "Adjusting Table Spacing.")

5. What attribute enables you to create tables that span the entire user's screen width? (See "Adjusting Table Space with the Percentages and Multiple Tables.")

Forms Add Function

Session Checklist

✔ Learn why it is important to work with forms and the role that the Web host and CGI play

✔ Create forms and add and manage form fields

✔ Further refine form fields by adding default values to them

✔ Create large text areas for less structured data

**30 Min.
To Go**

In this session, you learn how to design, create, and display forms inside your Web pages, as well as how to modify form fields. Forms enable your users to enter information in a structured format that you prefer. This session introduces the building process of standard forms. The next session shows you how to spruce up your form content with additional controls.

Working With Forms

Are forms useful? Consider what happens when you walk into a doctor's office for the first time. They hand you a form. What do you do every April 15th? Fill out a form. Forms provide an efficient and consistent method for gathering information. Although some forms are better than others, forms supply information that the form-taker wants. Instead of handing you a blank piece of paper in hopes that you'll write down the correct details, the form guides you as you complete the task.

Often, you need information from your Web site's users. More than anything else, forms help enable you to collect the data that you require. Consider the contact page on IDG's Web site, as shown in Figure 13-1.

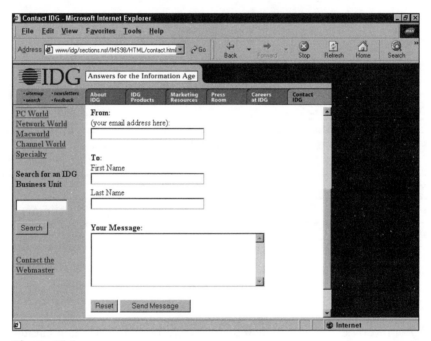

Figure 13-1
Web site forms request the correct information.

 If you do not use forms, your Web site is just a one-way street. That is, you can send information to your users, but your users cannot send information to you, except by unstructured means such as sending you e-mail when you place an e-mail hyperlink on the page.

The areas on a form are called *fields* or *text fields*. Figure 13-1 shows four fields: three that are one-line fields and one that is a multiple-line field labeled Your Message. The fields hold information that your users enter. In programming terminology, such fields are known as *text boxes*. However, a text box is not just for text; the users can enter numbers, dates, and any kind of information as well.

In addition to the fields, many forms supply *command buttons,* often just called *buttons*. Figure 13-1 shows two buttons: a Reset and a Send Message button. By clicking the appropriate button, the user can clear the current Web page form fields or submit the form to you. All form elements such as form fields and command buttons are called, collectively, *controls*. You can use other standard Windows-like controls, such as check boxes, radio buttons, and list boxes as well. Your users generally will be familiar with your Web page controls because your users are used to working with the common Windows controls.

Session 14 explains how to add check boxes, radio buttons, and list boxes to your Web pages.

Never put the text Click Me or Click Here To... on a button. Think about the buttons on a soft drink machine. They don't read, Click Here for SuperLime! The button's graphic or logo indicates what the button produces, and the user is smart enough to push the button. Assume the same about your Web site users.

Figure 13-2 shows a form that contains several kinds of controls. Again, all of these controls, which will be familiar with most users, can be added to make your forms more interactive.

Your Web host must help

Unlike all the HTML commands you've learned so far, you must contact your Web hosting company to determine exactly how to set up forms on your site. The Web host, who generally owns the server that serves up your Web site, doesn't have to help you with your HTML code but must somehow get the user's information from your form fields to you. Think about the data the user enters into a Web page form. Where does the data go? You, with your HTML knowledge up to this point, don't have any means to collect the information or transfer that information to your computer. Your host will provide the necessary details, such as path names for CGI scripts, that you will reference on your site.

As you learn more about forms, keep in mind that the form data goes directly to your Web server. You must somehow gather that information from the Web server, as the next few sections explain.

Text fields   **Check boxes**

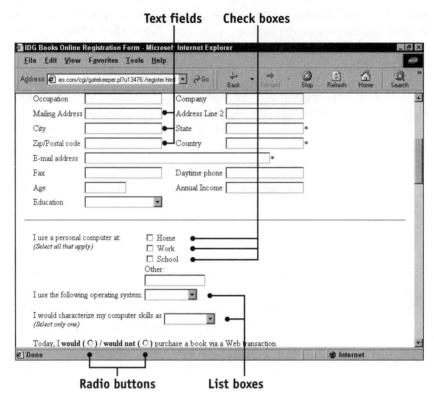

Radio buttons   **List boxes**

Figure 13-2
A Web form with several kinds of controls

CGI retrieves your data

Session 4 introduced the term *CGI* to you. The Common Gateway Interface is one of the languages of commercial Web sites because of the information that such sites collect. Think of an eCommerce transaction that might take place as the result of a customer ordering a product from your online catalog. Such an order system is nothing more than a set of forms that collect order information, including the products wanted, address, and payment information.

You don't have to run an eCommerce site to require forms. As shown on the contact page of IDG's Web site, you may need to collect information from your users that is noncommercial but still critical to your site's future direction.

The CGI script that runs on the server, in conjunction with your Web page, determines where the form information goes. Following are some common targets of form information:

- A database located on your Web server
- A nondatabase file, such as a simple text file, located on the Web server

The goal, obviously, is to get this information back to you from the Web server. You and your Web server have a relationship that enables you to retrieve such information. You have every right to the information that your site gathers, and your Web server wants to make that information available to you.

Never use a Web server that cannot make CGI scripts available to you. Otherwise, you'll never be able to utilize forms on your Web pages. Fortunately, most Web servers support the use of CGI scripts.

You can get around the CGI requirement, however, by requesting that your site e-mail you back the information that the user entered. The section on adding fields to your forms discusses how to do this.

20 Min. To Go

Creating Forms

The `<form>` and `</form>` tags surround the form's definition. Inside the `<form>` tag, you must include the `method=post` attribute, which tells the browser to post the form at the location of the path you specify. In addition to the method, you must supply the path, given to you by your Web host, for the Web server's CGI script that collects your form's information from your users and properly routes that information to you. Use the `action=` attribute to specify the CGI script location, such as:

```
<form method=post action="/cgi/info.pl">
```

Several different variations exist on posting forms, but `method=post` is probably the most common attribute that specifies the way that the data is written to the CGI program. The posting connects your form to the host's site. The form is now set up on the Web page, but nothing appears on the form. That job comes next.

One way that you can bypass the CGI script on the Web server is to have the Web page e-mail you the form's information. Instead of entering a script, you can enter the e-mail protocol inside the `<form>` tag, as follows:

```
<form method=post action="mailto:dataCollector@MyDoman.com">
```

Adding text fields

To add a text field to your form, you must label the field with a description. The description can appear to the left, above, to the right, or below the text box, but the description often appears to the left of the field. Therefore, after the opening `<form>` tag, you can enter something like the following text:

```
<p>Please type your full name:
```

You now have the form's first *prompt*. A prompt is a word, sentence, or special character that indicates what the text field that follows should hold. Leave a space after the colon so that the text field that you are getting ready to request will not jut right up to the prompt.

Never add a text field to your form without labeling that field with some kind of prompt. Otherwise, your users won't know what to type in the field. If you want the user to follow a specific format, you might even include that format in the prompt, like this:

```
<p>When were you born (mm/dd/yyyy)?
```

To place the actual text box that will receive the prompt's information, you must use the `<input>` tag. The `<input>` tag requires these two attributes:

`type=`	This specifies the type of control. The `type=` attribute specifies one of several different controls, many of which you'll learn throughout the rest of this and the next session.
`name=`	This names the data value so that the CGI script can keep the data separated from the other fields.

If the user is to enter text, as is often the case, use the `type=text` attribute. The following code includes the setup of a form, two prompts, and two text boxes that go with that prompt:

```
<form method=post>
<p>Please type your full name: </p>
<input type=text name=fullName>

<p>Please type your address: </p>
<input type=text name=address>

</form>
```

Figure 13-3 shows the form that these lines produce. Obviously, the form is overly simplistic and needs more fields and formatting, but it works well and is simple to produce.

Text fields

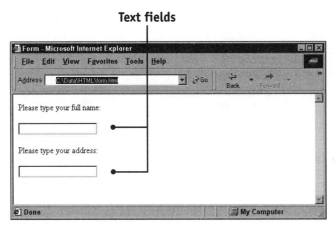

Figure 13-3
Creating this simple form is easy.

If you have the form mail the data to you instead of using a Web server CGI script to process the data, you'll get an e-mail message with each field labeled and the value typed by the user into that field. For example, for a two-field form such as the one in Figure 13-3, the e-mail you receive might look something like this:

```
fullName=John Freeport
address=917 S. Post Oak Road
```

If your form contains many named fields, the e-mail will also contain many named fields with the entered data assigned to each field.

Use a monospaced typeface for your field prompts. With this typeface, every letter takes the same width on the screen, meaning that you can control the spacing and alignment of fields on your forms. Figure 13-4 shows how the following code that uses a monospaced typeface aligns the prompts so they all end at the same location, making the input boxes align down the page:

```
<form method=post>
<p>
<font face="Monospace">
Please type your full name:
<input type=text name=fullName></p>
```

```
<!-- The nonbreaking spaces ensure that the fields align -->
<p>  Please type your address:
<input type=text name=address></p>

</font>
</form>
```

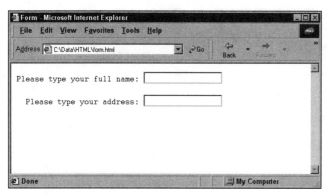

Figure 13-4
By using a monospaced typeface, you can align form fields.

Managing form fields

Use these two attributes, `size=` and `maxlength=`, to control how the user enters information into text boxes. The `size=` attribute determines how wide the text box, in characters, will be. You can further limit the user's input (by characters) by specifying a `maxlength=` attribute. Therefore, the following code displays a ten-character field box, but the user can only enter eight characters in the field:

```
<form method=post>
<p>
<font face="Monospace">
Please type the product code:
<input type=text name=fullName size=10 maxlength=8></p>
```

In addition, you can specify a `tabindex=` attribute to control the tab order of input boxes that the user's cursor jumps to as the user presses Tab. Assign a unique and sequential number, beginning with zero, to each field to control the tab order between the fields. Without the `tabindex=` attribute, the tab order should be the same as the order of fields on the screen.

Keep in mind that the tabindex= **is a relatively new HTML attribute and not all recent browsers support it. However, it doesn't hurt to specify a tab order.**

Sometimes, you'll want your users to enter a secret code in a field. Perhaps you want a password, credit card, or other data that the user may not want to appear on the screen. Someone might be looking over the user's shoulder, so you should hide the data as your user enters that data.

The type=password attribute, as opposed to type=text, inside the <form> tag handles passwords and other secret data for you. When you use a form with a password field, asterisks (*) appear on the user's screen as the user types the characters in the password.

The following code contains a password field:

```
<form method=post>
<p>
<font face="Monospace">
Please type your full name:
<input type=text name=fullName></p>

<!-- The nonbreaking space codes ensure that
     the fields line up -->
<p>  Please type your address:
<input type=text name=address></p>

<!-- The password will be hidden -->
<p>   Please enter a password:
<input type=password name=UserPassword size=10 maxlength=8> </p>
</font>
</form>
```

The password field is not only set so that asterisks appear as the user types, but the field is also limited to ten characters wide, and the user can enter only eight characters maximum. The extra spacing adds some padding that looks better on the screen than if you allowed a width that was the same limit as the password's maximum length. Figure 13-5 shows the resulting form.

Figure 13-5
Hide passwords in Web page form fields to protect your users.

Further Field Refinement

**10 Min.
To Go**

You cannot control exactly how your users enter data. In other words, no form can be perfect because no user is perfect. You might want an address, but the user enters a phone number. Therefore, you'll have some data validation to perform once you receive your data. Check to make sure, for example, that your user didn't enter a negative age or a state abbreviation that's not one of the 50 states. The problem is that you cannot validate data inside HTML.

> The CGI script that you or someone else writes for your Web server can perform some data validation. For example, if the user enters too few digits for a social security number, the CGI script can inform the user of the bad value and display the form again with the social security field blank.

Although you cannot perform true validation, you can help guide users by pre-filling some fields for them. For some fields, you know the user's value in advance. For example, the city and state might almost always be your own city and state if your program collects data from local residents only, or if you are writing HTML Web pages for a company's intranet where all users reside at the same site. For such fields, you may want to supply *default values* — values that appear in the fields that your users can keep, or change if the data happens to be incorrect.

Use the `value=` attribute to specify a default value. The following code does that:

```
<p>Please type your state:
<input type=text name=address value="CA" size=2 maxlength=2>
</p>
```

Default values require the quotes around the default value that you specify in the HTML code.

As Figure 13-6 shows, the state abbreviation CA automatically appears as the default value, but the user can change the state if another happens to be correct. By supplying a default with the most likely value, you speed up your users' data entry and accuracy.

Figure 13-6
Supply common data values for your users.

Large Text Areas

You do not have to limit input fields to a single line. Your input fields can span several rows and columns. These *text areas* enable users to enter freeform text. Such text may be beneficial for getting a user's input in sites such as:

- Sites that ask for user feedback on the site's design
- Customer service sites that require an explanation when the user requests a return authorization

- Message board sites that ask the users for their opinions

A large text area might also be needed on sites that request specific contact information, such as name and address requests, to give the user an area for special instructions, such as the name and address form shown in Figure 13-7.

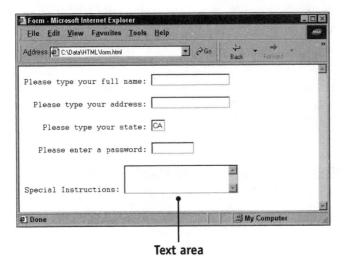

Text area

Figure 13-7
A large text area for special instructions is provided on this form.

 The text area's scroll bar becomes active when the user types more lines of text than will fit inside the text areas that you set up. The text will fit once the scroll bar becomes active.

The `<textarea>` and `</textarea>` tags enclose the field you want to specify as a text area. The `<textarea>` tag supports the following attributes:

`name=`	Names the text area field so that the CGI script or e-mail that comes back to you can identify the text area value.
`rows=`	Specifies the number of screen rows that you want to provide for the text area.
`cols=`	Specifies the number of screen columns (characters) that you want to provide for the text area.

wrap=   Determines whether or not the text automatically wraps within the text area. Without the wrap attribute, the browser may or may not wrap complete words within the text area.

You can also specify default text within a large text area by putting text between the <textarea> and </textarea> tags. For example, the following tags create a text area that spans 3 rows and 25 columns and displays Mailing information as default text in the text area:

```
<p><textarea name=mailinginfo rows=3 cols=25 wrap>
Mailing information
</textarea>
```

Done!

A read-only attribute exists (specified as readonly=readonly**) for text areas where you want to display text but not allow the user to enter new text. You, thereby, show default text that the user cannot change. Depending on the user's settings, you may want to offer the text area as a read-only for some users or for some of your Web pages. The read-only text area maintains the form's appearance while displaying the read-only text for your users. At a later time, or in another Web page, the same form might appear without the read-only attribute.**

REVIEW

- Forms allow you to obtain structured and ordered answers from your Web page users.
- The <form> and </form> tags create the form.
- The user enters data in the form's fields.
- You control the name of the fields and their descriptions so you can distinguish the fields from one another when the data returns to you via e-mail or CGI script.
- Although you can't perform true validation on forms, you can pre-fill or add default values to some fields to help prevent the inputting of invalid data.
- Text areas hold large amounts of information.

QUIZ YOURSELF

1. True or False: The CGI script runs on the Web server's computer. (See "CGI Retrieves Your Data.")

2. What appears on the screen in a password field? (See "Managing Form Fields.")

3. Where do you send your form for user accuracy validation? (See "Further Field Refinement.")

4. What is a default value? (See "Further Field Refinement.")

5. What is the difference between a text field and a text area? (See "Large Text Areas.")

Adding Form Elements

Session Checklist

✔ Create check boxes for your forms

✔ Place radio buttons on your forms

✔ Display selection lists, including pick lists, on your forms

✔ Learn how to create the submit and reset buttons to enable users
    to either submit the form's data or redo the form

**30 Min.
To Go**

This session expands on the previous session's lesson about forms. In this session, you will learn additional controls that you can place onto forms that enable your users to indicate choices and select optimum options. You'll learn how to place controls such as check boxes, radio buttons, selection lists, and reset and submit buttons, all of which are common to most users of graphical user interfaces such as the Macintosh- and Windows-based platforms.

Creating Check Boxes

Figure 14-1 shows a form with check boxes. When you set up check boxes, you can place one or more check box items on a form. In addition, you can check one or more of the items by default so the user doesn't have to change anything if he or she wants to accept the default values. By clicking a check box, the user either selects or deselects the check box item. Generally, you'll use check boxes when your user must choose zero, one, or more items from a list of several items.

selected check boxes

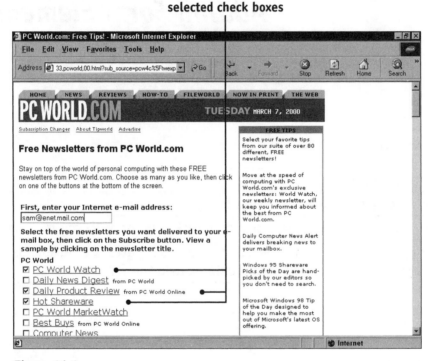

Figure 14-1
The user selects one or more newsletters to receive by clicking one or more check boxes.

Notice that a check box has a description and a box to the right of the description. When checked, the box displays a checkmark that indicates the user's preference.

To set up a check box, inside a `<form>` tag pair, insert the following `<input>` tag:

```
<input type=checkbox name=nameOfCheckbox value=groupName>
```

In the preceding tag, `nameOfCheckbox` is a name you supply so that the subsequent CGI script can store the value in a unique location, or so that the e-mail you receive from the form will have a name to assign the user's value to. The `value=`

attribute is the value assigned to that name in the CGI script or the e-mail that comes back to you from the form. In addition, the `checked=checked` attribute lets you set up default values in your check boxes.

Consider the following code that sets up six check box options:

```
<form>

<br><br>Please select your favorite vegetables:
<br><br><input type=checkbox name=Veggies value="Potatoes"
checked=checked> Potatoes
<br><input type=checkbox name=Veggies value="Cabbage" > Cabbage
<br><input type=checkbox name=Veggies value="Corn"
checked=checked> Corn
<br><input type=checkbox name=Veggies value="Carrots" > Carrots
<br><input type=checkbox name=Veggies value="Legumes" > Beans
<br><input type=checkbox name=Veggies value="Peas" > Peas

</form>
```

Figure 14-2 shows the form with check boxes that results from this code. Potatoes and corn have default checks set up, as indicated by the `checked=checked` attributes. Although you don't have to assign a value to the checked attribute, doing so ensures that your Web site will be compatible with future browsers that might require the assignment for consistency.

At first, it may seem strange that the name attribute values for each of the check boxes is the same and that the `value=` attributes are all different. Also, the `value=` attributes seem to match the text that appears on the screen next to the check box.

The `name=` attribute indicates the name that appears in the CGI script or e-mail that comes back to you, and the value assigned to that name is the value following `value=`, as mentioned earlier. Therefore, if the user selects all six of the vegetables, the values that the form will produce are:

```
veggies=Potatoes
veggies=Cabbage
veggies=Corn
veggies=Carrots
veggies=Legumes
veggies=Peas
```

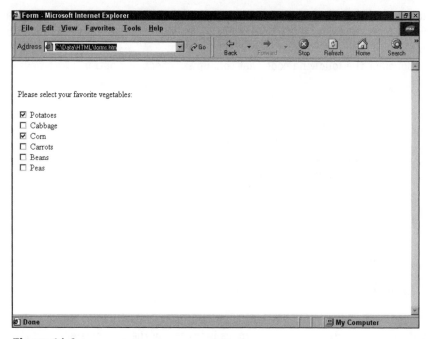

Figure 14-2
Producing the check boxes is a simple task.

Notice that the fifth value assigned is Legumes, the same value as the value= attribute for that item. The description that appears on the screen, however, is Beans because Beans is the description that follows the <input> tag and that's the value that appears as text next to the check box.

Creating Radio Buttons

Once you master check boxes, radio buttons are extremely easy. They are almost exactly the same as check boxes except that radio buttons allow only zero or one choice from the entire group of radio buttons.

In older cars, radios had push buttons that selected one and only one radio station at a time. When you pushed one button in, whatever button that was pushed in previously popped out. Radio buttons act the same way on forms.

Although the user can select only one radio button from a group of radio button selections, you can display more than one group of radio buttons on a Web page at the same time. Therefore, the user can select a maximum of one radio button from each group, but on the whole Web page, multiple radio buttons will be selected.

To set up a radio button inside a `<form>` tag pair, insert the following `<input>` tag:

```
<input type=checkbox radio=nameOfRadioButton value=groupName
[checked=checked]>
```

The optional (and seemingly redundant) `checked=checked` entry on one of the radio buttons makes it the default button in the list. Only one radio button can be the default. The following code produces the survey shown in Figure 14-3. The form contains three sets of radio buttons.

```
<form>
<H2>Computer Survey</h2>
<input type=radio name=machine value="PC"> PC
<input type=radio name=machine value="Mac" checked=checked>
Mac
<br>   <hr>   <br>
<input type=radio name=RAM value="Under64M"> Under 64 Meg
<input type=radio name=RAM value="64to128M"> 64 to 128 Meg
<input type=radio name=RAM value="Over128M"> Over 128 Meg

<br>
 <hr>
<br>

<input type=radio name=disk value="Under3G"> Under 3 Gig
<input type=radio name=disk value="3Gto7G" checked=checked>
3 Gig to 7 Gig
<input type=radio name=disk value="Over 7G"> Over 7 Gig
</form>
```

You'll notice that a dot appears next to a selected radio button, whereas a checkmark appears next to a check box. Also, if a button is selected and the user clicks another radio button within the same group, the first selected radio button will become deselected. Notice that in Figure 14-3 two of the radio buttons are selected already by default because of the `checked=checked` attribute.

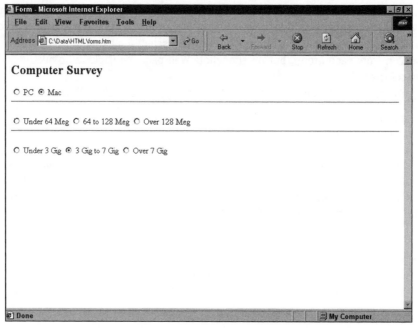

Figure 14-3
One and only one radio button can be selected from any group of radio buttons.

The name= **attribute determines which set of buttons go together in a group.**

**20 Min.
To Go**

Creating Selection Lists

Selection lists, also known as *list boxes, dropdown lists, scrolling lists, pick lists,* and *pull-down lists* depending on their style, offer the user a list of choices from which to choose. Unlike check boxes or radio buttons, selection lists can consume very little screen space while still offering the user a large list of alternatives.

You've seen selection lists before. Figure 14-4 shows one Web site with a series of selection lists. One of the lists is open because the user clicked that list's down arrow to view the options in the list. The remaining lists stay closed and save screen room.

selection lists

click to open list

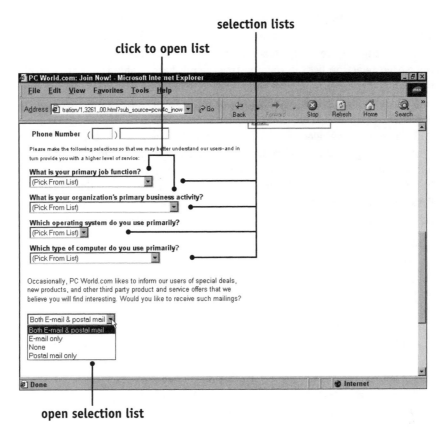

open selection list

Figure 14-4
Selection lists open to display the list of available choices.

Technically, a pick list is a selection list where the user can select one and only one item. In a way, a pick list is a replacement for a set of radio buttons: You can display a pick list or a list of radio button options when you want your user to select a single item from a list of items. A selection list, like a list of check boxes, allows for the selection of multiple items from the list.

Displaying a selection list

To set up a selection list on your form, you must enclose the list inside <select> and </select> tags. The <select> tag informs the browser that a selection list is about to appear. In addition to the name= attribute, you should specify a size= attribute that determines how many items appear in the list on the screen at one time. A list may have 40 options but may only show three on the screen, inside the closed selection list, at any one time. Scroll bars enable the user to scroll through the choices three at a time. You might choose to display only one item from the closed selection list. The closed selection lists in Figure 14-4 display only one item.

Each item in the selection list must appear between an <option> and </option> tag pair. The following code produces two selection lists, one with four options always appearing on the screen and the other with only one line appearing. The user can display all the values of the second selection list by clicking the list's down arrow and viewing the rest of the options. The first item in each list is already selected because of the selected=selected attribute.

```
<form>
<h2>Peripheral Order</h2>

<h3>Printer Selection:</h3>
 <!-- This list spans 4 rows -->
<select name=printers size=4 multiple=multiple>
 <!-- first option is selected by default -->
 <option selected=selected>PH LasetPrint 4EZ</option>
 <option>OKY DOKY InkJet 949</option>
 <option>Panamount InkJet Series a3</option>
 <option>Canyon BCJ 3 </option>
 <option>Pioneers LaserQuiet </option>
 <option>Sonny 54 DaisyWheel </option>
 <option>Blue Moon Ribbonless </option>
</select>
<br>  <hr> <br>
<h3>Storage Selection:</h3>
<!-- This list spans one row -->

<select name=storage size=1 multiple=multiple>
 <!-- first option is selected by default -->
 <option selected=selected>Jazzy 2Gig removable</option>
 <option>Cheata 5 Gig</option>
 <option>MaxStorage 3.9 Gig</option>
 <option>MaxStorage 8.7 Gig</option>
```

```
   <option>SlowMoving Tape System 4.1 Gig</option>
   <option>BroadStore 9 Gig removable</option>
   <option>One set of hole-punch cards</option>
  </select>
</form>
```

Figure 14-5 shows the two selection lists that appear from this code.

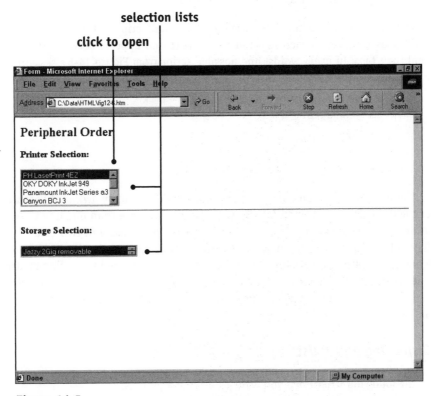

Figure 14-5
Two selection lists, one with four options displayed and another with only one option displayed

The `multiple=multiple` attribute enables the user to select multiple items from the selection list, unlike a pick list that would not contain this attribute. Most browsers support just the multiple attribute without the redundant `=multiple` assignment, but for future compatibility, you should assign the attribute.

The user should keep the following things in mind when selecting multiple list items:

- Hold the Ctrl key while clicking on each item.
- When selecting items that appear together, click the top item, scroll down to display the final item, hold Ctrl and Shift, and click the final item. The browser will select all items between the first and final items inclusively.
- Click on a selected item again to deselect it.

The values returned from the form's e-mail or CGI script will be the selection list's name assigned to each selected value's text that appears between the `<option>` tags. In other words, one possible script from Figure 14-5's session might contain the following data:

```
printers=PH LaserJet 4EZ
printers=Canyon BCJ 3
storage=Jazzy 2Gig removable
storage=Cheata 5 gig
storage=SlowMoving Tape System 4.1 Gig
```

The one-line selection list shown in Figure 14-5 is actually awkward because of the extremely small scroll bar. By not allowing for more than one line to show at one time, the `size=1` attribute severely limits the usability of this control. Without multiple lines, the user has a difficult time determining how many items are actually selected. Perhaps the control should be expanded to display multiple lines at one time, or perhaps the data better fits a pick list where only one item can be selected from the list at one time. The next section explains how to set up a pick list.

Displaying a pick list

In the following situations, you want to display a pick list:

- You want to devote only one line of the screen to the entire selection list, except when the user opens the list by clicking the down arrow.
- The user can select one and only one item from the list.

You can display a pick list and still specify a size attribute greater than 1. A scroll bar appears, and the pick list spans more than a single row. The user, however, will not be able to select more than one value if you do not specify the `multiple=multiple` attribute.

If you do not initially set up the pick list with a `selected=selected` attribute specified, no option will be selected when the user first sees the list, but as soon as the user clicks the down arrow to open the list, the browser will select the first item in the list by highlighting that item. The user then can select a different item. Once the user selects an item by clicking on that item, the pick list closes back to a one-line selection list, and the clicked item becomes the item that appears in the one-row selection list box.

The following code displays the storage items as a pick list, and Figure 14-6 shows the resulting pick list open with one of the items selected by the user.

```
<h3>Storage Selection:</h3>
<!-- This list spans one row -->

<select name=storage size=1 >
 <option>Jazzy 2Gig removable</option>
 <option>Cheata 5 Gig</option>
 <option>MaxStorage 3.9 Gig</option>
 <option>MaxStorage 8.7 Gig</option>
 <option>SlowMoving Tape System 4.1 Gig</option>
 <option>BroadStore 9 Gig removable</option>
 <option>One set of hole-punch cards</option>
</select>
```

Submitting the Forms

Once the user finishes entering all the form's control values, the user is ready to submit the form's data. You should supply a *submit button* at the bottom or on the side of your form that your user can click to submit the form for processing. Before clicking submit, however, the user might spot some data-entry errors. Therefore, the user may want to make changes to the form. You can give the user a way to reset the form completely, setting all values back to their initial default state, by offering a reset button. The following sections explain how to create both kinds of form buttons.

open pick list

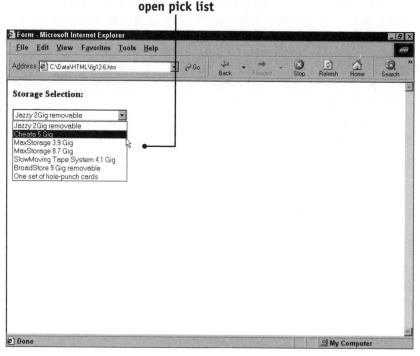

Figure 14-6
The user can select one and only one item from a pick list.

Creating the submit button

**10 Min.
To Go**

The submit button sends the form's data to the Web server's CGI script, or to you via e-mail, depending on how you set up your form's action. By clicking the submit button, your user tells the browser to ship the form's data to its intended recipient.

When you're ready to place the submit button on your form, enter the following command that uses an <input> tag:

```
<input type=submit value="Finished">
```

The button contains whatever text the value= attribute specifies, which, in this case, is Finished. Although you don't have to put quotation marks around the attribute if you only want to label the button with a single word, it's standard practice to do so. As stated in earlier sessions, some HTML programmers put quotes around *all* attribute values, even numbers. Figure 14-7 shows the submit button at the bottom of a form.

Submit button

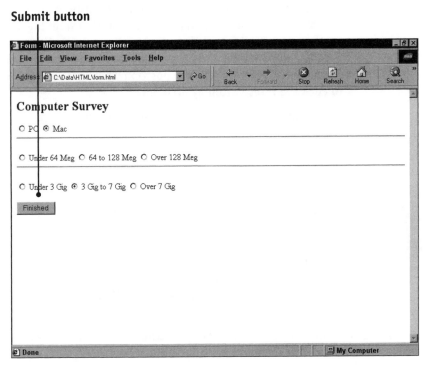

Figure 14-7
The submit button sends the form's data to the Web server.

As with most buttons inside graphical user environments, the submit button has a three-dimensional appearance that changes when the user clicks the button so it looks as if the button were actually depressed.

Creating the reset button

The opposite of the submit button, the reset button clears all the values in all the form's fields, resets all selection lists back to their original default values if any are specified, and enables the user to redo the form completely from the beginning. Often, a submit button appears next to a reset button.

Be careful where you place the reset button. The top-to-bottom, left-to-right nature of Web pages can encourage users to click the reset button when they mean to click the submit button, if the reset button appears too close to the final field on the form. As a matter of safety, separate the reset button from the submit button and from the rest of the form with a vertical line made from a graphic image. Then place the reset button within easy reach of the form, but not in a position where the user is likely to click the reset button by accident.

You should also use the `<input>` tag to create a reset button. The type will inform the browser of the kind of button you're requesting. For example, here is the code to include a reset button:

```
<input type=reset value="Erase all data - Start new form">
```

The browser handles both the resetting of fields and the submitting of data when the user clicks either the reset or the submit button. No further coding, other than the `<input>` tag that sets up each of these buttons, is required on your part. Once you place a reset button, for instance, you know that the form will reset when the user clicks the button without you having to do anything else.

Done!

As with the submit button, the reset button's text will include all the text between the quotations in the `value=` attribute that you specify.

REVIEW

- Display check boxes when you want to give users a list of choices from which they can select zero, one, or more options.
- Radio buttons allow for *mutually exclusive* selections; that is, the user can select no more than one choice.
- Selection lists save screen space because they scroll and open when requested.
- You can fix a selection list at a specific number of rows, or you can specify a one-row selection list that opens when the user clicks the list's down arrow.
- A pick list does not allow for multiple selections, only one at a time.

QUIZ YOURSELF

1. How does a user deselect a check box? (See "Creating Check Boxes.")

2. How do you know which check box options the user selected? (See "Creating Check Boxes.")

3. Is it possible for a user to view a Web page and not select a radio button? (See "Creating Radio Buttons.")

4. What is the difference between a one-line selection list and a one-line pick list? (See "Creating Selection Lists.")

5. What resets fields when the user clicks a reset button? (See "Creating the Reset Button.")

Transparent Imaging

Session Checklist

✔ Understand the basics of transparent images

✔ Use a graphics program that produces transparency

✔ Learn about the problems associated with anti-aliased graphics

✔ Create a one-pixel transparent image

✔ Specify low-resolution images

**30 Min.
To Go**

This short session returns to the graphical aspects of your Web pages. Although much of this session deals indirectly with HTML, most of the focus is on graphic design and creation. Your Web page creation involves much graphic creation for images, buttons, and other Web page elements, and no HTML coder gets very far without a mastery of graphics and how graphics work best on Web pages.

One of the most important imaging concepts that you can learn is transparent imaging — that is, creating images with backgrounds that are invisible so that the Web page shows through. When you place a transparent image over another image, or over text, or over a Web page that contains a background image, the transparent portion of your image allows the items underneath to show through. Only the non-transparent portion of your image remains on top of the rest of the page.

About Transparent Images

Although you can make transparent JPEG images, many of today's browsers do not yet support them. Transparent GIFs, on the other hand, are popular and have been for years. Most popular graphics programs enable you to create transparent images. In addition to graphics programs, some Web page-creation programs such as Dreamweaver and FrontPage 2000 also enable you to convert a transparent image to a nontransparent one. Nothing you do in HTML, however, can make a nontransparent image appear transparent in a browser.

You may wonder why transparent images are so important. Without transparency, your images take on a rectangular shape. Figure 15-1 shows the difference. The image on the right side is an example of a transparent image. The image on the left side is an example of a nontransparent image. Notice the white rectangular outline around the nontransparent image. Such images are somewhat unwieldy and add too much bulk to your Web page. With most users still using low resolutions and 17-inch screens and smaller, you want all the screen real estate that you can get, and nontransparent images take far too much away from your page.

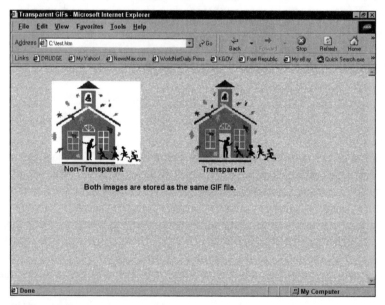

Figure 15-1
A transparent image does not carry with it a rectangular background that the nontransparent image has.

From the very beginning of the GIF image's initial design, you could specify one color as a transparent color. In other words, that color takes on the color of whatever is under it when you place the image on the screen.

As with *chromo key,* a process in television where actors stand in front of blue backgrounds that are later removed by the camera and replaced by a different background, a transparent color will fade to nothing when presented against another image.

The only real trick in making a GIF image transparent is to decide which color should be the transparent color. Generally, this color will be the color in the image's rectangular background area.

Transparency can only be applied to one color, which means that an image with a multi-colored background works poorly as a transparent image.

Making Images Transparent

Unfortunately, you cannot make a GIF image transparent with HTML code. You must use a graphic image-editing program or a Web page-creation program that supports the creation or conversion of transparent images. The steps for turning a GIF image into a transparent image are similar for almost all graphic image-editing programs.

Many freeware and shareware programs exist that can perform GIF transparency. To find out about the available programs, check out *Transparency* (http://www.macshare.com/graphic-to.html/**), the *GIF Construction Set* (**http://www.mindworkshop.com/**), and *LViewPro* (**http://oak.0akland.edu/simtel.net/win95/graphics.html**).**

Most of the editing programs follow the same procedure for converting an image to a transparency, although they do use different menu options and screen controls.

To give you an idea of the steps required, the following procedure details how you would make a GIF image transparent in PhotoDraw 2000:

1. Load the GIF image into PhotoDraw. The image should come into the program as a rectangle, possibly with a white background, as shown in Figure 15-2.

Non-transparent background

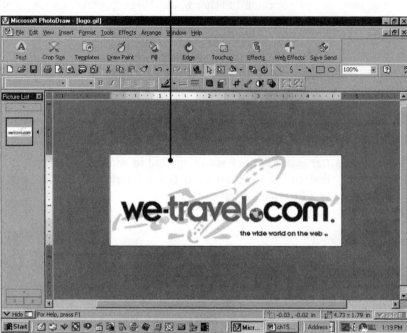

Figure 15-2
The GIF image to be made transparent

2. Select the transparent color. To do this, make sure that you know the exact color of the image's rectangular background area. (White will be the background color of Figure 15-2.) You can select the background color from the graphics program's color palette and draw a line over the background to make sure you've got the correct color. For white backgrounds, the selection of the background color is simple. For other colors, the color palette typically displays all colors in the image so that you can choose the color you desire.

3. Once you know the exact background color, select the Set Transparent Color tool (all graphics programs that support transparent GIF images will have such a tool or one similarly named). The cursor should change to a crosshair.

4. Click an area of the background color that you want to be transparent. The program should change the background color to show that the transparency is made. You won't be able to see the transparent effect just yet.

5. Save the image under a new name, perhaps with the filename suffix trans, such as logo-trans.gif, so you have both the transparent and the nontransparent image intact.

In addition to the transparent GIF image file, save the transparent image file using your graphics program default extension. This ensures that you have the highest resolution possible in case you want to edit the image later.

The $\langle$img$\rangle$ tags are explained in Session 7.

When you place the transparent GIF onto your Web page using the $\langle$img$\rangle$ tag, any images already at that location, including the background if you've supplied a background image, will show through your transparent region. Figure 15-3 shows the logo in Figure 15-2 as it appears after its background is made transparent.

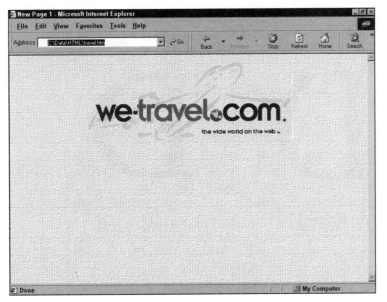

Figure 15-3
The GIF image's background now shows through the transparent region.

Never use the same image's background color inside your image. If you do, the color becomes transparent everywhere it appears. Your image might show through the middle as well as around the edges if the middle section's color matches that of the background.

20 Min. To Go

Transparency Problems Caused by Anti-Aliasing

If your image is an *anti-aliased* image, making the image transparent might be more difficult. Anti-aliasing is sometimes used to smooth the edges of certain images. The anti-aliasing process occurs during the image's design and creation, or perhaps later in an editing session with a graphics program that can perform anti-aliasing.

Figure 15-4 shows how anti-aliasing can help make an image look rounder than it really is. The figure presents the letter *D* both in a regular and anti-aliased close-up pattern. Although the difference is minor when the image is viewed at normal screen size, distance, and resolution, anti-aliasing's smoother edges can make small text or lines within a drawing appear more natural.

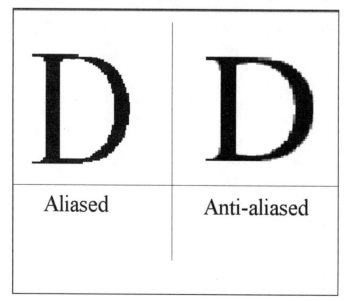

Figure 15-4
The right letter is anti-aliased for a smoother line set.

Notice that shading using a color like that of the actual image (in this case, the "image" is the letter *D*) is used to fill in the gaps to produce the rounder anti-aliased image. Once the image is reduced to its regular size and resolution, the shaded color fools the eye into thinking that the image is smoother than it really is.

Anti-aliasing can confuse your transparent GIF images if you use anti-aliasing anywhere within the image's background, because of the multiple shades it uses. When you pick a background color, several more shades may help comprise the background, and you'll miss those. Your transparency will look incomplete. You'll have to edit the image as best you can and apply a uniform color throughout the entire background. The image may look somewhat jagged around the edges, but it's the best you can do.

Another problem associated with anti-aliasing is that a halo effect often appears around transparent images that are anti-aliased. You must edit these images pixel-by-pixel inside your graphics editing program if you want to ensure a total elimination of the halo, but that might compromise the smoothness of the image. Anti-aliasing represents one of many trade-offs that you make when creating Web pages. Although most graphics programs enable you to save an image with either aliasing or anti-aliasing, the default is probably anti-aliased images.

The One-Pixel Transparent Image Trick

This session's title makes the subject sound much more fascinating than it is. As a matter of fact, many HTML programmers state, publicly, that they do not approve of this trick. Then, with doors closed, they use it in their own pages!

A one-pixel image is a picture you create in a graphics program that consumes only a single pixel of space. By stretching such a small image, you can blank out a large area of a Web page without adding download and space overhead to your page other than the single pixel.

Here's what you do to create a one-pixel transparent image:

1. Start your graphics program.
2. Draw a large white box with the edge white as well.
3. Make the image's transparent color white. This converts the entire image to a transparent image.
4. Adjust the size of the image to one pixel-by-one pixel.
5. Save the file as a GIF file to your images directory.

You now have an empty space that is a single pixel square. Keeping in mind that the `<img>` tag supports attributes that stretch and lengthen GIF images, you can place this one pixel throughout your Web pages wherever you need spacing. Although tables are great tools for aligning text and pictures, a transparent one-pixel image, stretched so a uniform size is left between all your Web page elements, makes laying out your pages much simpler.

Figure 15-5 shows a Web page with its second group of numbered items indented to the right. The background contains a pattern so that a transparent pixel, stretched to the width of the indented text, provides a simple way to indent the text. By inserting the pixel and enlarging it as the code in Listing 15-1 demonstrates, you shift the second group of text lines to the right by the width of the image.

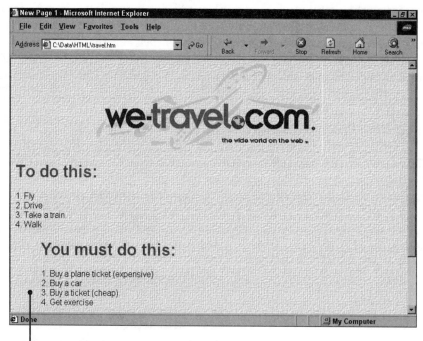

enlarged transparent pixel image is here

Figure 15-5
A one-pixel transparent image is useful for spacing.

Listing 15-1
You can use a transparent pixel image to indent a group of text.

```
<h1>To do this:</h1>
1. Fly
<br>2. Drive
<br>3. Take a train
<br>4. Walk
<br><br>
<!-- Without the align=left, the image would appear
     between the two lists. -->
<img src="images/trans.gif" width=45 height=250 align=left>
<h1>You must do this:</h1>
1. Buy a plane ticket (expensive)
<br>2. Buy a car
<br>3. Buy a ticket (cheap)
<br>4. Get exercise
```

**10 Min.
To Go**

Specifying a Low-Resolution Prototype

High-resolution images are graphic image files that are large, contain lots of colors, and show high detail of picture clarity. Many modern digital cameras shoot high-resolution photographs. Generally, a monitor is limited to 72 dpi (dots per inch), whereas most high-resolution images take much more than 72 dpi of resolution. Therefore, such an image is much larger than needed for a Web page; the extra resolution goes unused.

If you absolutely must use a large graphic image, consider making two images: one the regular image and the other a scaled-down version with a much lower resolution and fewer colors. The <img> tag supports a special lowsrc= attribute that will bring in a lower-resolution image that you supply and, once that image is loaded, will begin loading the higher-resolution image.

The low-resolution image might contain just enough detail for the user to see what is being loaded next. Perhaps you use a black-and-white version of the larger, colorful image as the low-resolution picture that takes the place of a higher-resolution photo. The low-resolution attribute works something like a dithered image in that the user sees a portion of the real image immediately and then the high-resolution becomes visible once the full image loads.

Your low-resolution image must match the high-resolution image in pixel size or the second image will not replace the first one properly.

Once you create a scaled-down version of a high-resolution, slow-loading image, you can specify the low-resolution image with the use of the `<img>` tag, as follows:

```
<img src="images/company.jpg" lowsrc="images/companyLight.gif"
width=350 height=350 border=3 alt="Company Personnel">
```

The `lowsrc=` attribute displays the low-resolution version of the image. That low-resolution image displays while the higher-resolution image, specified by the `src=` attribute, loads in the background. When the browser finishes loading the high-resolution image, the browser replaces the low-resolution image with the better graphic.

Session 10 explains how thumbnail images are used.

Done!

A low-resolution image, specified with the `lowsrc=` attribute, is not the same thing as a thumbnail image. With a thumbnail image, you have to take action to see the larger and higher-resolution image. With the low-resolution image specified with the `lowsrc=` attribute, the Web browser automatically loads the lower-resolution image first and then replaces that low-resolution image with the high-resolution image as soon as the larger image finishes arriving from the Web server.

REVIEW

- Transparency creates a see-through effect for GIF image backgrounds.
- You need to use a graphics program to convert a GIF image to a transparent GIF image.
- Anti-aliasing can cause extra colors to interfere with transparency.
- Keep a transparent one-pixel image handy to act as a filler when you need exact spacing between text and graphics on your Web page. The image gives you more precise control than tables do.
- A low-resolution image can load much faster so that your users can view something until the higher-resolution equivalent image loads and appears.

QUIZ YOURSELF

1. How many colors can be transparent at one time in a typical transparent GIF image? (See "About Transparent Images.")

2. True or False: You can make an image transparent with HTML. (See "Making Images Transparent.")

3. What does an alpha channel do? (See "Transparency Problems Caused by Anti-Aliasing.")

4. When might a halo effect appear? (See "Transparency Problems Caused by Anti-Aliasing.")

5. Why are images that are specified with the lowres= attribute not considered thumbnails? (See "Specifying a Low-Resolution Prototype.")

Advanced Color and Imaging Techniques

Session Checklist

✔ Understand that Web-safe black-and white-colors may be safe but do not always produce great results

✔ Keep your site less crowded by utilizing whitespace

✔ Create navigation bars to give your users a familiar way to traverse your site

✔ Create banners to divide your site so that users can easily distinguish between common areas

✔ Master graphics tips and shortcuts to make eye-catching Web pages

30 Min. To Go

As Session 8 explained, you should use only the 216 Web-safe colors if you want to maintain consistency across the range of browsers used today, and you should use colors that work well together, which is not always easy given the 216 Web-safe color limits. In this session, you learn some additional color issues and tips to consider when designing Web sites. You also learn some additional graphics techniques, namely creating navigation bars and banners.

A Problem with Displaying Black-and-White Photos

The problem with using only Web-safe colors is the low number of Web-safe colors available: 216. If you do not want a user's browser to substitute another color for a color you desired, stick with the Web-safe colors. Although the user's resolution might make your Web site look different, at least the colors are safe and will come across to the end browser properly.

A problem occurs when you limit your Web page design to 216 colors but you attempt to display black-and-white photos on your page. As the artist Ansel Adams proved, black-and-white photography can be beautiful and can convey tones and feelings that get lost in color photography. Perhaps you have black-and-white photos of relatives from long ago that you want to put on your site. Your site may be a historical site that shows Old West pictures or mobster bosses from the roaring twenties.

If you put the pictures on your Web page, you'll soon see that they have a color problem. The black-and-white pictures can appear grainy. At first, this makes no sense because the colors black and white are a part of the 216 Web-safe colors. Black uses the hexadecimal color #000000, and white uses #FFFFFF. Black and white are even among the 16 named colors that you can assign to backgrounds and text. The following code, which changes the color of specific text, is allowed and should work in all browsers your users use:

```
<font color=black>
<font color=white>
```

Nevertheless, a black-and-white photo contains many more colors than black and white. It may contain hundreds of shades of grays, working as black-and-white transitional colors. Table 16-1 lists the only four shades of gray that the 216 Web-safe colors include.

Table 16-1
Browser-Safe Shades of Gray

Decimal	Hexadecimal Equivalents
51-51-51	#333333
102-102-102	#666666
153-153-153	#999999
204-204-204	#CCCCCC

The answer is, no good answer exists. If you *must* use black-and-white photography, you are stuck with lousy pictures due to the limited color rendition, or you must increase the number of colors you use and hope for the best when the user browses your page. Use JPEG images and not GIFs, as JPEG grays render better than GIFs.

Never make assumptions about color substitution. If you offer a picture with multiple shades of gray on your site, browsers are free to turn your light grays into pink if the browser should deem it necessary.

Design Tip: White Works Well

Your Web page design could benefit from *whitespace,* also called *negative space,* which, basically, is blank space between elements. Ample whitespace in your Web page is crucial so that your pages don't take on a too-busy appearance. (However, keeping your Web page free of clutter isn't always possible due to the lack of screen real estate for which you must design.) White is a tremendous design tool that is underutilized by many Web masters. But don't limit whitespace just to the color white, because whitespace is more of a concept than a color. Use whitespace to group items together or to keep items spaced apart. For example, instead of keeping borders around every cell of every table you create, and instead of overusing the horizontal rule, consider doing nothing but separating your Web page elements with blank space.

Consider the simple Web page shown in Figure 16-1. The message is simple, the page is simple, but the page contains too much of something. What can it be?

The answer is that the page contains too much of *everything.* Too much *non-whitespace* exists. The page is overly busy. Even with the browser's toolbars and status bar turned off, the page doesn't completely fit the browser window in spite of the small amount of information presented. Obviously, this is an extreme example, but consider what happens when one does away with the fluff while still keeping the message. Figure 16-2 shows a much simpler example, yet it works very well. The graphics are spaced better, the background doesn't consume the message, the design and layout are slightly underdeveloped but far less busy, and the page is hands-down a better Web page. Even with the status bar and toolbar on, the page fits well.

Figure 16-1
Does a design problem exist with this Web page?

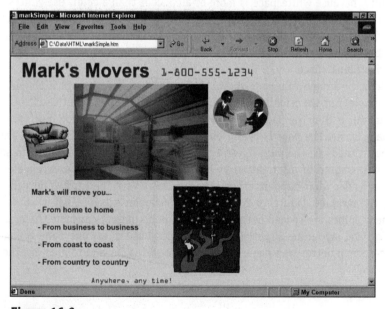

Figure 16-2
*Separating elements with nothing more than whitespace improves
this Web page.*

Creating Navigation Bars

One of the most useful places for GIF-based *icons* is in *navigation bars*. An icon is a small image that represents something else, such as the images you see next to the Windows Start menu options. A navigation bar works like a menu for your Web page, containing a series of icons that appears across the top of the screen or along the edge of the screen.

Figure 16-3 shows a navigation bar that can appear at the top of a Web page. The user clicks an icon, and that icon's page, represented by a hyperlink, loads and displays on the user's screen. The nice thing about navigation bars is that you will probably use the same navigation bar or parts of the same navigation bar in several of your site's pages. You'll insert the navigation bar code at the top of each page on the site so that the user can easily traverse the site with the familiar bar.

Navigation bars can help reduce your site's page-loading time if you put the navigation icons in your images folder. Don't be afraid to use the same image twice on your Web site. Many of your site's pages, for example, may share the same navigation bar or parts of the navigation bar. By using the same GIF image, and by putting all your images inside the site's images folder (as discussed in Session 7), you ensure that the user's browser only has to download your graphic images once even if the images appear multiple times throughout your site.

Here is the code that produced the navigation bar in Figure 16-3:

```
<!-- Navigation bar follows -->
  <a href=Breads.html>
    <img src="MaryBread.gif" border=0 hspace=35 alt=Breads></a>
  <a href=Fruits.html>
    <img src="MaryFruit.gif" border=0 hspace=35 alt=Fruits
width=87 height=87></a>
  <a href=Desserts.html>
    <img src="MaryDessert.gif" border=0 hspace=35
alt=Desserts></a>
  <a href=Coffees.html>
    <img src="MaryCoffee.gif" border=0 hspace=35 alt=Coffees
width=70 height=73></a>
  <a href=Coffees.html>
    <img src="MaryToGo.gif" border=0 hspace=35 alt="ToGo
Information" width=70 height=73></a>
```

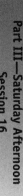

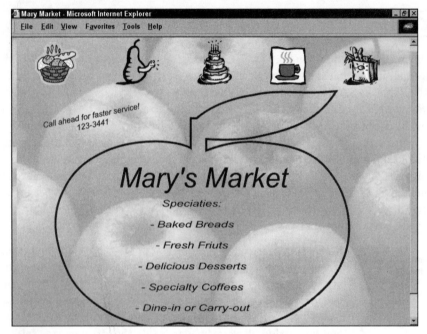

Figure 16-3
Navigation bars offer the user a method to traverse the site.

Never create a navigation bar without adding alternative text titles with the `alt=` **attribute. If you were to supply a navigation bar without the alternative text, any user who has turned off the display of graphics will not be able to use your navigation bar unless they know beyond a shadow of a doubt what Web pages your icons are supposed to represent.**

Web pages that use frames often contain navigation bars across the top frame or along the left side of the page. The remaining frames hold the remaining contents of the page.

See Session 18 for a discussion of navigation bars in frames.

**10 Min.
To Go**

Creating Banners for Style

The HTML programmer's world includes the HTML editor, as well as one or more graphics programs. Adding just the right touch to a Web site may be difficult. Often, you will create the graphics that you use in your site, because not only do copyrights restrict your use of images you'll find elsewhere, but also matching an image to the tone of the Web site seems impossible at times.

Therefore, you'll don your *chapeau* (that's French for hat and all the famous artists seem to wear them) and design images that complement your sites. HTML newcomers find that creating artistic banners that run across the top of a page or down a side is extremely easy. A *banner* can be just about anything that lies across your entire Web page or that takes space on the side or at the bottom. Many commercial Web sites use banners for advertisements. The banners must be eye-catching, use Web-safe colors, and load quickly, quite a challenge for such a small image space. Many banners take advantage of the capability to animate GIF images but consume very little page-loading time.

The following sections conclude this short session by describing guidelines you'll want to follow when generating banner graphics with programs such as Adobe Illustrator, PhotoShop, PhotoDraw, or Paint Shop Pro.

Bordering banners

Place band (or bordering) banners that you want spread across the entire screen in a table consisting of a single cell, and set the cell width to 100 percent. The banner will stretch to the user's screen. Obviously, if your banner includes a picture or text or both, such stretching won't work. A stretched banner does work well, however, for a formatted set of bars and designs that run across the screen to add a ceiling to your page such as the one in Figure 16-4.

Session 12 explains how to work with tables.

Bands don't have to cross the top of your Web page. Many fall down the left or right side of the page and separate a navigation bar or hyperlinks from the body of the Web page. To create vertical banners, a simple trick that you can use in almost any graphics program is to first create a rectangle with some pattern, such as the gradient fill shown in the Paint screen in Figure 16-5.

Part III—Saturday Afternoon
Session 16

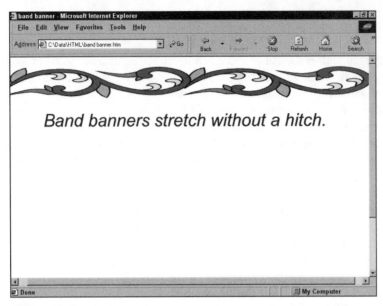

Figure 16-4
Stretch band banners across the screen in a table cell.

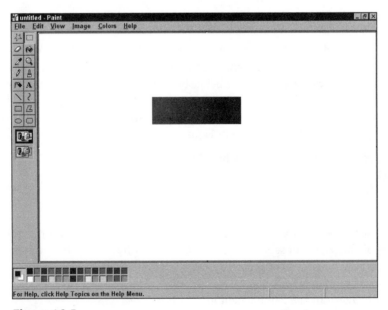

Figure 16-5
This simple rectangular image will help produce fantastic vertical banners.

Once you save your rectangle pattern, you can create a table on your Web page that begins in the upper-left corner and falls down the left side of the page. In other words, make the cell's height 100 percent. By coloring the page's background with the color on the right side, you instantly create an attractive theme-like Web page background even if you're not an artist, as Figure 16-6 shows. The page now includes a vertical banner on the left side of the screen that you can use for a navigation bar's background or for other kinds of hyperlinks.

Session 8 explains how to change the background color.

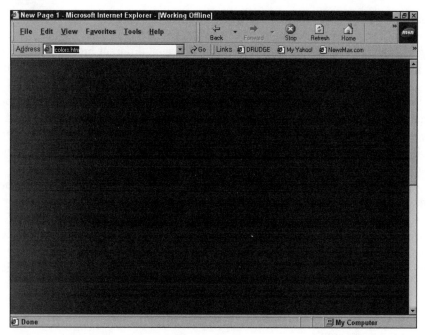

Figure 16-6
The page now includes a vertical banner.

Instead of putting the image in a table cell, you can create the image with a huge height, something like 2,000 pixels. You can stretch the image to 2,000 pixels using most graphics programs. If the image is a GIF image, it consumes an extremely small amount of storage and takes hardly any time to load. When several pixels of the same color appear in a GIF file, the GIF algorithm squeezes the size of the file dramatically. Instead of storing all those same-colored pixels, the GIF file stores only the color and the number of pixels required at that point in the image.

Advertising and headline banners

So many sites use advertising and headline banners that a site almost seems lost without them. Because banners often contain text, created as a graphic image, you'll want to test the banners you create in several different browsers using several different resolutions to ensure that the banner looks like you want it to look.

Make banners accent the page, not distract from the page's content. They should consume a reasonable amount of space. At the same time, you want a banner that contains your company logo to be seen and recognized, and you want your advertising banners to be noticed as well: You want the click-through credit often given for such banners, or if the advertising banner is your own company's, you want the banner to generate sales of a product.

Keep the banner's size limited to approximately 300 pixels wide. Keep the banner's height limited to around 100 pixels tall. Center the banner on your Web page or place the banner inside a table's cell that falls in the upper-center of the Web page or that remains in one of the corners. If you let the banner appear freestyle without any placement instructions, the banner can end up off-center on many browser screens. To make the banner appear quickly, reduce the number of colors (assuming the banner is a GIF file), even though you're sticking to Web-safe colors to make the banner load quickly. As always, add alternative text tags to the banner so that the user who is viewing your page with graphics turned off knows what the banner represents.

Most of today's Web-aware graphics programs will create a properly sized layout for banners that you want to produce.

Final Graphics Tips

After learning about Web page graphics and color techniques throughout this session and the previous ones, keep the following tips in mind:

- Always design and create your graphics using your graphics program's highest resolution. You have more control over the image's specifics. Only when you finally save the image for your Web page using the GIF or JPEG format will you decrease the resolution for the Web page.

- Utilize Web-safe colors. Generally, the graphics program will let you select a Web-safe palette so that only Web-safe colors are available to you.

- Save the image in the program's native format, as you design the image. For example, users of Microsoft PhotoDraw will create and save their images with the filename extension .mix. By saving with the program's native extension, you keep the image intact and maintain important layers that you'll further refine as you develop the image.

- Save a copy of the image in the Web page format and desired resolution once you've created the design in the high-resolution and native file format. If the image doesn't render properly on your Web page, you can always edit the high-resolution file.

Done!

- Graphics programs enable you to save fancy text as a GIF image so that your user's font selection won't change the look of the text.

REVIEW

- Even the black-and-white Web-safe colors can damage the look of JPEG files in many user's browsers.

- Ample whitespace keeps your site less cluttered and easier to navigate and maintain.

- Navigation bars, which work like a menu and contain icons, provide a uniform traversal path for your site's users.

- Banners, which can spread across and down the left or right side of your Web page, provide colorful separating areas.

- You should maintain the standard size guidelines when putting advertising and logo banners at the top of your sites.

Quiz Yourself

1. How do the Web-safe colors affect blank-and-white photographs? (See "A Problem with Displaying Black-and-White Photos.")

2. How does the use of whitespace improve your site's tone? (See "Design Tip: White Works Well.")

3. How does a user traverse your site's navigation bar if the user has graphics turned off? (See "Creating Navigation Bars.")

4. True or False: When creating images and banners in your graphics program, you should save the file in the GIF or JPEG format as you work to keep the image in its most optimum Web page format during the process. (See "Creating Banners for Style.")

5. How does a 2,000-pixel-high GIF banner load quickly? (See "Bordering Banners.")

PART

III

Saturday Afternoon
Part Review

1. What protocol opens the user's e-mail program?

2. What happens if the user doesn't have an e-mail program set up when the user clicks an e-mail link?

3. What tag encloses an HTML comment?

4. What code would you have to write to display the following text in the browser window?

   ```
   The <p> tag is an HTML paragraph tag.
   ```

5. True or False: Tables form from top-to-bottom and right-to-left.

6. What tag specifies a table row and what tag specifies a table cell?

7. How does a `<th>` cell differ, in appearance, from a `<td>` cell?

8. What is the difference between the `cellpadding=` and the `cellspacing=` attributes?

9. True or False: A cell with a `width=` attribute of 100 percent spans 100 percent of the row on the browser window.

10. What are the two ways to specify table cell widths?

11. What is the difference between a field and a field label?

12. What are the two common methods that a user's form data returns back to you?

13. What tag specifies a text-input field?

14. What character appears in a password field?

15. What is the difference between a text field and a text area?

16. When do scroll bars appear in a text area?

17. What is the difference between check boxes and radio buttons?

18. Why does antialiasing hinder transparency?

19. Describe the process that the `lowsrc=` attribute creates when the user displays a Web page.

20. What is a navigation bar?

PART

IV

Saturday Evening

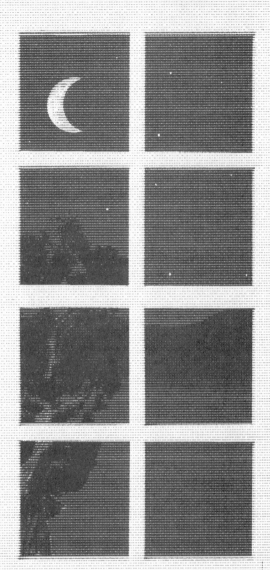

Marketing Your Web Site with HTML

Session Checklist

✔ Use meta tags to describe your site to search engines and get it noticed

✔ Understand how to push-market a Web site that works best as a pull-market product

✔ Learn other methods besides meta tags to get your site noticed

✔ Don't resort to HTML trickery to get your site noticed

30 Min. To Go

N o tutorial on HTML would be complete without some discussion about marketing your Web site, or, in other words, how to get an audience for your Web site. This session continues your HTML tutorial by teaching you how to use meta tags, the tags that determine how search engines locate your site. This session also discusses how to ensure that your site gets noticed by search engines in other ways without resorting to bait-and-switch techniques that will turn off your users and get your site booted from the search engines.

Getting Your Site Noticed with Meta Tags

A *meta tag* (`<meta>`) is a tag that appears in the header section of your Web page that contains general information about your site. Place your page's meta tags after the `<title>` and `</title>` tags but before the `</head>` tag that terminates the header section. As you can see, no end meta tag exists.

Here is an example of a meta tag:

```
<meta name="description"
  content="Your best resource for water-related activities and
fun! We sell boats, fishing gear, and skis online and we'll ship
anywhere!">
```

Current standards dictate that meta tags follow the `<title>` tag pair. Nevertheless, many HTML programmers and even Web page generators insert meta tag information before the `<title>` tag pair. For example, FrontPage 2000 always inserts the following code at the top of all Web pages:

```
<head>
<meta http-equiv="Content-Type" content="text/html;
charset=windows-1252">
<meta name="GENERATOR" content="Microsoft FrontPage 4.0">
<meta name="ProgId" content="FrontPage.Editor.Document">
<title>New Page 1</title>
</head>
```

At first glance, meta tags seem to hold information that could appear inside comment tags. For example, FrontPage's meta tags in the preceding code describe the version of FrontPage that generated the Web page, as well as the character set used for the text. Other more cryptic information also appears in the tag used internally by the FrontPage editor.

The advantage to using meta tags over comments for some information is that search engines utilize your page's meta tags to determine how to index your page inside the search engine. In other words, if you want your page to appear on one of the many Web search engines, you need to include search information inside meta tags in your page.

Never rely solely on meta tags for search engine inclusion. Many ways exist to get listed in search engines. You'll learn more ways to get your site noticed later in this session.

Tip

Many Web sites utilize *usability studies* to determine the best meta tags for their Web pages. A usability study has several people sit down and perform routine searches and navigation of Web sites. All the while, the study's researchers are looking at the ways that users search for things, the ways that they use the mouse and keyboard, and the ways that they click some areas more often than others. Usability studies have found that users may or may not notice something as simple as a Help button. When users get confused, they are likely to switch to another site, meaning that the site's Help button is not obvious or that the site is too boring. No matter how much you love your site's design, your *users* should determine how it performs. A usability study is one of the best ways to learn what typical users enter in a search engine to locate a given Web site.

The name= and content= attributes

The name="description" attribute specifies what the meta tag describes. The content= attribute tells search engines what your site is all about, in your own words. You'll want to be as specific and descriptive as possible. Describe the specific content of the site. If you sell technical books, the following tag would be too general:

```
<meta name="description" content="We sell books">
```

A better meta tag might be this one:

```
<meta name="description" content="We have tens of thousands of
rare technical books discounted for sale online">
```

Keep in mind that when you use a name="description" attribute, you also need a content= attribute to complete that tag and supply the description.

The bottom-line reason for specifying the name="description" and content= attributes is so that search engines will display your content in the first line in the search engine's results. So, when a search engine returns your Web site in a list of valid search hits, the content= value appears after your site's address. The user who views the search engine's results reads through the content values looking for a site that might be of interest.

Specifying keywords

Another meta tag attribute pair enables you to specify keywords about your site. Search engines look for key words in sites to match up against a user's search query. For example, if a user goes to Yahoo! (http://www.yahoo.com/) and types `online auction teddy bears`, Yahoo! would use the keywords *online, auction, teddy,* and *bears* to match against sites' keywords specified in meta tags.

Use the `name="keywords"` attribute, followed by the `content=` attribute, to specify keywords that relate to your site. The following might contain the keywords for your online technical book site:

```
<meta name="keywords" content="technical, books, book, online, bookseller, rare, inexpensive, overnight">
```

The keywords determine your Web page's ranking when a search engine returns your page along with other Web pages. Therefore, the more keywords you specify, the more likely your site will match closely with someone searching for a site like yours.

If you do a Yahoo! search with the search phrase, `hard disk drives`, Yahoo! performs a series of two searches. The first search passes over Yahoo!'s own internal categories. If a search phrase makes a good match on a Yahoo! category, that category appears at the top of the search engine's results. After Yahoo! displays the matched categories, Yahoo! then displays a more general Internet match list of sites. (Yahoo! makes sure that you know about its own sites before the general sites, which is fine, because Yahoo! is paying the bills for its free search engine.)

Study the results that appear when you perform searches yourself. Yahoo! returns not just hard disk sales, but also disk repair sites. The more specific that you are with your search query, the more specific are the results that the search engine returns. But much of that specific match centers on the meta tag contents the HTML programmers included in the Web page. The more descriptive the meta tags, the more likely your site will come up when it should.

Hiding from search engines

If you don't want to appear in a search engine's results, you can opt out of being included with the following meta tag:

```
<meta name="robots" content="noindex">
```

When a search engine indexes sites for inclusion in searches, the search engine sends something called a *gobot, robot,* or *spider* out to scout for correct matches. Your name="robots" and content="noindex" meta tags inform the search engine's robots that you are not to be included.

Many reasons exist for not being included in a search engine's results. Perhaps you have a new Web site that is not fully functional yet. Until your Web page is ready to be viewed on the World Wide Web, you might keep the page out of sight from search engines with the content="noindex" **attribute.**

20 Min. To Go

Channeling Your Product: The Web Site

Several methods exist for getting your site noticed. The foundation of site location resides in the search engines. You now understand how meta tags can get you noticed. As you'll see throughout this session, other ways exist that get your HTML-coded site into the hands of the users you want to target.

Keep in mind that your job as an HTML programmer works in an opposite direction from your users' job of finding, locating, and staying with your site. Your job consists of the following:

1. Create a Web site that loads quickly, looks good, stays fresh, and retains the user's interest.

2. Code meta tags so that the search engines not only find you, they find you using the criteria you specify.

3. Register with search engines.

You want to *push* your site. In marketing terminology, this is called *channeling your product.* You want your site to appear in front of the user so that the user cannot help but view your beautiful HTML-coded Web pages. When the user searches for a topic that you cover, your Web site should be first on the list! Nevertheless, the striking truth is that unlike just about any other medium, Web sites lie in *pull* channels. Your users don't ever have to go to your site just because it's there. Millions of sites sit in waiting, each one equally accessible to the user. Your site might come up as a result of a search, but your user still has many other options. Therefore, from a marketing standpoint, if you want visitors to your site, you must consider the marketing aspect separately from your site's creation. After all the work, sweat, and time you put into making your site the best-looking, freshest site on the Internet, all that work is in vain if users never know about your site, or never feel compelled to go.

Other Ways of Getting Your Site Noticed

Meta tags are not the only way to get your site noticed. Although a large audience at a site is the exception and not the norm for the majority of Web sites, you can greatly increase your chance at a large audience by following some guidelines outlined in the next few sections.

Understand how search engines operate

Ample use of meta tags is required but not always all that helpful. Without the meta tags, a search engine cannot index your site using the standard method used throughout other sites. Therefore, you must use meta tags as described throughout the previous sections of this session, in hopes of getting noticed, but the meta tags alone do not ensure that you'll rise to the top of a search engine list.

Whether you sell products or provide information, you want your site noticed, and a search engine is the primary method for locating new sites. The search engines are the table of contents for the Web. Some search engines, however, are picky about meta tags. If, for example, you repeat the same keyword over and over, some search engines will rank your site high in the list of found sites. Others will remove you altogether due to your overuse of the same keyword to get noticed.

Yahoo! is actually not a great example for explaining general Web searches because a site appears on Yahoo! if the site's contact person, most often the Web master, contacts Yahoo!, fills out a form, and gets accepted as a listed site. Yahoo! certainly also sends out robots all the time looking for new sites, but Yahoo! never hesitates to let you know that it ranks its own site categories before all others. That's okay — Yahoo! has many great categories of sites, and many of those sites paid for the privilege of being in a Yahoo! category, but other sites are so prominent and used by so many people that Yahoo! wanted to include them.

If a search engine requires that you fill out a form to get noticed, as Yahoo! and many others do, you'll be busy doing just that, registering. Many search engines exist, but the major ones require registration. But before going to the effort to register, you need to work on the most common and best standardized method for getting noticed, and that simply is supplying meta tags, as discussed in the previous section.

Registering with the common search sites

If you don't go to the trouble of registering with the common search sites, your site will be left out of the game almost every time. Eventually, the search engine's spiders will get around to locating your site, but being unregistered, your site is going to get low priority when it comes time to display your site in a list of other sites.

More than 30 search engines are in use at any one time on the Internet, but the ones in Table 17-1 are by far the most popular. If you do nothing else, take the time to register your site with all of these services.

Table 17-1
The Major Search Engines

Engine	Location
Yahoo!	http://www.yahoo.com/
AltaVista	http://www.altavista.com/
Excite	http://www.excite.com/
GoTo	http://www.goto.com/
Lycos	http://www.lycos.com/
InfoSeek	http://www.infoseek.com/
MetaCrawler	http://www.metacrawler.com/
Microsoft Network	http://www.msn.com/
America Online	http://www.aol.com/

MetaCrawler is an example of a search engine that searches the search engines! Instead of looking through the tons of Web sites, MetaCrawler scours the search engines in an attempt to provide users with an all-in-one place for locating what one needs. Each search engine is unique in the way it scouts for site matches, and each produces a different set of results. Engines, such as MetaCrawler, attempt to search the major search engines to return a collection of searches, with as little overlap as possible, that you'd get individually if you searched using each of the individual search engines. And after this session's description of meta tags, you now understand the intended pun in the name *Meta*Crawler.

Using e-mail: spam or attention-getter?

One of the most direct methods that you can use to market your site is through e-mail. Companies lease e-mail customer lists that you can rent. These lists are divided into target audience groups from which you can select. In today's world, however, people often say they get too much e-mail. One of the reasons for the oversized Inbox of most people is *spam,* the unrequested e-mail that arrives in the user's Inbox folder constantly.

Electronic mailing list servers, also called *listserves,* are more than just lists of e-mail addresses. A list server is an automatic router of e-mail to large groups of people who can choose to be on or off certain lists targeted to certain people. When scouring the ideas of Web site marketing, check into the list server options available to you.

Hiring outside help

Several sites exist that offer to do all the legwork for you. They will, for a fee, register you with the major search engines, offer to create and distribute banners to your site on other pages, put your daily, weekly, or monthly announcements in e-mail form for a list server, and so on. One of the most popular sites is bCentral (http://www.bcentral.com/), popular because Microsoft's connection with bCentral promises that bCentral should be around for a while.

**10 Min.
To Go**

Playing Meta Tag Tricks

Now that you've seen an overview of Web page announcement (the requirements needed to get your site noticed) you're ready to perform some HTML tricks (that do not always work) on the meta tags that get people to your site. But, first, it's important to know that search engines do not look *only* at meta tags.

Searching for content

Search engines do *not* only look at meta tags for sites. Search engines do their best to scan Web pages for content that the engine might be able to use. Scanning meta tags is the preferred way that search engines locate pages because the HTML author wrote the meta tags, most of the time, with the search engine in mind.

Therefore, the search engine can more safely use the meta tags to index the site, as opposed to the opening few paragraphs of text.

You must, however, keep in mind that search engines do look at other text to index sites. A heavily text-intensive site is more likely to appear in a search engine's results properly than a site that uses very little text and a lot of graphics. The graphics cannot convey the site's content, only text can, and many times the text is misleading. A news site, for example, might have this for its headline news of the day: "Insurance company lowers rating on automobile repair facility."

A search engine, when it happens to scan this site, might consider this to be a site that is insurance- or auto-related, when the site is actually a general news site. The meta tags, with appropriate keywords, will help keep the search engine on target, but the text on the page will play a role in the site's location within found pages.

Meta tag tricks

Because search engines do scan the page's text in addition to the meta tags, you can play tricks with the code. For example, a rather boring site such as that of a parts manufacturer could have embedded, in a blue background, blue text that reads, "Money Money-making free money sex get-rich weight-loss," in an attempt to appear in as many search engine requests as possible. The blue-on-blue text doesn't appear to the user, but the HTML code contains the words and a search engine might possibly pick up those words. When someone goes looking for the latest in weight loss, the parts manufacturer's site comes up in the list of hits and, possibly, gets a look from the unsuspecting users.

Other sites that sell specific product brands will hide competitor's names throughout their meta tags and embedded in hidden text throughout the site. Such sites hope that their site appears when someone looks for one of their competitors.

Today's popular search engines are sophisticated and will look for such bait-and-switch subterfuge. Many search engines are refusing to list sites that employ same-color text tricks to gain hits. Even if you are more accurate in placing hidden text on your page that correctly defines your site, you run the risk of being ousted from a search engine. Rely on good text and meta tags to do your search engine work, and properly register with as many engines as possible to get the word out about your site.

Done!

REVIEW

- A meta tag is a tag that appears in the header section of your Web page, which contains information about your Web site.

- When specifying the `content=` attribute, use a specific, accurate description of your site.

- You can opt to hide your Web site from search engines by applying the proper `name="description"` and `content=` attributes in the meta tag.

- Registering with the major search engines doesn't guarantee they will list your site, but your odds are much improved.

- HTML tricks often hinder your site's inclusion in the search engine's databases.

QUIZ YOURSELF

1. What are two common attributes that describe a Web site to a search engine? (See "Getting Your Site Noticed with Meta Tags.")

2. What is the difference between push channeling and pull channeling as it relates to the Web? (See "Channeling Your Product: The Web Site.")

3. How do usability studies help determine the best marketing methods for your Web site? (See "Understand How Search Engines Operate.")

4. Name two ways some sites try to apply bait-and-switch tactics to get users. (See "Playing Meta Tag Tricks.")

5. True or False: Search engines rely solely on meta tags to index sites. (See "Searching for Content.")

Page Layout with Frames

Session Checklist

✔ View different content on the same Web page with frames

✔ Learn about the problems associated with frames on a Web page

✔ Learn the steps for creating frames

✔ Generate frame-based HTML code for Web pages

**30 Min.
To Go**

In this session, you learn all about frames and how to plan for them and position them on a Web page. Frames separate Web page content from the navigation bar, banner, footer, and any other special area that you want to make distinct. In this session, you'll walk through the creation of an online auction Web site that uses frames to teach its users all about managing online auctions. Frames can be confusing, both from the user's as well as the HTML programmer's standpoint.

Frames Separate Web Page Content

Frames separate the content of a Web page into different areas on the screen. Figure 18-1 shows a Web page with four separate frames. The figure presents the most common uses of frames. Frames are often used for displaying the following Web page sections:

- The header, which often contains a site banner
- A navigation bar that runs vertically down the left side of the page
- A footer section with contact and other supporting information
- A large body area that holds the details of the site

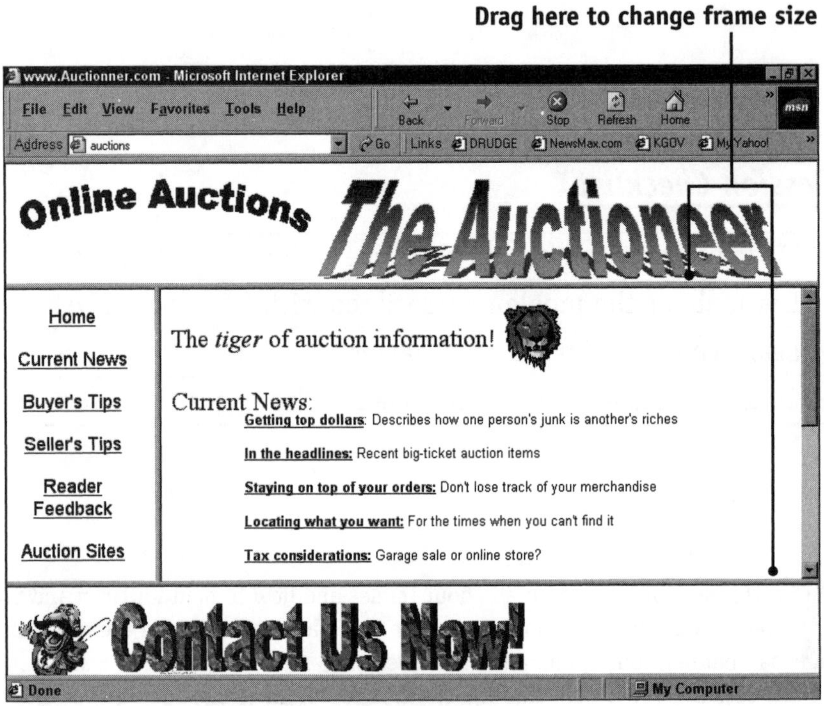

Drag here to change frame size

Figure 18-1
Frames divide the Web page into several sections.

At first, frames look no different from tables. And if you generate a table with a border that contains the same four sections that the Web page in Figure 18-1 contains, the table will look identical to a page that displays frames. The difference between tables and frames, however, is great. Unlike table borders, which can be invisible, frame borders usually appear, and the Web page that uses frames always keeps the sections distinct, whereas a table might format rows and columns that flow together imperceptibly. When the user clicks a link inside one frame, the contents of a completely different frame can change. You are in control of which frames change by controlling the hyperlinks. The user can drag a frame's corner to resize the frame borders, or you can fix the borders so that the user cannot resize the frames.

The advantage to using frames is that when frames appear on a Web site, each frame contains a unique Web page. Therefore, when four framed sections appear, the user is really viewing four different Web pages. The information from one frame cannot overflow into other frames as it can from table cell to cell. The frames keep the information distinct, such as a navigation bar kept in the left frame while the user scrolls one of the other frames. While the user works inside one frame, scrolling and reading, the other frames remain as they were.

Although frames offer features not found in tables, such as the freeze-frame effect of all the frames except the user's active frame, the bottom line is that HTML programmers generally prefer tables over frames. Tables aid in formatting because most tables are presented without borders. The Web page can contain a strict and structured format thanks to a table, without the user noticing a bordered frame structure. The user virtually always sees the frames.

New additions to HTML, included in HTML 4.01, are *inline frames,* which enable you to embed scrolling areas of content together with stable banners and navigation bars without resorting to messy frame borders. It will take a few years for the majority of browsers to implement inline frames, so don't use them yet.

When a user's screen is too small to hold the contents of a frame, the browser automatically attaches scroll bars to the frame windows so that the user can scroll within that frame. As the user scrolls, the rest of the frames remain stable.

A navigation bar in a frame, whether textual (as in Figure 18-1) or graphics-based, remains constant as the user views different content inside the main content frame. The beauty of navigation bars is that they remain fairly constant throughout the entire site, and frames help ensure that consistency.

Problems with Frames

As you can see, frames offer several advantages, such as the scrolling frame windows and the consistent framing of the header, navigation bar, and footer windows as the user views differing content inside the main content frame. Frames do come with their own set of problems, however, and you need to be aware of them.

Not all browsers in use today support frames. Perhaps you've been to Web sites that include a link that read, Non-frame version. The site is offering a version of the site without frames for users whose browsers do not support frames. Although browsers have supported the use of tables since HTML's earliest versions, frames didn't come along until later.

Some users always choose the non-frames version of a site by preference and not because their browsers require the non-frames site.

In spite of the lack of 100-percent browser support, realistically, *most* of today's browsers probably do support the viewing of frames. If you want to address the widest possible audience, however, you'll offer two versions of your site: one with frames and one without. The site without the frames might turn out to be more heavily visited than your frame site if you don't keep your frames simple and relevant.

Keep in mind that frames do have drawbacks as well as advantages. Frames are sometimes confusing. The various scroll bars can clutter the screen. Web sites exist with too many frames, and the user tires of all the scrolling that has to be done. In addition to requiring excessive scrolling, Web sites with too many frames waste screen real estate on the frames and scroll bars and take too much room away from content.

Never create a Web site with frames that you don't test with several different browsers and at several different screen resolutions. Screen resolution can greatly affect the look of a frame-based Web site. At a low resolution, the site can have little content and lots of scroll bars. At a high resolution, the site can have too much blank space and appear empty of content.

In addition to adding clutter and not being fully supported, frames add another layer of confusion when the user attempts to bookmark a page. Depending on how the frame document loads, the user's browser's URL may not properly match the page the user is viewing. Perhaps the URL corresponds to only one of the frames.

Frames even disable the needed Back button in some browsers! The Back button is one of the most commonly used browser features. When frames disable the Back button due to poor implementation by the browser's authors, confusion results and usually your site is not revisited by the user.

Frame Creation Steps

20 Min. To Go

The steps in creating a frame-based site depend on the content of the frames. This section reviews some common elements found in frames and describes the steps you will most likely follow to create a site with frames.

Step 1: Planning the frame-based page

Before creating frames in HTML code, sketch your site's pages so that you know which frame will hold which content. The following guidelines are not set in stone, but consider them as a starting point:

- Put your company or site logo in the banner frame at the top of the screen. If you center the banner, the frame will look nice, but if you left-align the banner, even the lowest-resolution screen will be able to show the entire banner along with the rest of the page.

- Save the largest frame for the most important and detailed content.

- If older information is to be available to your readers, regularly archive your content by storing older data in separate frame pages that the user can call up by clicking a list at the bottom of the current main contents frame. Figure 18-2 shows such an archive list. The user scrolled down the main contents frame to see the past articles that may be of interest. By archiving in this way, you reduce the amount of information inside the main contents frame.

archived articles

Figure 18-2
Archive older frame material that you want to make available to users.

Step 2: Creating the frame's pages

After you sketch your basic frame document, you're ready to begin the HTML coding. You must create each frame separately, in its own Web page. In other words, every window in a frame is a complete, stand-alone Web page. You must create the banner frame, the navigation bar frame, the detailed window frame, and the footer frame if you want a footer at the bottom of the page.

A frame window such as the banner window shown in Figure 18-3 comprises a complete Web page including a header section enclosed by the <head> and </head> tags, meta tags, a body section, comments to make the page easy to maintain, and all the other Web page constructs discussed in the earlier sessions of this course. The window can contain animated GIF images, form elements, and anything else.

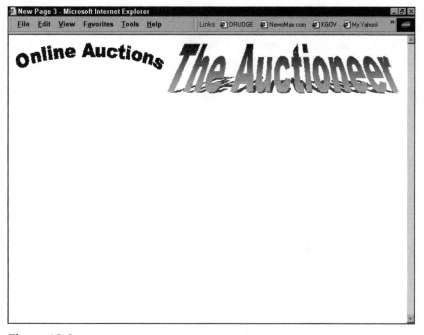

Figure 18-3
The banner frame in this Web page is a complete Web page.

Never lose sight of the ironclad Web page creation rule: The faster your page loads, the more likely users are to wait for your page to load and the more likely they are to return to your site. When you create three or four separate windows for three or four frames, you must add the load times for *all* those window frames to determine the actual page-loading time needed by the frame document as a whole.

Once you put all the Web pages together into the complete frame document, you'll make adjustments to the individual Web pages. You'll find that some colors won't blend well, some window sizes will not work, and some Web pages simply don't work well as a frame.

Step 3: Generating the frame holding page

A Web site that contains frames uses not only separate Web pages for each frame window but also a background Web page that holds the format of the frame itself.

The user never sees the background frame page (or the frame-holding page), but it's the page that holds the others together.

The frame background page determines the structure of the site and includes the number of frames on the page, the size of each frame, whether or not the user can resize any of the frames, and the name of the Web page that appears in each frame. No information for the user resides in the frame page. You will probably assign a base name to this frame page, such as auction.htm or auctionframe.htm, so that you can easily locate all the site's pages in a group file listing.

The frame page is the actual page that the browser loads to display the frame windows all together. In other words, once you create an auctionframe.htm page, the user will load auctionframe.htm, which performs the task of loading all the appropriate pages into the correct frame windows.

**10 Min.
To Go**

Frame-Based HTML

You do not need any help with Step 2, creating the individual frame window pages, because they are nothing but regular Web pages. They might be narrower or wider than usual depending on the frames they reside in, but they do not contain any special frame-related HTML, except perhaps a hyperlink reference to another frame, which you'll learn about later in this section. To learn how to generate a frame-based Web page, you need to know how to carry out Step 3, creating the background frame page that contains the structure of the frame, and how to link the frames.

Background frame page

Here's how to create the background frame page that contains the structure of the frame. In HTML terminology, you are creating a *frameset,* and the <frameset> and </frameset> tags handle the job nicely. Listing 18-1 begins the creation of the structure frameset.

Listing 18-1
The beginnings of a frame structure

```
<html>

<head>
<title>www.Auctionner.com</title>
</head>
```

```
<!-- Notice that the frameset tag goes in the header area -->
<frameset   ???>
   <!-- The frame structure goes here -->
</frameset>
  <body>

  </body>
</frameset>

</html>
```

Notice that the `<frameset>` tag in Listing 18-1 is incomplete. You must supply other information within the tag, as indicated by the `???` in line 8 of Listing 18-1. You must convey to the browser, through the `<frameset>` tag, the information that describes the rows and columns in the frame structure. The different `<frameset>` and `</frameset>` groups describe each frame in the document. How to finalize a frameset is explained in the following sections.

If a row is to be variable — that is, if the row will contain a growing amount of information and most likely will require scroll bars — use the wildcard character, *, for the row height. The browser will adjust that row as needed. You may also specify frame row (and column) sizes as percentages of the browser window.

Specify the rows with the `rows=` attribute to set the height in pixels of each row. To create the auction site's three rows, you would use the following HTML:

```
<frameset rows=115,*,85>
```

This tag tells the browser that the first row is 115 pixels high, the third row is 85 pixels high, and the middle row is variable and should consume all that's left.

As with tables, you must view the frames from top to bottom and left to right. Therefore, you must finish the first row's information before working on the columns in the second row. For a frame to hold a Web page, you must name the frame and specify the Web page that resides in that frame. The following tag does that:

```
   <frame name=top scrolling=no target=contents
src=auctionbanner.htm>
```

The name must be unique. Other windows will reference the frame document, as well as the individual frames by their names once you begin setting up the site's navigation. For example, many people use *banner* for the name of the top window frame. The `scrolling=` attribute determines whether or not you want your user to be able to scroll the window frame. Your banner window should fit within the pixel height you specified.

Obviously, you'll need to tell the frameset where the columns fall. To do so, add the `cols=` attribute as follows:

```
<frameset cols="150,*">
```

This `<frameset>` tag informs the browser that two columns are to appear next: the first 150 pixels wide (this is the navigation column) and the second as wide as the screen allows, with scroll bars appearing if necessary.

You've just created a second frameset within the first. Therefore, you'll need two `</frameset>` tags before the closing `</html>` tag.

You must then inform the browser of the Web pages inside each column, as follows:

```
<frame name=contents src=auctionnav.htm scrolling=auto>
<frame name=main src=auctiondetail.htm scrolling=auto>
```

By specifying `scrolling=auto` as opposed to `scrolling=no`, you are informing the browser that scroll bars are to appear *if needed to fit the information within the frame window.* The browser will not waste space with a scroll bar if one is not needed.

Terminate the column frameset with the end tag, as follows:

```
</frameset>
```

You must now complete the final row, the footer frame window, and then terminate the frameset. The following does that:

```
<frame name=bottom scrolling=no src=auctionfoot.htm>
</frameset>
```

Linking the frames

The code shown so far for the auction site's frames is almost complete. You must make sure that all the frames reference other frame windows. In addition, any links within the navigation bar must change the detail window but no other window.

You will use the `target=` attribute inside the `<a href>` anchor hyperlink tag to specify which frame window changes when the user selects the hyperlink. In addition to using the `target=` attribute in hyperlinks, you must use the `target=` attribute inside the frameset tags as well.

Perhaps the easiest place to begin describing the `target=` attribute is to see the entire frameset Web page's HTML. In the previous section, you saw the fundamentals of the frameset HTML, but a little more is needed to complete the framework. Listing 18-2 contains all the code necessary for the auction site's frameset.

Listing 18-2
The complete HTML code for the frame structure

```
<html>

<head>
<title>www.Auctionner.com</title>
</head>
<!-- Notice that the frameset tag goes in the header area -->

<frameset rows=115,*,*>
  <frame name=top scrolling=no target=main src=auctionbanner.htm>
  <frameset cols=150,*>
    <frame name=contents target=main src=auctionnav.htm
scrolling=auto>
    <frame name=main src=auctiondetail.htm scrolling=auto>
  </frameset>
  <frame name=bottom scrolling=no target=main src=auctionfoot.htm>

  <body>
  </body>

</frameset>
</html>
```

Each of the frames described in Listing 18-2 contains a `target=main` attribute. Actually, unless you put a hyperlink reference inside each of the frame windows, not every frame needs the `target=main` attribute, but coding the attribute means you will have less worries if later you do decide to add a link to one of the frames.

By specifying `target=contents`, you tell the browser that any hyperlink reference from that particular frame should *not* change the current window but should change the window named *contents,* which is the detailed window in the large, central portion of the Web page. The window named *contents* does not require the `target=contents` attribute, because without the attribute, it follows whatever hyperlink is clicked inside that window frame.

You must edit each of the Web pages in each of the frames to ensure that they update the proper window frames — most usually, the frame holding the content window. In other words, you now must edit the navigation page's HTML so that the hyperlinks all refer to the contents window. One possible cross-reference might appear as follows inside `auctionnav.htm`:

```
<br><br>
<a href=article3-21.htm target=main>Check out last week's
auctions</a>
```

Other frames can change

In many instances, the contents frame is not the only frame that should change as the user navigates the site. For example, links or buttons that perform links in the banner area might produce a completely different set of navigation links if you've placed a navigation bar in the left frame. Therefore, you can set the `target=` attribute to the name of any window frame on the Web page. When the user clicks a link in any frame, any other frame, referenced by name, can change. Your Web page determines how your site's frame windows cross-reference each other.

Just because a Web site uses frames does not mean that you are limited to frames for the hyperlinks. Open links inside frame windows or open a brand new window (using the `target="_blank"` attribute as you learned in Session 10) if the information resides better in its own frameless window. The user can always close the new window and return to the frame-based site.

Help for non-frame browsers

If you want your users without frame-aware browsers to understand why they don't see anything when they visit your site, you can add some content to your frameset HTML. Enclose a message to the users inside the `<noframes>` and `</noframes>`

tags. If the browser supports frames, that browser ignores the <noframes> tag contents, so you won't mess up the users whose browsers are frame-aware.

Listing 18-3 shows simple code you can add to all your frame-based Web pages that inform the frameless browser users why the site is otherwise vacant.

Listing 18-3
Using the <noframes> tag in HTML for users who cannot display frames

```
<html>

<head>
<title>www.Auctionner.com</title>
</head>
<!-- Notice that the frameset tag goes in the header area -->

<frameset rows=115,*,*>
  <frame name=top scrolling=no target=main src=auctionbanner.htm>
  <frameset cols=150,*>
    <frame name=contents target=main src=auctionnav.htm
scrolling=auto>
    <frame name=main src=auctiondetail.htm scrolling=auto>
  </frameset>
  <frame name=bottom scrolling=no target=main src=auctionfoot.htm>
</frameset>

  <!-- Inform the users without frames why they cannot
       see the site -->
  <noframes>
  <body>
   <h1>Sorry.</h1>
   <br><br>Your browser does not support frames which this
           uses. An <a href=noframeauction.htm>alternative
           frameless version</a> of this Web page is now
           available for you to use.
  </body>
  </noframes>
</html>
```

Done!

REVIEW

- Frames, which offer a way for you to separate areas of a Web page, are used for displaying headers, navigation bars, footers, and a large content area.
- Frames differ from tables in that frames usually appear and one frame's links can control the contents of another frame window.
- You can overuse frames to the point that the frames begin to clutter the user's screen.
- Before creating frame-based HTML, sketch your Web site's pages so that you know which frame will hold which content.
- After sketching your Web site's pages, create all the frame window pages before working on the frameset itself.
- The `<frameset>` and `</frameset>` tags determine the rows and columns of a framed page.
- Although you don't want to put content in the body section of your frameset HTML, you can include code for those users who cannot display frames.

QUIZ YOURSELF

1. Name two ways that frames differ from tables. (See "Frames Separate Web Page Content.")

2. When will scroll bars appear inside a frame? (See "Frames Separate Web Page Content.")

3. What is a frameset? (See "Frame-Based HTML.")

4. What attribute controls the appearance of scroll bars? (See "Frame-Based HTML.")

5. What attribute opens a new window inside one of the page's frames? (See "Linking the Frames.")

Activating Pages with Multimedia and Rollovers

Session Checklist

✔ Speed up your multimedia processes with bandwidth

✔ Add sound to your Web site

✔ Add video to your Web site

✔ Learn how to code the rollover effect, thereby offering movement
to Web pages

**30 Min.
To Go**

Why would you want to add multimedia elements to your Web pages?
To make the pages more enjoyable, to make them stand apart from the
crowd, to give them *zing!* Why would you *not* want to add multimedia
elements to your Web pages? After 18 sessions, you know the answer: Extras will
slow your page-loading time and lose viewers. In this session, you learn how to
add multimedia and changing content while still maintaining quick-loading pages.

Speeding Up the Multimedia Process with Bandwidth

Fortunately, you have time on your side. *Bandwidth,* the avenue of speed on which Web pages travel, is only getting faster, not slower. The faster the average user's bandwidth becomes, the more successfully you can add multimedia to your site. Still, you need to be conservative a while longer, because most users are still tied to modem technology and will be for a few more years.

Some Web sites require more multimedia than others. For example, you may want to present audio information in a radio show format. You might create a Web page for a movie production company that wants to embed previews on the site. Such sites can be slower than normal for the slow-bandwidth users because these users know what to expect. This session describes the multimedia options you have for Web pages.

Adding Sound to Web Pages

Sound is perhaps the easiest form of multimedia to add to a Web site. You can play a Windows-like intro clip as someone first views your site. In addition, you might want to put a list of recorded conferences from your company meetings on the site.

Table 19-1 lists the most common audio formats that you can store on a Web page. By far, the most popular formats are MPEG for music files and RealAudio for radio and voice files.

 You can learn more about these two formats at http://www.mp3. com/ **and** http://www.real.com/. **Both sites offer players you can use to preview audio clips, and both provide much content for your enjoyment.**

Many sites use short WAVE sound clips to welcome a user to the Web page. Short clips don't consume much load time, although they certainly impact the load time. If you want to use a sound clip, you can find several by searching your computer's disk drive for those that your operating system utilizes for its messages. In addition, http://www.wavecentral.com/ offers several WAVE files you can use, both royalty-based and royalty-free, for sound effects.

Table 19-1
Common Audio Formats

Name	Extension	Description
MIDI	.mid	Individual instrumental sounds
MPEG	.mp3	Songs and online radio broadcasts, often used for storing audio CD content on computers
RealAudio	.ra or .rm	Songs, voice, and online radio broadcasts
WAVE	.wav	Sounds such as those produced by Windows

Sound with HTML

A sound clip requires very little effort to include on a Web page. Basically, you create a hyperlink to the sound file just as you might create a link to another Web page. Consider the HTML code in Listing 19-1, which describes and provides the Windows 98 start-up sound on a Web page. Figure 19-1 shows the Web page that this short HTML code produces.

Listing 19-1
Providing the Windows 98 start-up sound on a Web page

```
<html>

  <head>
  <title>Starting Windows 98</title>
  </head>

  <body>

    <h1>Windows 98 Tutorial</h1>
      <h2>The Start-up</h2>
      <font size=3 face="Arial">Once you start a computer running
          Windows 98, the computer performs a self-test and then
          <br>Windows 98 loads. Toward the end of the loading,
          you'll hear the <a href=Start.wav>Windows 98
```

Continued

Listing 19-1　　　　　　　　　　　　　　　　　　　　　　　　　*Continued*

```
        start-up sound</a>.
     </font>
  </body>
</html>
```

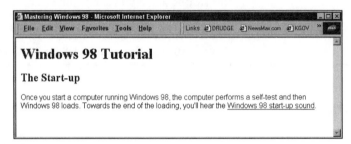

Figure 19-1
When the user clicks the hyperlink, the sound plays.

Just as you save your site's graphics in a single images directory, save your sounds in their own folder as well, named "sounds." If a sound appears twice throughout a site, the user's browser only has to load the sound once. If the same clip appears in multiple directories, the browser has to load the same sound twice. Once you create video content, as explained in the section named "Adding Video to Web Pages," you should store the video in its own folder called "videos" as well.

Better sound management

When offering sound or any other kind of multimedia event, be sure to provide the size of the clip, perhaps in a ToolTip message. Give the user some idea of the length of the clip and the size of the file. Otherwise, the user may have to wait longer than expected for the clip to load.

By adding the following title to the hyperlink in Listing 19-1, you enable the user to rest the mouse cursor over the link to preview the sound parameters before deciding to play the sound:

```
<a href=Start.wav title="The start-up sound will play, 4 seconds,
676K">Windows 98 start-up sound</a>
```

Not only does such a title help warn the user that a long delay may be waiting ahead, but also, users without sound equipment and hearing-impaired users will know what the link produces from your description.

Depending on the type of sound file, your user may or may not be able to play the clip without some kind of accessory program. Although most users can play WAVE files, not all users have an MPEG or a RealAudio player on their system. If they do not, and if another sound player such as Windows Media Player or the Mac's Quick-Time player does not support your sound file's format, the user will not hear the audio. You may want to provide a link to the format's home site, such as the Real-Audio Web site, so that the user can go there to download the proper player before clicking on your sound's link. The problem is that the users will often move on to another site rather than spend the time downloading the right player. Fortunately, MPEG and RealAudio formats are so popular today that you can usually assume that users have the correct players needed for your clips.

Adding Video to Web Pages

20 Min. To Go

If sound adds pounds to a Web page, video adds tons. Even short video clips consume massive amounts of storage and bandwidth. Nevertheless, more and more sites are providing limited if not full video capabilities for their users. Movie sites provide film previews, training companies provide online walk-throughs, and news services frequently provide news clips of the top stories on their home pages. The advent of the video connection port for many of today's new computers also means that more personal home pages will be putting up more and more videos of the family and pets.

Obviously, preparing the user for a possibly long wait is extremely important if you provide video clips. Tell the user exactly how large the file will be and how many seconds or minutes of playtime the file consumes.

 You can provide some video, as well as audio such as RealAudio files, in a *streaming* format. Instead of the user having to wait for the entire clip to arrive in the user's browser, the clip begins playing after a few seconds. As the user watches or listens to the clip, the rest of the clip loads in the background.

Table 19-2 lists three common video formats you'll run across as you create Web pages. They all play video content that includes motion and sound. As with the audio formats, your users must have the appropriate players to play these files.

Part IV—Saturday Evening
Session 19

Fortunately, these video formats are becoming so common that most users have players installed that will take over when such a clip is loaded in the browser.

Table 19-2
Common Video Formats

Name	Extension
AVI	.avi
MPEG	.mpg and .mpeg
QuickTime	.mov

Two forms of Web page video exist. They are external video and internal video.

Specifying external video clips

An external video clip is a clip that plays, when the user selects the appropriate link, using a program that is external to the browser. For example, when an external QuickTime video clip is requested, the browser idles while the user's QuickTime player program automatically starts and plays the video sent to it. When the user closes the player window, the Web page appears on the screen in the same state it was in before the user clicked the link, except that the link's color will now reflect the fact that the link has been visited.

To specify an external video, simply hyperlink to the video file. The user's browser is responsible for sending a request to the operating system to start the external player that will play the clip. Here is some HTML code that produces such a clip by inserting a link to the AVI file:

```
<br>
<a href="window.avi">This window video</a> (1.02 Meg AVI, 11
seconds)
shows the many analogies between the physical
<br>windows you open and close and your operating windows.</font>
```

When the user selects the clip, the user's default player for that video format begins, as shown in Figure 19-2.

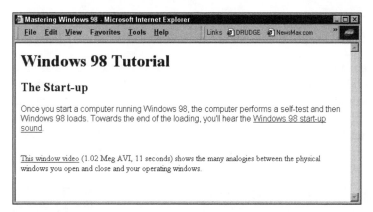

Figure 19-2
When the user clicks the video's hyperlink, the external player begins.

Many browsers will not instantly start the clip but will give the user a chance to save the clip instead of opening, or running, the clip. Rarely, computer viruses can reside inside multimedia format, although clips from known Web sites should be safe to load. By saving the clip, the user can better control how the clip plays.

As with all hyperlinks, you can make an image a link as well as text. Perhaps a still image from the video would make a good hyperlink because it offers a preview of the clip the user is about to see.

Specifying internal video clips

Instead of letting an external video player begin, you can specify that the video play directly inside your Web page. Although the AVI video format is the format best supported, most of today's browsers support the other video formats as internal video clips as well.

When you specify an internal video clip, you can control the following aspects of the video:

- The location of the video play
- Whether or not the video begins as soon as the page loads or only when the user clicks the Play button

- Whether the video repeats continuously or plays only once
- The width and height of the embedded video player

The `<embed>` tag controls the internal playback of AVI videos. As a matter of fact, the `<embed>` tag is useful for embedding any file of any type in a Web page, but the file is to remain hidden unless the browser has the correct *plug-in,* a helper application program that can open files of that type. Most modern browsers have ample plug-in support for all the popular multimedia file types described in this session, but not all users use modern browser versions that support all these files. Therefore, use `<embed>` with discretion.

The `<object>` tag is a standard that began with HTML 4 that enables you to embed a file of any type in a Web page; if the proper plug-in is available, that file will activate properly. The `<embed>` tag is better supported, however, by Netscape and Internet Explorer, still the two most popular browsers.

Listing 19-2 contains a simple but complete Web page that plays a video clip internally.

Listing 19-2
Embedding a video inside the Web page

```
<html>

<head>
<title>Mastering Windows 98</title>
</head>

<body>

    <h1>Windows 98 Tutorial</h1>
      <h2>The Start-up</h2>
      <font size=3 face="Arial">Once you start a computer
         running Windows 98, the computer performs a self-test
         and then
      <br>Windows 98 loads. Toward the end of the loading,
         you'll hear the <a href=Start.wav>Windows 98
```

```
        start-up sound</a></font>.
<br><br>
<h2>Familiarizing Yourself With Window Operations</h2>
<font size=3 face="Arial">
The beauty of a windowed environment is that this
environment uses familiar terminology. You open a window,
<br>you close a window, you select one of the window's
    panes.
<br><br>
As you learn the process of window management, consider
how you work with windows in the real world.
<br>
<center>
  <!-- The video plays internally in a 300x200 window,
       not starting until the user clicks the play
       button, and repeating continuously -->
  <embed src="window.avi" width=300 height=220
     autostart=true loop=true>
</center>
<br>This window video (1.02 Meg AVI, 11 seconds)
    shows the many analogies between the physical
<br>windows you open and close and your operating
    system windows.</font>

   </body>
</html>
```

Figure 19-3 shows the Web page that results from Listing 19-2's HTML code. If you don't want the video to start until the user clicks the Play button, set the autostart= attribute to false. If you want the video to play only one time, set the loop= attribute to false. One final attribute, hidden=, determines whether the user sees the video or only hears the sound. Because you can embed files of any data type using <embed>, you can embed a sound file with <embed> and set the hidden= attribute to true to hide the audio player but still permit the user to hear the audio.

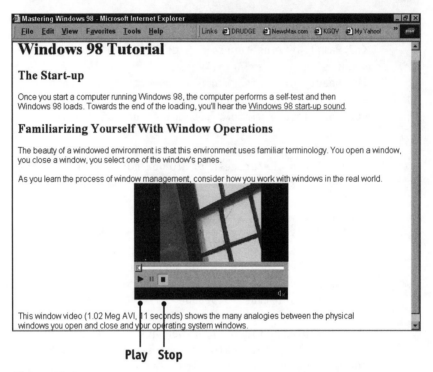

Play Stop

Figure 19-3
The user can stop the video and replay it by clicking the appropriate
control buttons.

**10 Min.
To Go**

The Rollover Effect

One of the most impressive features of any Web page is the *rollover* effect that causes a button or label to change when the user runs the mouse over the button. The button's text may change color or the font may grow, but whatever happens, the rollover effect provides the user with active feedback that shows exactly what the mouse pointer is pointing to.

Rollover effects have nothing to do with typical multimedia features such as sound and graphics, although you certainly can generate a sound within a rollover effect if you want to. You achieve rollover effects by writing a mini-program using the JavaScript language. In a way, JavaScript is a language within HTML, another language. A Web page can become extremely tactile, offering feedback as the user mouses around the screen, making the Web page seem to come alive. The great thing about rollovers is that they add very little to a page's overhead, unlike the typical multimedia elements described in the earlier parts of this session.

Therefore, you should spend a few moments learning how to produce your own rollover effects. Even though rollover effects are not strictly multimedia elements, they fit well as a closing topic for this session because of their active nature. Figure 19-4 shows a Web page that supports the rollover effect. As the user moves the mouse over a button, that button changes in color to show that, if the user clicks the mouse, that button will activate.

Rollover in effect

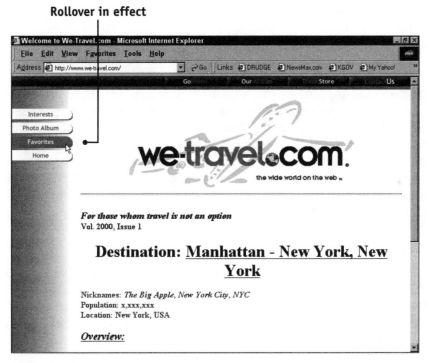

Figure 19-4
Rollover effects help add a useful, dynamic effect to items on a Web page.

JavaScript-enabled

As you learned back in Session 1 and 4, JavaScript is a scripting language, as opposed to a programming language. Although the purists would argue the point, HTML is, in a way, a scripting language of sorts because the browser interprets the HTML commands you write as it reads the commands. Unlike a more traditional, nonscripted programming language that must be compiled to be understood by the computer, JavaScript is interpreted and acted upon line by line.

Netscape developed JavaScript a few years ago as a competitor to Microsoft's ActiveX technology. With JavaScript, Netscape's browsers were able to dynamically respond to the user's actions, leading to the term *DHTML* or *Dynamic HTML*. JavaScript has grown so popular that now all the browsers, including Microsoft's, support JavaScript commands.

A quick rollover example

Although there is not enough time in a weekend course to teach both HTML and JavaScript and anything more than raw HTML at that, you might be able to pick up enough in an example to piece together your own rollover effects if you decide to use them. Therefore, here you will look at the creation of a single rollover effect. You will take one of the buttons from Figure 19-4, which is actually nothing more than a GIF file sized to a button, and see how to create a simple Web page with only that button and the button's rollover effect. This example will move fast and will not explain every last detail, but your appetite to learn about rollovers will be amply whetted once you reach the end of this session.

Create the Graphics

For each rollover effect in your Web page, you need to produce two separate GIF files. Figure 19-5 shows the two buttons, each saved in its own separate GIF file. The button with the white background is saved under the name button.gif, and the button with the dark background is saved under the name buttonM.gif, meaning that is the button that is to appear when the mouse points to it. This button will change colors when the mouse moves over it.

Now that you have two buttons that will represent both sides of the rollover effect, you are ready to create the Web page.

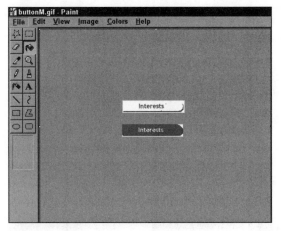

Figure 19-5
The two buttons represent both sides of the rollover effect.

Code the Initial HTML

You can now create a Web page that is a simple page containing only the single button. Listing 19-3 contains a simple HTML program that places the regular button
towards the top of the Web page, using the <img> tag, as shown in Figure 19-6. The
button's image file is named button.gif.

Listing 19-3
Creating a single Web page with one regular button

```
<html>

<head>
  <title>Rollover Effect</title>
</head>

<body bgcolor=#808080>

  <!-- Create some space from the top of the screen -->
  <br><br><br><br>
```

Continued

Listing 19-3 *Continued*

```
<!-- Add a light background to further emphasize rollover -->

<center>
 <img border="0" src="images/button.gif" width=119 height=23>
</center>

</body>

</html>
```

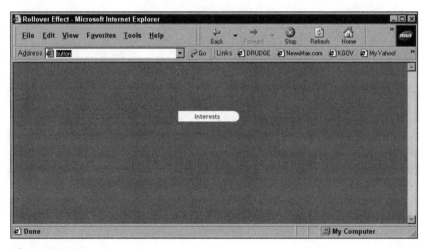

Figure 19-6
The button will change colors when the mouse moves over it.

Writing the JavaScript

Now things get a little crazy. At least, the first time you're exposed to JavaScript, they seem crazy. You now must write the JavaScript code, in the JavaScript language that you do not know, that will store the two versions of the button and make them available when needed — that is, when the user moves the mouse pointer over them and then off once again.

In the header section, you must place the JavaScript that defines the two graphic images, assigns names to them, and makes the images available later in the HTML code. In the body of the page, you must name the button with the name= attribute and add two new *events* to the button's hyperlink reference: ONMOUSEOVER and ONMOUSEOUT. An event is something that happens in a Windows session, usually as the result of the user clicking or moving the mouse or pressing a key. A specific event's code triggers whenever the user performs that event. Therefore, when the user moves the mouse over the button, the ONMOUSEOVER event triggers. When the user moves the mouse away from, or out of, the button's image, the ONMOUSEOUT event occurs. Listing 19-4 shows the complete code that enhances the button with the rollover effect.

Listing 19-4
Creating JavaScript code to store the buttons and make them available

```html
<html>

<head>
  <title>Rollover Effect</title>

  <!-- JavaScript goes next -->
  <script language="javascript1.1">
  <!--
    firstimage=new Image()
    firstimage.src="images/button.gif"
    secondimage=new Image()
    secondimage.src="images/buttonM.gif"
    <!-- Add more dual images for each button on your page -->
    <!-- Therefore, if you have 3 buttons, you'll have a pair
         of entries for thirdimage, etc. -->

//-->
</script>

<script>
<!--
  function changeIt(imagename,objectsrc)
    {
      if (document.images)
```

Continued

Listing 19-4   *Continued*

```
        { document.images[imagename].src=eval(objectsrc+".src") }
        <!-- No change no matter how many buttons you have -->
    }
//-->
</script>

</head>

<body bgcolor=#808080>  <!-- Sets background to gray -->

    <!-- Create some space from the top of the screen -->
    <br><br><br><br>

    <center>
      <!-- Uses the button's name to swap picture -->
      <a href="somewhere.htm"
       ONMOUSEOVER="changeIt('Interests','secondimage')"
       ONMOUSEOUT="changeIt('Interests','firstimage')">
       <!-- A third is ONMOUSECLICK if you want a third effect -->
       <img border="0" name="Interests"
        src="images/button.gif" width=119
        height=23></a>

    </center>

</body>

</html>
```

Notice that the code stores each of the two images, and then the event, in the body of the code, swaps the button with its opposite image. The changeIt routine requests that the button named Interests be swapped with the other image. You might also notice that JavaScript appears completely inside comments. Therefore, any older browsers will ignore the JavaScript and will just display a regular button. Older browsers also ignore unrecognized attributes, such as the ONMOUSEOVER and ONMOUSEOUT events.

Done!

"How am I supposed to know what to code?" you may be asking. When your Web page contains ten buttons, what do you do differently? The answer is, start with this code and simply add to it. Where this code stores two button images, your code will store ten pairs of images. This code is the skeleton for most of the rollover effects in use today. Don't expect to decipher and understand every line of the preceding JavaScript. It is the foundation for future expansion as you learn more about JavaScript and DHTML.

REVIEW

- Although bandwidth is increasing, limit your use of multimedia to present fast-loading Web sites.
- You can add sounds with the simple hyperlink tag.
- Sound and video clips should be stored in their own directories to limit the multiple loading of the same file that appears several times on a site.
- Video clips can request an external player or appear inside the Web page itself.
- Rollover effects help to activate your page with DHTML.

QUIZ YOURSELF

1. Name two popular audio formats for Web use. (See "Adding Sound to Web Pages.")
2. True or False: The user can start and stop a sound you embed in a Web page using the ⟨a⟩ tag. (See "Sound with HTML.")
3. What is the difference between a Web page video and a Web page streaming video? (See "Adding Video to Web Pages.")
4. What is the difference between external video and internal video? (See "Adding Video to Web Pages.")
5. What language supports rollover effects? (See "The Rollover Effect.")

Part IV—Saturday Evening
Session 19

SESSION

20

Be Uniform with Style Sheets

Session Checklist

✔ Learn why style sheets are needed and their advantages and disadvantages

✔ Learn the format of a style in a style sheet and the most popular styles

✔ Prepare a style sheet for an individual Web page or one for an entire site

✔ Perform advanced work with styles, such as specifying classes

**30 Min.
To Go**

I n this session, you learn how to format using an approach that differs from the individual formatting you've learned so far. You learn how to format with style sheets. Style sheets should revolutionize the way programmers write HTML code. In this session, you learn the why and how of style sheets. Although you won't learn every style sheet detail, you will begin to see why style sheets promise to change the way programmers create Web pages in the future.

Introducing Style Sheets

Perhaps you've used styles in word processors. When you create a style for a paragraph, for example, you specify that paragraph's margins, fonts, and spacing, as well as any other details you want that paragraph style to achieve. You name the style for easy reference. Then any paragraphs you later write will take on that style's requirements when you apply the paragraph style's name to those paragraphs.

By defining a style once, you don't have to reissue the same formatting commands every time you want that style. You only need to begin writing without regard to any formatting. When you finish, you then apply the style, and the word processor formats the paragraph properly. HTML supports style sheets as well. The HTML style sheets are called *Cascading Style Sheets* (or *CSS*), and they work in a manner similar to those in your word processor.

Before you continue . . .

Before this session continues, please understand that the analogy between word processor style sheets and HTML style sheets is an imperfect one at best. Whereas most word processors are *WYSIWYG* (*What You See Is What You Get,* which is the concept that the screen looks like the finished, printed product will look), most HTML style sheets do *not* represent what appears on the final user's screen. HTML's style sheets are merely recommendations to the end-user's browser as to how to format the Web page. This is because of the vast array of Web viewing equipment on the market. You can create a fantastic heading style that wows the masses when your screen is the only game in town, but consider a list of just *some* of the hardware that users may use to view your Web page:

- A 21-inch, high-resolution, plasma, flat-panel, 1200×1024 pixel, 16-million color monitor
- A 15-inch, 640 × 480 pixel, 256-color monitor
- WebTV
- Black-and-white portable Internet-ready displays, such as cell phones, that display 40 characters per line and up to 10 lines of a Web page at any one time before requiring scrolling (such screens come on devices called *PDAs, Personal Data Assistants*)

With such an array of hardware, how applicable is your style that defines a paragraph as a boldfaced blue Times Roman 12-point font whose first line is indented 5 characters, with a maximum line width of 80 characters? You have absolutely no assurances that the target browser will be able to respect your style wishes.

Yet, you cannot throw out Web page material without any formatting, right? You have the choice of applying all the individual formatting commands you've learned so far, applying a style sheet to your page, or combining the two.

Why use style sheets

Style sheets have had some impact on HTML coding but have a long way to go. Just about everybody agrees that style sheets are necessary to ensure a site's consistency and maintainability. The problem is that not all browsers support styles and style sheets themselves are going through a maturation phase, having two sets of standards: CSS1 (or CSS Level 1) and CSS2 (or CSS Level 2). Until the style sheet standard settles a little more, and until HTML programming handles style sheets more consistently, the use of style sheets will remain more theory than practice.

Nevertheless, you must maintain proper coding techniques, and to do so, you need to understand style sheets and how they benefit you as you do HTML programming. Depending on your audience, you may want to offer your entire site with style sheets. If you write for a company's intranet that has standardized on a browser version that supports style sheets, it is safe to use them and you are encouraged to use style sheets. A company-wide style sheet helps ensure that your company's Web pages remain consistent.

Another reason to learn about style sheets is that they are a part of HTML and are growing with each new release. HTML 4.01 supports both the CSS1 and CSS2 standards of style sheets, and in the future, no browser is likely to be released that does not conform to these standards. As the world begins to use styles more, so will you.

The added advantages of CSS

To wrap up the CSS introduction, consider this list of features and advantages:

- You can speed the formatting of your Web pages by defining a style in one place and then applying that style to all Web page material that should use it.

- You can change the look of your entire Web site by changing only the style sheet's styles.

- Style sheets support formatting that straight HTML does not support. For example, you can remove the automatic underlining from hyperlinks and place text and graphics at an exact pixel position on the page.

- You can save time when creating new pages for your Web site if it has its fundamental styles defined.
- You can create a style sheet for an individual page or for all the pages on one Web site.

Introducing HTML Styles

Just about any formatting you've already mastered has a style sheet equivalent. In style sheet terminology, you'll be specifying *characteristics* as opposed to the attributes you specify when issuing individual tags. The format of the typical style and some of the popular style characteristics are covered in this section.

Typical style format

Here is the format of the typical style:

Tag{characteristic1; characteristic2; ...; characteristicN}

Here is a sample tag:

```
h1{font-family: "Arial", "Schoolbook"; color: blue}
```

The <h1> tag is the primary heading tag that you've already mastered. The characteristics (you can list as many as you need to list) follow the tag inside the braces. This style says that all h1 tagged paragraphs in the page (or on the entire site depending on how you set up the styles) are to use the Arial font, and if that's not available, a font named Schoolbook. In addition, the second characteristic states that all h1 text is to be blue. Any characteristics of the tag that you do not explicitly state will take on the tag's default characteristics. Therefore, text formatted with this <h1> attribute will be boldfaced because <h1> normally boldfaces the heading text and the style does nothing to override that boldfacing.

That's really all there is to creating styles. The remaining sections of this session explain how to apply the styles to a Web page or to your entire site, and explore more ways to present the styles.

Useful style characteristics

**20 Min.
To Go**

As previously noted, just about any formatting you've already mastered has a style sheet (or style sheet characteristic) equivalent. In this section, you'll learn the more popular style characteristics.

To align text, use the `text-align` characteristic. Each of the following styles aligns a headline level differently. (By the way, this is for illustrative purposes only; don't try this at home! Giving the first four headline styles four different alignments would look disastrous at best and is likely to lose visitors to your site.)

```
h1{text-align: left}
h2{text-align: center}
h3{text-align: right}
h4{text-align: justify}
```

You can change the *weight* of a font, meaning you can use the `font-weight` characteristic to apply boldfacing to a font of a normal, nonboldfaced weight or apply normal weight to a font that is already boldfaced by default. The first of the next two styles removes the boldfacing normally found on the h1 (heading) font, and the second style applies boldfacing to the p (paragraph) style:

```
h1{font-weight: normal}
p{font-weight: bold}
```

Remember that all unspecified default characteristics will apply unless you override them. Therefore, the ⟨h1⟩ tag will appear with a normal weight due to the style but will still be in a large typeface because the ⟨h1⟩ tag will normally display its information in the large typeface.

To italicize text, use the `font-style` characteristic like this:

```
h1{font-style: italic}
p{font-style: italic}
```

Even though these examples specify only one characteristic at a time for each style, you can combine as many as you want, separating them with semicolons. I show only one at a time here so that you can more easily focus on each new characteristic.

Change the size of the font by specifying the `font-size` characteristic. You can specify an exact font size like this:

```
p{font-size: 14}
```

You can also specify a relative font size using one of these characteristics: `xx-small`, `x-small`, `small`, `medium`, `large`, `x-large`, and `xx-large`. The following styles each specify one of the seven relative font sizes, which let the user's browser resize the text on the page:

```
p1{font-size:xx-small}
p2{font-size:x-small}
p3{font-size:small}
p4{font-size:medium}
p5{font-size:large}
p6{font-size:x-large}
p7{font-size:xx-large}
```

Never, as a rule, specify a style with an exact font size if you want to please all your users all the time. Most of today's browsers enable the user to increase or decrease the text size on the page. The browsers might refuse to change any font size for which you've specified the exact point size. However, they often resize specified relative font sizes.

To specify a named text color, use the `color` characteristic like this:

```
h1{color: blue}
h2{color: red}
```

In addition to the named colors, you can also specify any color using a hexadecimal number such as this:

```
h1{color: #00cc00}
```

As you saw in the previous section, you can specify one or more font names you want the browser to choose from. The browser begins at the first font on the left and goes down the list, from left to right, until the browser sees a font that it recognizes. If all fonts in the style are unavailable on the user's machine, the browser does its best to guess, which is not always well.

Use the `font-family` characteristic to specify one or more fonts as follows:

```
h1{font-family: "Arial", "Schoolbook"}
```

To specify the maximum width of a style's paragraph, use the `width` characteristic followed by a pixel value, like this:

```
p{width: 400px}
```

You can also specify both the width and height of all images that use a specific tag with the `width` and `height` characteristics, like this:

```
img{width: 320px; height: 240px}
```

You can use the `line-height` characteristic to specify the exact line height, in pixels, like this:

```
body{line-height: 12px}
```

A nice style that often comes in handy where the regular formatting codes don't work well is paragraph indention. Use the `text-indent` characteristic to specify the paragraph's first line indention. You can specify the indention in exact pixels (px), inches (in), centimeters (cm), millimeters (mm), or points (pt), or else as a percentage (%). The percentage ensures that your paragraph indents well no matter how wide the user's browser screen appears.

```
body{text-indent: 3%}
```

The `margin-left`, `margin-right`, and `margin-top` characteristics determine how wide the margins around the text will be. If you want to set both the left and right margins to the same width, use the `margin` characteristic, like this:

```
body{margin: 12pt}
```

You've now seen the general fundamentals of styles that you can specify. You now need to learn how to prepare the style sheet for use. The last ten minutes of this session will then explore the more advanced characteristics that you can use.

Preparing One of Two Style Sheets

Keep in mind that HTML supports two style sheets: a style sheet for an individual Web page and one for an entire site. When you create a style sheet for a single Web page, you define the styles inside that page in the header section. When you create a style sheet for an entire site, the style sheet must reside in an external central location so that all the Web pages can link to the styles.

Generally, linking to an external style sheet is better site design than embedding styles inside each page. The single, linked style sheet puts all your site's styles inside one location for easy access. Nevertheless, if a Web page does contain a special style element not found in any other page on the site, you might embed that single style in that one Web page. The style won't clutter the site's external style sheet. If, however, that style ultimately needs to appear on more pages, move the embedded style to the linked style sheet.

The next few sections explain both ways to set up the styles.

Style sheets for individual Web pages

Place your styles in the header section of the Web page you want those styles applied to. Begin with the <style> tag and follow that tag by all the styles you want to define. When you finish, close with the </style> end tag before completing the header section. The following code illustrates such a header section:

```
<html>
  <head>
    <title>Family Reunion</title>

    <style>
      h1{font-family: "Arial", "Schoolbook"; color: blue}
      p{font-family: "Arial"; color: black}
    </style>
  </head>
<!-- Rest of HTML file goes here -->
```

In the HTML body, any and all lines formatted with the <h1> or <p> tag would take on the style listed in the style section of the header. The default <h1> and <p> tags would take backseats. Therefore, the following heading would appear blue and the subsequent text black, both in the Arial font:

```
<body>
<h1>Come One, Come All!</h1>
<br><br>
<p>The McMullen Family Reunion is June 6th.</p>
```

Only those tags you've defined will be affected by the style. If you are creating a rather long Web page, define a style for each element that varies from default values and then forego all the subsequent formatting tags except for the start and end tags that specify which style to use.

Not all browsers support styles, but many in use today do. If you want to be absolutely certain that all users, including those with browsers that do not support styles, view your Web page without confusion, you can embed the styles inside comment tags. Browsers that can read the styles will realize that the styles lie inside comments and *will* follow those styles in spite of the comments. The comments, however, will protect the styles from those browsers that do not recognize them and that would otherwise display the style text on the screen.

To hide a style, add a comment directly on the line that follows the `<style>` tag, then close the comment once you finish typing the styles. The following code hides the styles from unsupported browsers:

```
<html>
  <head>
    <title>Family Reunion</title>

    <style>
    <!--
      h1{font-family: "Arial", "Schoolbook"; color: blue}
      p{font-family: "Arial"; color: black}
    -->
    </style>
  </head>
  <!-- Rest of HTML file goes here -->
```

Type the comment exactly as you see it here, and the browsers will follow or ignore the styles as needed.

One style sheet for multiple Web pages

As you surf through popular Web sites, consider why they are popular. Almost all the popular, most-visited sites have these elements in common:

1. They contain needed information or provide an enjoyable diversion.
2. They load quickly.
3. They retain a consistent look throughout the site.

One of the ways to achieve site consistency is to develop a style sheet for the entire site. Once you do, each Web page can then use those styles in a uniform manner.

Consider how much less cluttered your HTML code will be when you adopt style sheets. Instead of wading through all those tags and attributes, you can maintain all the styles in a single location, the rest of your pages containing primarily text and graphic elements. When you make changes to the site, such as updating some of the text, you won't be bothered with as many tags. When you add new text, grab one of the appropriate predefined styles in the style sheet that you have already set up.

To create a single style sheet for your site, you only need to create a text file and add the styles. Do not include tags. A file that defines styles such as those presented at the end of the previous section might look like this:

```
h1{font-family: "Arial", "Schoolbook"; color: blue}
p{font-family: "Arial"; color: black}
```

As you can see, the file is simple. You must save the file with the .css filename extension, such as salesite.css; the name before the extension can be any legal filename.

In each Web page that is to use the .css file's styles, you must link the header section to the style sheet file. Don't use the <style> tag, but rather use the <link> tag with this format:

```
<link rel=stylesheet type="text/css" href=filename.css>
```

Therefore, a Web page that uses styles from salesite.css might begin like this:

```
<html>
  <head>
    <title>4th Quarter Sales Site</title>

    <link rel=stylesheet type="text/css href=salesite.css>
    </style>
  </head>
  <!-- Rest of HTML file goes here -->
```

Advanced Work with Styles

Several more style factors exist that you can incorporate into your Web site. Although some are fairly advanced for this weekend introduction, such as style classes, you will have little trouble understanding the concepts presented here. Not enough room exists in a single session to explore style classes fully, but that's okay. It will take several years before every Web user can handle style sheets, and it will take even longer before all Web sites begin to use styles exclusively. Other advanced topics include specifying background images and colors, specifying exact pixel placement, and removing underlines from hyperlinks.

Specifying style classes

Classes add a layer of complexity to style sheets, and yet the need for classes will be obvious to you as you use styles. Classes enable you to specify two or more styles for a single tag element. In other words, you can specify two styles for the <h1> tag and three styles for the <body> tag if you feel the need to do so.

Obviously, the extra layer adds confusion because the Web page body is one entity and uses one tag, <body>, and yet two or more styles can be applied to the use of the <body> tag on the site. Actually, the implementation of classes is not as difficult as it may first sound. In some ways, the multiple levels of file directory structures that you have used for years are similar to those of style sheet classes.

When you define a class, separate the class name from the style with the dot operator (a period). The following style sheet defines three classes (i.e., normal, quoted, and vital, good names to use for such styles) for the paragraph tag:

```
<style>
  p.normal{margin: 12pt; text-indent: 3%}
  p.quoted{margin: 16pt; font-style: italic}
  p.vital{margin: 12pt; color: red; font-weight: bold}
</style>
```

Here you have three separate styles defined for the regular paragraph tag. Certainly you have regular paragraph text that takes on different formats. Listing 20-1 contains an HTML program that utilizes these classes. The regular text uses the normal class, quoted text uses long quotations, and the vital class sets apart important text from surrounding text.

Listing 20-1
Utilizing three classes in HTML

```html
<html>

  <head>
    <title>Classes</title>
    <style>
      p.normal{text-indent: 3%}
      p.quoted{margin: 45pt; font-style: italic}
      p.vital{text-indent: 3%; color: red; font-weight: bold}
    </style>
  </head>

<body>
  <h1>Investing Basics</h1>

  <p class=normal>Personal investing basics begins with your
    bills. How much do you owe? To whom do you owe? How much
    interest do your debts require? Consider the case of Jeff
    G., a homeowner who recently wrote into
    MoneyFinancesAndMe.com:</p>
  <p class=quoted>We want to look into investing. We have
    about $2,500 to invest. We own our home and have a
    mortgage. We also owe about $2,500 in credit card bills
    that require about 19% annual interest. Where do we
    begin investing?</p>
  <p class=vital>Jeff G, we can tell you how to earn 19% on
    your money instantly and risk-free! Pay off the credit
     card. Don't even consider putting your money in other
    investments until your card is handled. If you do
    not, you must make your investment earn 19% before you are
    one penny ahead!</p>
  <p class=normal>In many ways, a penny saved is worth
    <i>more</i> than a penny earned. When you earn money, you
    must pay taxes on that money. If, however, you save any
    amount, such as $10, you save that $10 after-tax. The
    IRS has not (yet) found a way to tax you on money
    you save by not spending that money on goods or high-debt
interest.</p>
```

```
    </body>
    </html>
```

Figure 20-1 shows the Web page produced by the classes in Listing 20-1. The quoted paragraph stands out from the rest of the text, and the second-to-last paragraph appears in red due to its important nature.

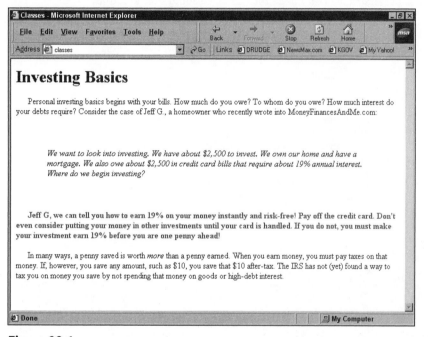

Figure 20-1
Distinguish similarly tagged paragraphs from each other with classes.

If you or your company use multiple style sheets, use the same class name for the same kind of style throughout your Web pages. If you do not, the similar styles with different names will be confusing at best and make maintenance difficult when you must make a change to one of those styles.

Specify background images and colors

Remember that you can specify just about anything inside style sheets that you otherwise would include in a formatting tag. You can add a background color or image to a style. One of the more interesting effects of adding color or a background is the appearance on the Web page. The rectangular text that appears inside the style is enclosed inside the color or graphic image, whereas the rest of the Web page is left in the default color.

A simple example will demonstrate how effectively you can use color and background images. Listing 20-2 sets up two heading classes. One specifies a color, and the other specifies an image for the h1 heading's background.

Listing 20-2
Adding background colors or images with styles

```html
<html>

  <head>
    <title>Classes</title>
    <style>
      h1{background: blue; color: white}
      h2{background: url("fire.gif"); color: white; font-weight: bold}
      p.normal{text-indent: 3%}
      p.quoted{margin: 45pt; font-style: italic}
      p.vital{text-indent: 3%; color: red; font-weight: bold}
    </style>
  </head>

<body>
  <h1>Investing Basics</h1>

  <p class=normal>Personal investing basics begins with your bills.
    How much do you owe? To whom do you owe? How much interest do
    your debts require? Consider the case of Jeff G., a homeowner
    who recently wrote into MoneyFinancesAndMe.com:</p>
  <p class=quoted> We want to look into investing. We have
    about $2,500 to invest. We own our home and have a mortgage.
    We also owe about $2,500 in credit card bills that require
    about 19% annual interest. Where do we begin investing? </p>
  <p class=vital>Jeff G, we can tell you how to earn 19% on your money
    instantly and risk-free! Pay off the credit card. Don't even consider
    putting your money in other investments until your card is handled.
    If you do not, you must make your investment earn 19% before you
    are one penny ahead!</p>
  <h2>Saving Money!</h2>
  <p class=normal>In many ways, a penny saved is worth <i>more</i> than
    a penny earned. When you earn money, you must pay taxes on that
    money. If, however, you save any amount, such as $10, you save that
    $10 after-tax. The IRS has not (yet) found a way to tax you on money
    you save by not spending that money on goods or high-debt interest.</p>

</body>
</html>
```

Figure 20-2 shows the headings as they now appear.

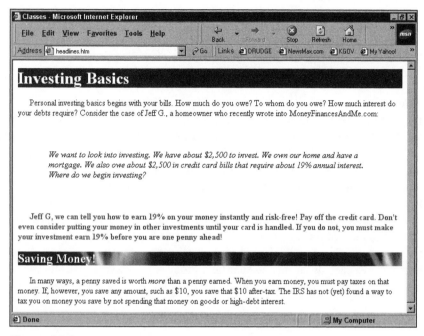

Figure 20-2
Background colors and images can accent headings.

If the GIF image is not large enough to cover the paragraph's rectangular area, the browser repeats the image.

Specifying exact pixel placement

Beginning with CSS2, supported only by some of the most recent Web browsers, along with HTML 4.01, you are able to specify the exact pixel placement of text or images on the page. Unfortunately, the huge lack of support for the feature means that you should not attempt to use these new styles for a few years.

In the meantime, you can use a trick to place an image or text exactly where you want. Remember that the `margin-top` and `margin-left` style characteristics allow you to begin a new element at a specific pixel. Therefore, to place an image at exactly 45 pixels from the top of the screen and 30 pixels from the left of the screen, you code this:

```
p.pic1{margin-top: 30px; margin-left: 45px}
```

Later in the body, you can position an image like this:

```
<p class=pic1><img src="myphoto.gif"></p>
```

Actually, this method works consistently, but it is crude. Besides, why would you want to place an image at an exact pixel location when so many monitors with so many different sizes and resolutions will be viewing your Web page? The answer is that you may need to exactly position an image or text, such as a small company's logo, in the top-left corner of the screen. With exact image positioning, you can even produce a shadow effect by positioning two versions of the same text offset from each other.

As you progress through your HTML coding career, keep your eyes peeled for signs of more conformance to the CSS2 standard that allows for this kind of text and image positioning, which works better than the older margin characteristics. New features such as layers and spanning produce the effects that one would want, but the cost, at least for today, is lack of compliance among browsers.

Removing underlines from hyperlinks

One way that some HTML programmers distinguish their pages with styles is to remove the underlines from hyperlinks. The hyperlinks still appear in their usual colors, and the mouse cursor changes to the hyperlink shape, but the typical underline does not appear. Too many underlines throughout a page may make the page look busier than it should appear. Then again, by removing the underlines, you remove one standard way of specifying hyperlinks. The trade-off between style and standard must be yours to make.

To remove the underlining, you only need to define a style for the anchor tag using the text-decoration characteristic like this:

```
a {text-decoration: none;}
```

In addition to removing the underline, you can also specify colors for the anchor like this:

```
a:link {color:#0000ff }
a:active {color: #cccccc }
a:visited {color: #ff0000 }
```

Done!

REVIEW

- Web page style sheets are similar to, but not the same as, word processor style sheets.
- Style sheets provide a uniform formatting for Web pages but do not ensure the pages will look the same on every user's screen.
- You must define styles, either inside the Web page or in a linked, centralized text file, before you can use styles on your site.
- Style characteristics define the styles.
- Classes enable you to format similar kinds of text in different ways.
- With styles, you can position text and graphics exactly where you want them as well as remove the underlines from hyperlink anchors.

QUIZ YOURSELF

1. Why don't style sheets ensure that all your users' Web pages look exactly the same? (See "Before You Continue . . .")

2. What is the difference between the `font-weight` and `font-style` characteristics? (See "Useful Style Characteristics.")

3. What advantage does a percentage indention offer over a fixed paragraph indention specified in pixels? (See "Useful Style Characteristics.")

4. Why would you ever need to embed a single style in a Web page's header section, while still maintaining a centralized, linked style sheet file? (See "Preparing One of Two Style Sheets.")

5. What is the difference between a class and an unclassed style? (See "Specifying Style Classes.")

PART

IV

Saturday Evening
Part Review

1. What displays on your Web page as a result of a meta tag?

2. In what section do you place meta tags?

3. How do search engines treat the `name=` and `description=` meta tag attributes?

4. True or False: You can make your Web page invisible from search engines.

5. Name three common Web page sections typically offered with frames.

6. How can frame borders and table borders differ?

7. Name two drawbacks to using frames.

8. Why is a general, nonviewable frame set Web page required when using frames?

9. What is the purpose of the `<noframes>` and `</noframes>` tag pair?

10. What multimedia item is the simplest to embed in a Web page?

11. Why should you tell the user how much space a multimedia element requires before the user elects to experience the multimedia element such as a video clip?

12. What is the difference between a streaming and nonstreaming video clip?

13. What is the difference between an external video clip and a Web page's internal video clip?

14. Why is `<embed>` still a better tag to use for embedded video clips than `<object>` even though `<object>` is the approved standard tag?

15. Describe rollover effects.

16. What is an event?

17. Why should you not specify fonts of specific sizes when using style sheets?

18. What is the equivalent style characteristic for margin-left and margin-right?

19. In which Web page section do you embed styles?

20. Write a style that colors a page's visited anchor tags gray and removes the underline from all hyperlinks.

☑ Friday

☑ Saturday

☑ **Sunday**

PART

V

Sunday Morning

Developing a Web Site from Scratch

Session Checklist

✔ Hire a team of developers to create a professional-looking Web site

✔ Explore all potential Web sites and strategies

✔ Consider the Web site's general content and make-up

**30 Min.
To Go**

Y ou now have learned all the HTML you need to know to create beginning
and even fairly advanced Web pages. Not only do you understand the HTML
behind the page, but also you've picked up many design tips along the way.
Now you are ready to follow the step-by-step creation of a Web site from design
to implementation. In the next 9 sessions, you will review the concepts you've
learned thus far and see most of them implemented in a building-block approach.
Along the way, you'll take detours to learn why one method or design was implemented over another.

The subsequent sessions are shorter than the previous ones to give you ample
time in 30 minutes to try some of the techniques shown to you. Think of these
next sessions as both a review and a hands-on guide, with extra tips and techniques
thrown in when needed to give you a feel for the real world of site building.

The Web Page Team

Implementing a Web site requires more than a single person in the majority of cases. When you run across a site that is conspicuously amateurish looking, that site is less than professional for one or two reasons:

1. The Web site author didn't understand Web-based design issues such as ample whitespace, fast-loading pages, and less-is-more when it comes to frames.

2. The Web site author is simply too burdened with the creation and upkeep of the site itself and cannot spend the time and resources needed to make the site work well.

Except for extremely simple personal Web sites, a professional Web site almost always requires a team of people. That team might include:

- Project Leader: Coordinates all the user interviews, the artwork (icons and other art), and the text, while maintaining constant contact with the users who want the Web site.

- Art Director: Maintains consistency of the site's artwork, plans much of the artwork, and directs the individual artists.

- Copy Editor: Keeps the grammar and spelling of the site correct and has Web-based skills to help manage the proper use of headings and overall tone.

- Programmers: Develop the JavaScript and CGI scripts, and write the HTML code.

Some of these jobs will overlap. The Project Leader might very well help code the HTML tables, and the HTML programmers might design icons under the direction of the Art Director. Allow your team members to perform cross-duties to keep the activity fresh and enjoyable, because the excitement will show through to the final project if the team likes the work.

Obviously, the term *user* takes on different meanings at different times. Company A may hire a team to develop a professional Web site. To the site designers, Company A is the client and the initial user of the Web site during the testing and implementation. The company's customers then take over the user role. You, the designer, must listen to the people paying your salary, Company A, but design ultimately for end users, the typical customers who may be viewing the site. You must tread carefully between the client, your design team, and the ultimate end users. Systems analyst skills are often vital if you are to function as a go-between between your client, who may know nothing about Web page construction, and your team, who may know nothing about business.

Consider the expense for a company that devotes resources to funding a Web team. The start-up costs of a major Web site are staggering. When I first thought of designing Web sites, I figured it would take little more than a word processor with pictures to move around. Was I ever wrong! Even a simple personal Web site such as the one created in the next few sessions takes time and, if available, personnel to design, lay out, create, implement, and maintain it.

Sites don't have to be elaborate to work well! As a matter of fact, most of the popular sites today have extremely simple formats. They load fast and offer elements the user can dig deeper for if desired. Consider the Yahoo! home page, one of the most popular home pages today. The Yahoo! home page contains virtually no graphics, text headings are nothing more than hyperlinks to the details behind them, and a search box enables users to look for topics. A couple of banner ads, unlike on many sites, do not distract from the page; they even add some freshness to the simplicity. Yahoo! works because it is simple. A ton of information resides just under the surface if the user wants to explore a link or perform a search, but the information is never forced upon the user in great amounts until (and only if) the user requests the information.

Suppose you don't have time or a desire to throw together a Web team! Obviously, you'll be following along, watching the sample site's development, as a one-person operation. Great! You want to be Project Leader, and that means that you have all the skills necessary to understand your team's needs when you lead a team. And if you are simply a sole Web designer and HTML coder who wants your own Web site for fun, kicks, family, friends, and possible profit, hang on and you'll learn the skills.

For more information on Web page design, take a look at *Web Design Studio Secrets, 2/E,* by Deke McClelland, et al, (IDG Books Worldwide, Inc.).

**20 Min.
To Go**

Exploring Possible Sites and Strategies

Given that you're working alone for the rest of the weekend, without a team, the site chosen for this cross-session tutorial will be simple but will contain as many elements as can be squeezed in without making the site look cluttered. You should see as much HTML and as many HTML features and techniques implemented as possible. And yet, a major Web site cannot be described, let alone created in a step-by-step manner, in ten sessions of a tutorial such as this without keeping the site simple.

Therefore, you will consider a family Web site for a professional HTML programmer. Such a site may seem a little too watered-down for an old HTML pro such as yourself (after all, you've spent twenty 30-minute hard- and fast-hitting sessions learning HTML). The site, however, will take on a fairly professional quality given the simplicity at which this tutorial must keep it, the time you have left in the weekend course, and the amount of HTML programming that you know.

Brainstorming with the team

So far, you've read about the goal and nature of the site, but you haven't seen anything. That's because you *won't* see anything until the first page of the site is created. When you sit down to design a site, or when you and your Web team first sit down, you don't have a copy of the Web page that you want to develop in front of you because the page isn't yet developed!

The first thing you'll do as a team is discuss the goals of the site. You will brainstorm about possible strategies such as an all-encompassing linked style sheet versus individual formatting tags. Who is the audience? Who wants the site built? If you are creating a Web site for your family, some of the answers are obvious. If, however, you work for a company, the customers of your Web site may be a division within your firm that needs a site for parts distribution, or it may be your sales staff, who need a sales analysis site. The customers may be individuals in the Web community who may order products from you. You may be a *B2B* (*business-to-business*) Web operation whose customers may be other companies that use your company's services.

As you can see, some customers pay for the site's creation directly (another department that wants a Web page), and some customers pay for the site's creation indirectly (as do end users in the community who might purchase a product from you or from one of your banner advertisers).

What resources are devoted to the site's creation and maintenance? If no resources are devoted to maintenance, you know to go right back to the customer to explain that the site will be static and customers will never return a third time. Explain how much time and effort is required to keep the site fresh. Ask who will supply the material to be put on the site periodically if the customer wants regular updates.

For a family Web site, you are probably the entire Web design team. You are probably paying for the site, paying for your own time (your payment is the opportunity costs that you lose by spending time on the site instead of on another project), paying the site domain name registration, designing the site, creating the site, gathering the artwork, implementing the site, and maintaining the site when a family member wants something changed or added.

Such a multi-hat job sounds horrible when put that bluntly! Nevertheless, such a site is perhaps the *best way* to hone your HTML and Web page design skills. Starting with a personal Web page means that you can mess things up with no major consequences. You can learn what works and what doesn't. If you spruce up the site and provide extras that only HTML coders would know, as opposed to the personal Web sites created on the fly in a Web-page creation program such as FrontPage Express, your site will stand apart in a crowd of personal Web sites and you'll learn fast.

Getting specifics from the client

You must know where you're headed before designing your site. You must interview the client, hold brainstorming Web team meetings, conduct more interviews, remain realistic about what works on the site, and hone the site's design. Specifics now are crucial, and as the Web page develops, you or the client will surely change some details later. When you are building a house, adding a bathroom between two existing walls is difficult, so the complete house plans must be made before construction. Adding a new page between two existing Web pages is simple. Nevertheless, if the client changes the design once you've began the site, you'll need to consider upping your charges. If you're building the site for yourself, change is not an issue.

Sticklers who insist on designing every single page element before going to the keyboard are stuck in the 1960's batch language world of mainframe computers. Today's computers give instant feedback. Make a change to your HTML, and you instantly see the result of that change inside your browser. However, if you're working for a client who wants a change, request that your client sign a change-order request that states the change and the added cost.

Assume that you've already interviewed the family. Therefore, you are ready to move on to deciding what content your family Web site will have.

The Site's General Content and Make-Up

Much more time could be spent describing the design process that Web teams go through and that Web masters perform when creating Web pages on a consulting basis. Nevertheless, you need to get started on the hands-on experience. Assume the kinks have been worked out of the design and that you have interviewed all the family members and know that they are happy. You have the general content just as you would at this point if you or your team were designing the site for a company. You know that someone's going to want things changed, and you don't have all the details but you have enough of a target to go to work.

Therefore, the rest of this session will describe the overall site contents of the family Web Site. In the sessions that follow, you will design the site described here.

General content characteristics

Being that the site is a noncommercial, family site, you'll expect to see all the usual: a familiar tone, lots of pictures, and family news. The parents want a forum to discuss issues that are important to them, the kids want a page to show off to friends, and even the three-year-old has to have something to show for her efforts. Your audience will be far-away family members who view the site every month to catch up on family news, coworkers who view the site because the parents tell them to read their take on a current event, and Web surfing strangers who happen onto your site because the site made it into a Web search engine eventually. Make the family members happiest. Give the coworkers something to talk about (don't they wish *they* knew HTML!), and as a bonus to yourself, attempt to keep that one-in-a-million (literally) surfer who stumbles onto your site reading your site for more than three seconds before jumping to another page.

A multipage site is required because a single Web page is only good for short, informational kinds of sites such as a relocation map that a company might put on the Web for a few months while customers learn the new location. As you develop a multipage site, establish page-by-page goals, as described in the section that follows.

Page-by-page goals

Although the home page is your starting point, you should consider your audience and site goals when you first design your Web site. One way is to lay out a detailed home page contents listing and then describe various pages that will link from that home page. The home page sets the stage for the others. The following sections show how you can go from the home page to the other pages, early in the design stages, without getting too wrapped up in specifics.

The Home Page

The details of the home page are:

- Introduction: Welcome the viewers to the family home page
- E-mail contact: Give others a chance to write to you for feedback and suggestions
- Family Logo: A simple eye-catching logo in the upper-left corner
- A navigation menu for the site
- Recent news (gossip)
- The date of the most recent update to the site

The friends and family who love you most will bookmark this page. Correction, *a few* of the friends and family who love you most will bookmark this page. The home page is the focal point of your site, the central location, the page you'll update most often.

After some discussion, the family members agreed on the following navigation bar items:

- Mom's Corner
- Dad's Corner
- Kids' Playground
- Family Pictures
- Favorite Movies
- Special Bulletins
- Family Travels

Each of these items will link to another page or set of pages.

Mom's and Dad's Corners

In Mom's Corner and Dad's Corner, the parents can say whatever they want announced to friends and family. Probably, each will discuss current events and their reactions, job news, and family gossip that pertains more to their individual interests than the family's interests as a whole.

Kids' Playground

The kids also have their page on which they, within reason guided by the parents, can put whatever they want. You may be surprised how many fairly young school-children now boast having their own Web pages.

Family Pictures

The Family Pictures will hold more photos than text. This might be a great place for the three-year-old's drawings. In the old days, parents would post their kids' drawings on the refrigerator door. Today, they post them on the Internet, a door for the whole world. By archiving such pictures, you can keep such memories alive, and as your children get older, they can see their earlier attempts at artistic fame.

Favorite Movies

The family loves movies, both at the cinema and as video rentals. As members of a heavy movie-watching family, everybody wants to talk about their likes and dislikes in this section.

Special Bulletins

The Special Bulletins section can contain just about anything. Depending on the topic, the Special Bulletins section may grow to include its own submenu on the navigation bar. The Special Bulletins will be more in-depth news that pertains to the family, perhaps hinted at on the Home page's central section.

Done!

Family Travels

The Family Travels section tells either about upcoming trips or recent travels, or both. All have agreed not to list exact travel dates for security concerns at the home!

REVIEW

- Web teams often develop and implement professional Web sites.
- By interviewing clients and users, and by brainstorming, a Web team decides what should and should not appear on a site.
- Users are not always the clients.
- When developing a Web site's content, it helps to outline page-by-page goals.
- The next eight sessions will design the family Web site with the entire family included.

QUIZ YOURSELF

1. Why do professional Web sites require such large teams? (See "The Web Page Team.")
2. Why do you not see a picture of the Web site that's going to be developed in the next several sessions? (See "Brainstorming with the Team.")
3. What's the first step in creating a brand new Web site (after the client hires you, that is!)? (See "Brainstorming with the Team.")
4. What does the term *B2B* mean? (See "Brainstorming with the Team.")
5. True or False: You should never change the site's design once you and the client agree to a design. (See "Getting Specifics from the Client.")

Making the Web Site Home Page Look Good

Session Checklist

✔ Create a logo for the Barkley home page

✔ Prototype the Barkley home page

✔ Decide whether to use tables, frames, or both

✔ Sketch the Barkley home page's table cells from the prototype

✔ Select a color scheme for the Barkley home page

**30 Min.
To Go**

This session focuses on designing the Barkley family's (the family whose Web site you are seeing being developed here) Web site's personal home page. When designing Web sites, you should always work on the home page first. The home page determines the look and tone of the remaining pages on the Web site. Table design forms the skeleton of the Web page. This session ends by showing you some tricks to move quickly to HTML-based tables from your page's initial design.

Creating the Logo

Every site needs a logo. The logo is placed on a Web site's home page. Some may debate this, but as you drive around town, look at the signs for all the businesses you pass. Each business has a primary logo. Logos quickly generate *brand recognition,* letting you and others know at a glance what you're looking at. No names please, but suppose you were traveling in a foreign country, didn't know the language, and saw a sign advertising the largest soft drink maker in the world. You'd know instantly what that sign was selling, wouldn't you? You cannot read the sign's language, but you know the logo.

Your site deserves no less. Create brand recognition. Who knows, your site might be the next Yahoo! Before working on the overall page, work on the logo. Although you may end up honing the logo somewhat over time, improving it as you go, spend some time planning your site's logo now so that you can provide that logo to other sites that might want to link to yours.

 Place your site's logo in the upper-left corner of the home page. You can put the logo anywhere on the page, but by putting the most important element where the user sees it first, no matter what the user's resolution and screen size values are, you ensure that your logo is seen.

A family Web site, such as the site the rest of these sessions develop, may not seem to require a logo. Some family sites grow to become more important sites, even developing into commercial ventures. Even if you have no desire for commercialism on your site, spend time on the logo so that your family and friends quickly recognize your site when it loads.

As you develop the logo, consider the following:

- Logos don't have to be fancy.
- Keep your logo simple.
- Keep your logo small enough to load quickly.
- Use Web-safe colors.
- Use a GIF file to speed the logo's loading time.
- Don't use an animated GIF; your logo should look the same on paper as it looks on the screen.

For extremely simple logos, logos that work just fine on family sites, consider converting your name to a logo. One of the easiest ways to create such a logo is to use an art program to create your logo from text. These applications often let you wrap text around a half-moon or grow the text from left to right and adjust the colors and the shape.

The *Barkleys,* the family whose Web site you are seeing developed here, created the image shown in Figure 22-1 from their name. This is the logo they will place at the top of their site.

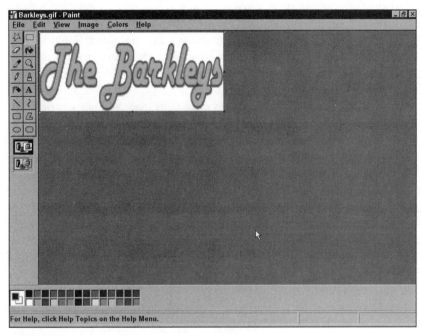

Figure 22-1
Converting text to art is a simple way to generate a logo.

Never lose site of your goal: to make a Web site that people visit, return to, and enjoy looking at. What does creating a logo have to do with HTML? Directly, nothing, but your HTML is only a structure that defines the shape of your site. The site's content is your goal, and HTML is the tool you use to achieve that goal. These last few sessions that show you how to develop a Web site focus on non-HTML elements so that as you do HTML programming, you can work with these other elements that are not straight HTML code.

**20 Min.
To Go**

Creating the Prototype

By now, you've seen the importance of using one or more graphics and design programs as you code with HTML. These programs are a must-have for you as you do HTML programming! No single graphics program does everything well, so you may add several to your HTML programming toolkit as you progress in your work.

Perhaps the single worst mistake you can make when first creating a Web site is to start with the HTML code. You cannot start with the HTML code anymore than a house builder can start with a hammer, nails, and wood. Begin by creating a prototype — a model — of your home page using the graphics program you feel most comfortable using. If you need to, lay out your site's home page on paper first and then move to the graphics program.

The graphics program enables you to place your logo; add mock article titles; draw placeholders for icons you'll fill in later; draw lines to separate sections; play with color schemes that collide, contrast, and complement each other; and add a navigation bar and other elements you'll want to place on your Web page. If the graphics program is fairly recent, you'll almost surely be able to request a Web-safe color palette so that you only choose from colors for the background and fills that come from the 216 Web-safe colors.

By sketching your site in the graphics program before coding any HTML, you can see more quickly what works well and what does not. Don't spend a lot of time on the prototype, but the more final your prototype is, the faster you'll turn HTML into a Web home page that looks like your prototype. Once you have that Web page, you won't need the prototype again.

Depending on how Web-aware your graphics program is, here are some things you can hope to do with its Web page prototyping tools:

- Create a background size to match the screen and resolution you want to target.

- Adjust the resolution to fit different monitors of the users who will visit your site to see the effect on your site.

- Determine the approximate load time for your general home page.

- Note the exact pixel location of the Web page elements to know how to place them with HTML.

- Size boxes that act as placeholders for graphics so that you can more accurately size the graphics from the placeholder pixel sizes when you code the HTML.

By designing the prototype, you are not locking in the design. Your prototype acts to save you time. You can drag elements around the prototype screen, but with HTML, you must change code every time you determine that a graphic image is better located elsewhere on the Web page.

Only after you complete the home page should you worry about any remaining pages on your site. Your home page sets the theme and the tone of the other pages. Often, subsequent pages will have the same header information, perhaps with your logo appearing on all the pages, as well as a navigation bar that keeps appearing throughout so that your users can navigate your site with ease.

Figure 22-2 shows the home page prototype that the Barkleys developed. Notice that the Barkleys left room at the top for the user's Web browser tools. Don't forget that your Web page has, at most, about 75 percent of the user's screen because the browser consumes the rest. Plan for the reduced screen real estate.

If you want to follow along on your own, consider starting your graphics program and designing such a page. Even if you use one of the generic drawing programs that comes with your operating system, such as Paint, you will more quickly achieve a good-looking HTML-based home page.

The design is fairly stable as you see it in Figure 22-2. Users with small screens or low resolution will still see most of the page because the page contents are skewed toward the upper-left corner of the screen. The green bars will span far enough to the right to extend across however wide a screen the user has.

As you develop your prototype, display the prototype in several screen resolutions to ensure that the design works under different conditions. You can often change your monitor's resolution settings, but many Web-aware graphics programs these days offer you the ability to view your creation in different resolutions.

Never allow your graphics program to generate a Web page from your prototype. Many more recent versions can convert your prototype into a Web page. Without exception, graphics programs seem to take your prototype and create a monster page, with too many table cells, too much overhead, and almost indecipherable HTML code. As with Web page development systems such as Dreamweaver and FrontPage, the generated HTML code is tricky to follow. Until these programs get better — and they will — stick with creating your page in HTML. At this point in your HTML career, the practice pays dividends.

room for navigation buttons

room for status bar

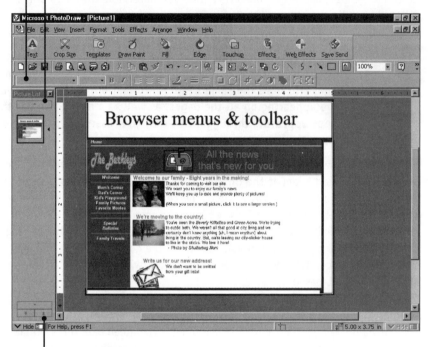

room for user's scroll bar

Figure 22-2
The Barkleys created this prototype for their home page.

**10 Min.
To Go**

Tables or Frames or Both?

Almost all but the simplest Web pages in use today contain tables, because they are so easy to format. Some Web pages use frames as well. The choice between tables and frames sometimes comes up during page design, but it is not a valid choice. You can choose to use both if you want. One does not eliminate the need for the other.

Nevertheless, as you learned in Session 18, frames are not always the best choice for Web pages for the following reasons:

- Frames can confuse users.
- The various screen resolutions can wreak havoc on frame-based pages.
- Frames can actually disable the Back button on some browsers.
- Frames make pages difficult for the user to bookmark.
- The frame borders and scroll bars consume real estate space that you might better use for content.

Despite the problems associated with frames, some simple content is easily presented with frames in a way that won't necessarily cause any problems for your users. For example, if you want the top header portion of a page to remain fixed while the user scrolls down the rest of the page, a frame probably will make such action simple.

The Barkleys decided not to use frames on the majority of their pages, but they use frames on the children's pages (covered in Session 26). Mr. Barkley, however, being an HTML programmer, understands that tables will help the design and lay-out of the page tremendously, as well as make it easy to change the table data as the site changes. Therefore, Mr. Barkley is using tables throughout the site.

Preparing for Tables

Your prototype defines the starting point for designing your home page's tables. One HTML-programmer trick is to print the prototype and draw lines indicating where table cells should be. Even better, use your graphics program to sketch table lines in the prototype, as Figure 22-3 shows. The lines enable you to determine where cells need to go and where they do not need to go.

Many Web-aware graphics programs, such as PhotoShop, virtually create tables for you. For example, once you create a prototype, create a new and empty layer and use the screen guides to create rectangular cells around the boxed areas that seem to demand cells. PhotoShop will display the height and width of each cell box. The total should add up to your projected screen resolution with possibly some overflow that you can adjust once you generate the table in HTML.

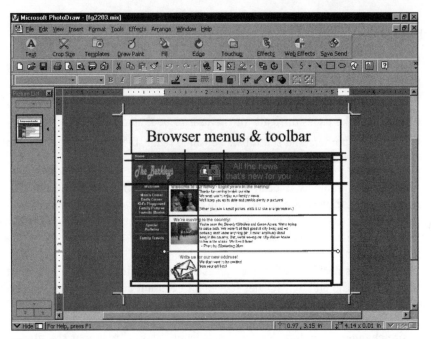

Figure 22-3
Use your prototype to draw table cell lines.

When you start out, you won't know exactly where to draw lines. Just about any place whose baseline holds text or a graphic image should be a cell in your table. Obviously, your Web page will change over time, but you should rarely change your overall structure except to make minor adjustments when content requires it. The Barkley Web site's home page will remain fixed as much as possible, and they will change only the content. Nevertheless, if they have a new baby or some other major news occurs in their lives, they will certainly skew the page's content toward this news, possibly even eliminating the regular article structure in favor of lots of pictures.

Use multiple tables if your Web page requires them. In Figure 22-3, the Barkley family's Web page will use two tables; one will define the header, and one will define three columns in the primary content area. The first column will hold the navigation bar's text, the second column will hold thumbnail pictures and the left part of the heading text, and the final column will hold the bulk of the detail.

Some cell lines will flow through words and sentences. You may have to split some words and sentences into two or three cells, as is done with the Barkleys' heading text. Each row can have a different number of cells, and each cell can have a different width. Nevertheless, don't conform your cells to the text on your initial home page; you don't want to have to change the table's cell arrangement every time you change your text. Better to fix the table arrangement now and then adjust text when needed, even if the adjustment requires that you split text between two or more cells.

Remember that HTML tables use pixel measurements. Therefore, you now must assign pixel widths and heights to the table. If your graphics program displays pixel widths for the various elements on your prototype page, your job is mostly done and you are ready to begin HTML coding. If you must determine pixel widths and heights yourself, you may need to first print the prototype onto paper. To use this method, convert your screen resolution to the most common screen size that you predict your users will use and then print the prototype once you've viewed the prototype in full-screen mode. You will custom-fit many cell pixel sizes to this printed prototype. For example, if you think your typical user will maintain an 800 × 600 screen, print the prototype from a screen of this resolution and estimate a pixel size for each cell using your prototype and drawn cell lines from Figure 22-3.

Selecting Color Scheme

Although your selection of colors is limited to 216 Web-safe colors, you must still ensure that the combination of those 216 colors that you select for various elements of your home page complement each other and not clash. Open a set of commercial art design texts, and you'll see hundreds of pages devoted to color combinations, complementary colors, and reasons that various color mixtures do or don't work for various applications.

The Barkleys decided upon a green with the Web-safe hue of #009900 for their home page's background color, but only for the header and navigation bar to the left of the primary content area. They want to stick with a white background for the majority of the page's content. Although some would argue that a white background is boring, the Barkleys know that a readable page is more important than a snazzy page that's hard to read.

Done!

Now that you've walked through most of the page's design process, the next session leads you into the HTML code. You've now seen how the table structure is best developed. In the next session, you follow along with the Barkleys as they write the initial HTML code to define their home page.

REVIEW

- Your logo, which loads first on your home page, forms the cornerstone of your site and generates brand recognition.
- After you design your logo, create a prototype for your home page before you write any HTML code.
- From the prototype, you can more easily create the home page's table structure.
- It's better that your home page's background color be boring and readable than snazzy and hard to read.

QUIZ YOURSELF

1. What considerations should one make when designing a site's logo? (See "Creating the Logo.")
2. What is a prototype? (See "Creating the Prototype.")
3. Why is HTML one of the worst places to begin a Web site's design? (See "Creating the Prototype.")
4. What tools can you use to create a prototype? (See "Creating the Prototype.")
5. How can a printed prototype enable you to structure your page's table? (See "Preparing for Tables.")

The Web Site Home Page's HTML

Session Checklist

✔ Use an HTML template to begin the Barkleys' home page

✔ Document the Barkleys' HTML code to help others understand it

✔ Create the Barkleys' header with a header table

✔ Complete the Barkleys' header by making its width span the entire screen

**30 Min.
To Go**

Now the fun begins! In this session, you follow the creation of the Barkley family's actual home Web page by watching the building of the HTML code. Remember, you've already been a part of the Barkley family site design in the previous two sessions. Without a proper design, the HTML code becomes a boggled mess. With a good design, the HTML code falls out easily, as you'll see here.

To display one of your own files, such as the Web pages you create in this weekend crash course, don't use the `http://` prefix followed by a Web page address in your browser's address bar. Instead, simply type your own computer's disk and directory. You might type `C:\html\Barkley.htm` to view the Barkleys' Web page that you've created, assuming the page resides in the HTML directory of drive C and that you've named the file Barkley.htm.

The Initial HTML Template

When building your HTML code for the Barkley family's home page, start with an initial HTML skeleton structure for your code. By creating such a template, you help ensure that you include all the important sections. Listing 23-1 shows the basic starting place for all HTML-based Web pages.

Listing 23-1
Starting the HTML-based pages with a template

```
<html>
 <head>

  <title>Window title goes here</title>

 </head>

 <body>

  <p>
  The body of the Web page, text and graphics, appears here
  </p>

 </body>

</html>
```

As you add to your HTML file, the sections begin to run together. You might easily insert body code in the header section. In addition, some indention will help you keep the sections together. To separate the template's sections better, consider adding comment lines, as shown in Listing 23-2.

Listing 23-2
Adding separating comment lines to help distinguish sections

```
<html>
 <!-------------------------->
 <!-- The header begins here -->
 <!-------------------------->
 <head>
```

```
<title>Window title goes here</title>

</head>
<!------------------------->
<!-- The body begins here -->
<!------------------------->
<body>

 <p>
  The body of the Web page, text and graphics, appears here
 </p>

  <!------------------------->
  <!-- Any footer goes here -->
  <!------------------------->

</body>

</html>
```

Document the HTML Code

Add initial documentation to the code (in the form of comments) that explains the purpose of the HTML file, contains your name and contact information (especially if you work on a team that is developing several Web pages, so that other team members can contact you when they need to link to your set of pages), and includes the date of the initial HTML design. This documentation will help both you and others who may edit your Web page's HTML. In a printed listing of several HTML Web pages, the comments will enable you to determine which listing produces which Web page.

Never include contact information that you don't want others to know about, because your Web page's HTML source code is available for others. If you develop Web pages for your company's intranet, and your pages remain within the company's servers, document your name and contact information so that others in the company can locate you if a change must be made. If your site goes out to the entire World Wide Web, do not reveal personal contact information. Your company's physical mailing address is appropriate to include, however, so that others can write to the company about the site.

Generally, you'll provide some way on the Web page for users to contact you (e.g., your e-mail address and public phone numbers). With personal Web sites, an e-mail address is generally the only contact information that you need to provide.

The Barkleys didn't want to put their phone number or address in their HTML code for the Web site because the site is intended for enjoyment by family and friends and they will be the only people modifying the code. Nevertheless, they understand the purpose of good documentation, as well as good meta tags that may get their site found by a search engine. Their initial HTML code, before adding any specific Web page tags, appears in Listing 23-3.

Listing 23-3
The Barkleys' starting HTML code

```html
<html>
    <!------------------------------------->
    <!-- The Barkley Family Web site    -->
    <!-- To relate news to family and   -->
    <!-- friends around the world.      -->
    <!-- Created: June 4, 2003          -->
    <!-- Last modified: August 15, 2003 -->
    <!-- Write wBarkley@ourweb.net if   -->
    <!-- you have questions.            -->
    <!------------------------------------->

    <!--------------------------->
    <!-- The header begins here -->
    <!--------------------------->
    <head>

        <title>The Barkley Family Web Page</title>

    </head>
    <!------------------------->
    <!-- The body begins here -->
    <!------------------------->
    <body>


    <!------------------------->
    <!-- Any footer goes here -->
    <!------------------------->
```

```
</body>

</html>
```

Starting the Header Table

**20 Min.
To Go**

The header section of the Barkley home page will contain the top table on their page; it will top the other pages on the site as well. You might want to reference Figure 22-3 in the previous session, where the Barkleys used a graphics program to lay out their home page and draw the table guidelines for two tables: one for the header and the other for the home page contents. Figure 23-1 shows the finished header section, which is the goal of this section and the section on completing the header, which immediately follows.

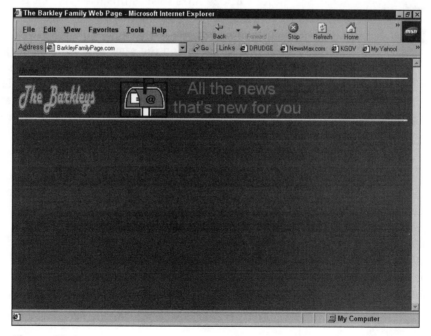

Figure 23-1
A table defines the Web page's header section.

The elements of the header all form a table. The table is beneficial because it enables the Barkleys to add elements, change the artwork, and add more links at the top of the page easily by inserting these items in cells, adding new cells, and resizing cells that need to be resized. Without the table's format, modifying one item in the header may negatively affect the formatting of the other items, and simple changes will become difficult.

The added benefit of the table-based header is that the header's colors and lines can span the user's screen no matter what the screen width is.

The header shown in Figure 23-1 contains five rows and three columns. Not all the columns will be used on each row, but the three columns enable you to align all the data properly. For example, the first row contains only the hyperlink Home. On subsequent pages, Home will form a link back to this page. On this page, the link simply reloads the current page.

Some Web masters utilize links such as this Home link on every page in a Web site, but they leave the link _dead_ on the home page (meaning the text appears but no hyperlink is defined). Clicking a dead link keeps you on the same page, but clicking the link on subsequent pages returns the user to this home page. If you define the link, even on the home page, the page will reload, showing the user the purpose of the word. If the user clicks on the link but nothing happens, the user may not know to click the link on subsequent pages where the link is active. Therefore, consider activating all links, even same-page links.

The second row is a thin strip of white that separates the first and third rows. Table rows are rarely the same height except when they contain numerical data in a spreadsheet-like format.

The third row in the header table more obviously shows the three cells that make up the header. The cells will hold, from left to right, the family logo, the mailbox (which is a hyperlink to the family's e-mail address in case anybody clicks the mailbox), and a gold-colored message that the Barkleys can easily change by altering the contents of the cell.

This tutorial's CD-ROM contains all the graphic images used in the Barkley Web site.

Two more rows in Figure 23-1 contain two additional lines: one white and one golden. The golden text and lines work well with the green background of this Web site. You won't be able to distinguish the bottom two lines very well in this text's figures, but if you follow along and create the HTML, you will see how well the colors work together.

To create the initial table, the Barkleys used the following code:

```
<table width=100% cellpadding=0 cellspacing=0 border=0
bgcolor=#009900>
```

The table will span 100 percent of the user's screen without any padding or spacing between the cells or any border lines around the table. The table's cell background colors will be green (#009900) unless overridden with a `bgcolor=` attribute set in one of the table's `<td>` or `<tr>` tags.

Browsers determine a lot from a table by scanning the complete set of command tags from `<table>` to `</table>`. If the first row contains a single cell but the third row contains three cells, the entire table will be assumed to have three cells. Given that this page's header will require three cells in the third row (the row with the logo), you might as well code the two extra cells on the first row of the table. Doing so makes it more obvious that the table contains three cells per row.

The following code defines the first row with the `Home` link:

```
<!-- First row is only a Home hotspot -->
<tr>
  <td height=21 width=179 align=left>
    <font face=Arial size=2>
    <a href="http://www.BarkleyFamilyPage.com/">
    <b><i>Home</i></b></font></a>
  </td>
  <!-- Table needs two more cells defined -->
  <td width=169 height=21>
  </td>
  <td width=788 height=21>
  </td>
</tr>
```

The thin separating line between the first row and the third is specified in this code:

```
<tr>   <!-- Blank Line as a thin row -->
  <td colspan=3 bgcolor=white width=100% height=2 align=left>
  </td>
</tr>
```

The `width=` attribute is huge to ensure that the line spans the entire width of the user's screen.

The rest of the code that you'll add defines the row with the logo and mailbox. This is the most detailed row in the table, as the next section explains.

Completing the Header Table

The rest of the header fills in the remaining three rows of the header table. The third row is the most complex because the row holds the logo, mailbox, and opening message. To the user's eye, this row becomes the actual header; the rest of the rows are just decoration except for the lone Home hyperlink in the corner.

The logo falls into the first cell easily with this code:

```
<tr align=left>  <!-- Logo -->
<td align=left width="179" height="24">
   <img src="barkleys.gif" width=149 height=66
align="absmiddle" alt="Family Logo">
   </td>
```

As is virtually always true for graphics on your site, you should include the image's width (`width=`) and height (`height=`) attributes so that the browser does not have to slow down to compute the dimensions. In addition, the `alt=` attribute ensures that something appears even when the user has turned off graphics in the browser. The `alt=` attribute also yields a pop-up ToolTip that reads Family Logo if the user rests the mouse pointer over the logo.

The next cell holds both a graphic image of the mailbox and a hyperlink to the family's e-mail address. Although the Barkleys plan to add an e-mail link elsewhere, one here is nice and the GIF image performs a dual role: It acts as the hyperlink image and also conveys the idea "Here's a Web page with Barkley news delivered to you."

The following code defines the cell:

```
<td width=169 height=24>
  <p align=center>
         
  <a href="mailto:Barkleys@email.mn.net">
   <img border=0 src="mailbox.gif" align=middle width=120
height=77 alt="Mailbox">
   </a>
 </td>
```

The four nonbreaking spaces add some room to the left of the mailbox. Although the mailbox could be fit there through other methods, such as justifying the mailbox to the right edge of the cells, the nonbreaking spaces enable you to place the picture more accurately. Although you won't add hyperlinks to this page until Session 25, the Barkleys' e-mail hyperlink (mailto:Barkleys@email.mn.net) is simple to add here before the mailbox graphic (src="mailbox.jif").

Finally, the remaining cell that holds the text, All the news that's news for you, very simply closes out the row by placing the gold text on the green background. The nonbreaking spaces enable the Barkleys to adjust the spacing around the text to look somewhat centered.

Listing 23-4 shows the complete HTML code for the Web page as it now stands. The header is complete.

Listing 23-4
The completed header table code

```
<html>
 <!------------------------------------>
 <!-- The Barkley Family Web site   -->
 <!-- To relate news to family and  -->
 <!-- friends around the world.      -->
 <!-- Created: June 4, 2003          -->
 <!-- Last modified: August 15, 2003 -->
 <!-- Write wBarkley@ourweb.net if   -->
 <!-- you have questions.            -->
 <!------------------------------------>

 <!--------------------------->
 <!-- The header begins here -->
 <!--------------------------->
 <head>

  <title>The Barkley Family Web Page</title>

  <table width=100% cellpadding=0 cellspacing=0 border=0
bgcolor=#009900>
```

Continued

Listing 23-4 *Continued*

```html
<!-- First row only contains a Home link -->
<tr>
  <td height=21 width=179 align=left>
    <font face=Arial size=2>
    <a href="http://www.BarkleyFamilyPage.com/">
    <b><i>Home</i></b></font></a>
  </td>
  <!-- Table needs two more cells defined -->
  <td width=169 height=21>
  </td>
  <td width=788 height=21>
  </td>
</tr>

<tr>   <!-- Blank Line as a thin row -->
  <td colspan=3 bgcolor=white width=100% height=2 align=left>
  </td>
</tr>

 <tr align=left>  <!-- Logo -->
  <td align=left width="179" height="24">
    <img src="barkleys.gif" width=149 height=66
align="absmiddle"
      alt="Family Logo" border=0>
  </td>

  <td width=169 height=24>
    <p align=center>
           
    <a href="mailto:Barkleys@email.mn.net">
      <img border=0 src="mailbox.gif" align=middle width=120
height=77>
    </a>
  </td>

  <td height=24>
  <font face=Arial size=6 color=#CC9900>
       All the news<br>
```

```
         that's new for you</font>
      </td>

   <tr>   <!-- Blank Line as a thin row -->
      <td colspan=3 bgcolor=white width=100% height=2 align=left>
      </td>
   </tr>

   <tr>   <!-- Golden Line as a thin row -->
      <td colspan=3 bgcolor=#CC9900 width=100% height=2 align=left>
      </td>
   </tr>
</table>
</head>

<!------------------------->
<!-- The body begins here -->
<!------------------------->
<body bgcolor="#009900">




<!------------------------->
<!-- Any footer goes here -->
<!------------------------->
</body>
</html>
```

Done!

The second table that will appear on the page will be the body of the page that holds the navigation bar, and home page content comes next. You'll follow the next session and create the Barkley family's home page's body from this remaining table.

REVIEW

- An HTML template helps you get your Web page started.
- Documentation makes your HTML code clearer and easier to maintain.

- The header is often a table that spans the user's entire screen width.
- Contact information in a header hyperlink enables users to contact you about your site.

Quiz Yourself

1. What can happen if you place undivided comments throughout the sections of an HTML Web page? (See "The Initial HTML Template.")

2. Why should you not always include your address and phone number in the opening comment section of your Web page? (See "Document the Code.")

3. What width advantage can a table provide for the header? (See "Starting the Header Table.")

4. What is an advantage to activating same-page hyperlinks? (See "The Top Table.")

5. Why do you often see nonbreaking spaces scattered throughout HTML code? (See "Completing the Header Table.")

The Web Site Home Page's Text and Graphics

Session Checklist

✔ Understand the table that creates the Barkleys' home page contents

✔ Create the Barkleys' navigation bar from a table

✔ Remember to create simple Web home pages

✔ Create the Barkleys' thumbnail images and text from a table

***30 Min.
To Go***

In this session, you continue building the Barkley family home page that you began in the previous sessions. The page is coming along nicely. Here, you'll put the header that is now complete at the top of all the site's Web pages, and you'll add some new elements as well. The rest of the home page includes a single table that holds the navigation bar and the primary page's content. If you are following along, load the HTML code that you created from the previous session and begin.

The Home Page's Bottom Table

As noted in the previous session, the Barkley home page consists of two tables: one for the header and the other for the navigation bar and the contents. The graphics program mark-up lines, repeated in Figure 24-1, show the three cells of the lower table and how the cells hold and help place and align their contents. The three cells contain the navigation bar, thumbnail images, and text.

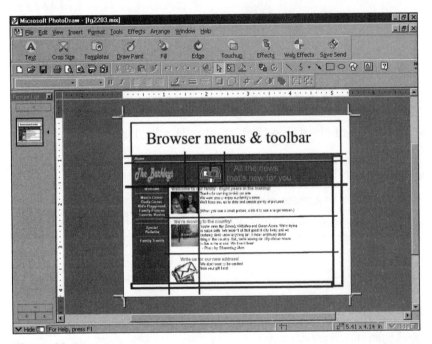

Figure 24-1
The table's cells enable you to manage a Web page more easily.

Although the Barkleys chose white on green letters for the heading and the navigation menu down the left side of the page, they wisely decided on a white background for the central content's table background color. All the Web site's content appears in this large, central area. Nothing works better than a white background. Other colors will make your users hesitate somewhat because the eye does not adjust well to many text and background color combinations. Some color combinations can slow the reading of a Web page by 10 percent or more. To be safe, use a white background.

Make sure that your table background colors match those of the Web page's background on which the tables lie or that the tables are as wide as the entire Web page. Otherwise, the browser will leave a border around the outside of your tables. For example, Figure 24-2 shows what happens when the Web page's background color is white but the heading is green. Because the header's tables do not take the width of the Web page, the page's white background creates a white border around the heading. By specifying a green page background, the heading and other tables are not outlined.

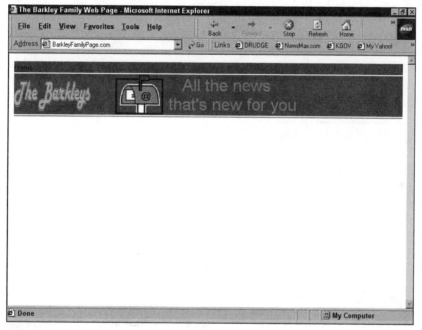

Figure 24-2
Don't outline your header table by specifying a different body background color.

The following statement defines the table that comprises the bottom of the home page:

```
<table border=0 width=2000 height=3 cellspacing=0 cellpadding=0>
```

Why isn't a width of 100 percent used, as was used for the header table in the previous session? Problems sometime arise with percentage width measurements in tables. The left-hand table column is squeezed down to fit any other columns whose widths are specified in pixel measurements. In other words, the center column of the table must be exactly 105 pixels to ensure that enough room appears for the thumbnail pictures the Barkleys want to put before most of their announcements on the home page. Given that this column is a fixed width, the 100 percent would mean that the browser would adjust other columns if necessary. It would turn out that the browser would adjust the left column in this situation, making the navigation bar thin and squeezed and messing up the spacing of the text. By specifying all three columns by an exact pixel measurement, and by keeping the total width less than the screen size of most computers in use today, you can keep your columns an accurate size. By giving the far right table a width of 2,000 pixels, you ensure that the heading will fill the entire Web page no matter how great the user's screen resolution is.

Remember that this bottom table begins the body of the home page. The header section holds the table that you created in the previous session.

The Navigation Bar

**20 Min.
To Go**

This Web page's navigation bar would have been a great use of a frame; the window with the navigation bar remains on the screen while the user scrolls the content in the large window. You already know the frame feature's problems and limitations. Given the problems with frames, such as the fact that some browsers still in use don't even support frames, the Barkleys decided that their home page should stick with tables, which have been around since the first version of HTML. Fortunately, the Web page looks much better without the frame.

Except in extremely advanced sites developed by graphics and Web specialists, frames can make even a good site look amateurish. Not all sites that use frames look amateurish, but frames add an element that detracts from almost any page.

The cell on the left of the page's bottom table will hold the navigation area for the page. The left column consists of a single cell. This cell must span three rows because the rest of the page uses three rows by design; the Barkleys want their top two messages to their friends and family to appear in the large content area of the body and other notes to appear throughout other pages on the site.

The Barkleys are wise to keep their home page text to a minimum. The rather large header already consumes much of the site. Although the header is not one that overshadows their content, the Barkleys must keep the content on the home page simple and let the navigation bar take users to more detailed points of interest.

Listing 24-1 shows the navigation bar portion of the body. The cell is the first cell in the row, so a <tr> tag must inform the browser that a new row is beginning.

Listing 24-1
Creating the navigation bar's code

```
<tr>
 <td width=140 height=382 bgcolor=#009900 align=center valign=top
rowspan=3>
  <font face=Arial size=2 color=#FFFFFF>
  <b><i>Welcome</i>
   <hr>
   Mom's Corner
   <br>Dad's Corner
   <br>Kid's Playground
   <br>Family Pictures
   <br>Favorite Movies
   <hr><hr>
   <i>Special
   <br>Bulletins</i>
   <hr>
   Family Travels</b>
   </font>
  </td>
```

The <hr> (horizontal rule) tags draw a horizontal ruler line across the cell. To separate the two large sections of the navigation bar, the Barkleys used two horizontal rules. The first section, the Welcome section, will remain fairly static, and the Barkleys have no plans to change the structure. The second section, the Special Bulletins section, may hold from one to 10 items depending on how important the family considers each new item to be. As it stands now, only one Special Bulletin, the recent family travels, appears in the navigation bar's second section.

The rowspan=3 attribute informs the browser that this cell is to extend as far down as needed to hold its contents. Without the rowspan=3 attribute, the browser would make the rest of the navigation bar only as wide as the first cell. Figure 24-3 shows the Barkleys' home page as it now appears.

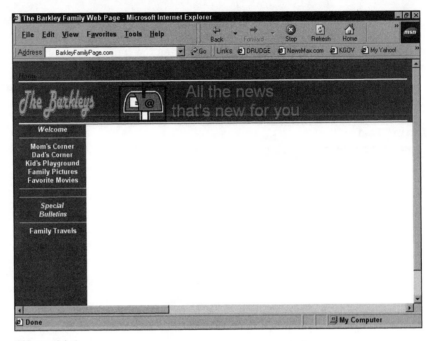

Figure 24-3
The navigation bar spans three rows to extend down the page.

Obviously, the navigation bar requires links to pages. In the next session, you will add hyperlink anchor tags to each of the navigation entries.

**10 Min.
To Go**

The Final Two Columns: Images and Text

The two final columns are rather simple to add. The middle column's primary job is to hold thumbnail images the Barkleys will use next to their home page announcements. In addition, to make heading text run across the top of the center column's graphic and into the third column where most of the text content lies, the middle column will hold the first few letters of the headings, as you'll see here. The two columns of cells in the white, content section finish out the three columns that the bottom table displays. In other words, the large section below the heading is just a three-column table, with the first column being the navigation bar and the second and third holding content.

Listing 24-2 contains the code for the top cell in the first row of the middle column. It holds the thumbnails and some heading text.

Listing 24-2
Creating the top cell in the table's first row

```
<td width=114 height=1 bgcolor=white valign=top align=right>
<p align=right>
<font face=Arial size=3 color=#CC9900>
<b>Welcome to o</b><img border=0 src="ourfamT.jpg" align=top
width=105 height=82 alt="Our Family">
</font>
</p>
</td>
```

The key points to Listing 24-2 are simply that the background color is now white (bg=white) and the cell's contents are aligned vertically to the top of the cell (valign=top) and horizontally (align=right) to the right so that the headline text can be continued into the next cell.

Finish entering the text in the third cell before viewing the page. Listing 24-3 contains the contents of the third cell.

Listing 24-3
Creating the third cell in the table's first row

```
<td width=2000 height=1 bgcolor=white valign=top align=left>
<p>
<font face=Arial size=3 color=#CC9900>
<b>ur family - Eight years in the making!</b>
</font>
<font face=Arial size=2 color=black>
<br> Thanks for coming to visit our site.
<br> We want you to enjoy our family's news.
<br> We'll keep you up to date and provide plenty of
pictures!
<br><br> (When you see a small picture, click it to see a
larger version.)
</font>
</td>
</tr>
```

Figure 24-4 shows the Barkleys' home page as it now appears. The final cell helps fix the spacing properly for the page. The third column maintains the white background and continues the gold headline that began in the previous column.

The middle column's align=right attribute ensures that the text, Welcome to, appears above the graphic, and the third column's align=left attribute ensures that the remaining text, our family - Eight years in the making!, completes the headline. By the way, the align=left attribute is the default alignment, but specifying it here helps show your intention of merging the heading together and spanning two cells with the heading. The remaining text falls under the heading and uses nonbreaking characters to add some needed spacing between the thumbnail pictures and the text.

HTML programmers often break text across table cells, starting in one and completing in the next one.

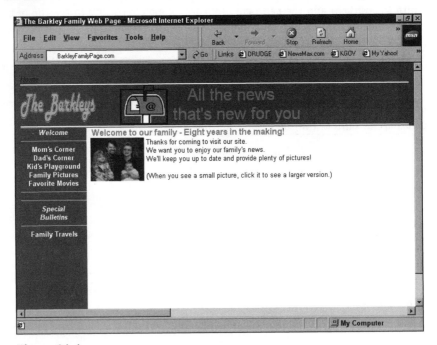

Figure 24-4
The top row of the navigation bar and content area is now complete.

The remaining two rows of the content table are just more of the same. Fortunately, the same format and spacing are required, and you will format the remaining cells just as you did the cells in the first row. By keeping this structure, the Barkleys help keep their Web site consistent and familiar to users who view the site on a regular basis. Listing 24-4 lists the rest of the page's body. You should have no trouble understanding the rest of the code.

Listing 24-4
Creating cells in the remaining two rows

```
<td width="114" height=80 bgcolor=white valign=top align=right>
 <font face=Arial size=3 color=#CC9900>
  <b>We're movin</b><img border="0" src="ourhousT.jpg" align=top
   width=105 height=82 alt="Our New Home">
 </font>
</td>
<td width=2000 height=80 bgcolor=white valign=top>
<p align=left>
<font face=Arial size=3 color=#CC9900>
 <b>g to the country!</b>
</font>
<font face=Arial size=2 color=black>
<font face=Arial size=2>
<br> You've seen the
<i>Beverly Hillbillies</i> and <i>Green Acres</i>. We're trying
<br> to outdo both. We weren't all that good at city living
and we
<br> certainly don't know anything (uh, I mean anythun')
about
<br> living in the country. But, we're leaving our city-
slicker house
<br> to live in the sticks. We love it here!
<br>   - Photo by <i>Shutterbug Mom</i></font></p>
 </font>
</td>
  </tr>
  <tr>
 <td width=114 height=80 bgcolor=white valign=top align=right>
  <font face=Arial size=3 color=#CC9900><b>Write us f</b><img
border=0 src="lettersT.gif" align=top width=105 height=82
alt="Send us mail!">
  </font>
 </td>
```

Continued

Listing 24-4   *Continued*

```
<td width=2000 height=80 bgcolor=white valign=top>
<p align=left>
<font face=Arial size=3 color=#CC9900>
 <b>or our new address!</b>
</font>
<font face=Arial size=2><br> We don't want to be omitted
<br> from your gift lists!</font></p>
</td>
</tr>
```

Figure 24-5 shows the completed home page. Notice that each figure includes alternative text, with the alt= attribute, that appears even when the user's browser's graphics are

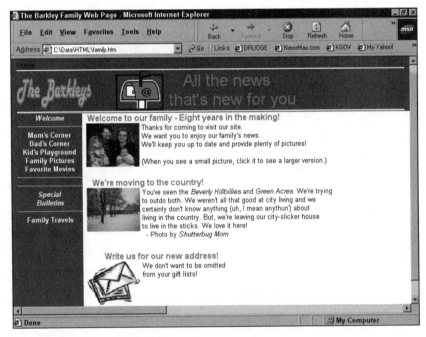

Figure 24-5
You've just completed the layout for the home page.

The Barkleys are not using a footer section on their Web pages.

Done!

The Barkley's home page will contain simple colors, fonts, and graphics that are not overbearing. You may be surprised to note that the site uses only three colors — green (for the heading and navigation bar tables' backgrounds), gold (for the heading and greeting message), and white (for the home page content table's background) — for its primary elements and layout. Only minor exceptions here and there exist when the page's graphic images utilize more colors.

You are keeping the fonts simple as well. The only font used is Arial, and almost all browsers that have ever been developed substitute a similar sans-serif font if Arial is not found. The logo contains rather fancy text, possibly even too fancy for the page so far, but it does not look so dominant once you finish the home page, as you'll do in the next section. By keeping the home page simple, you do not overload the user's eyes and you make the site welcoming.

REVIEW

- Maintain a high contrast between text and background colors to make your site easy to read.
- Use the same table background color as your Web page's body unless you don't mind a border appearing around your tables.
- Utilize tables throughout your site to help format your Web page properly and consistently.
- Once you create the home page, connect the linked pages to it.

QUIZ YOURSELF

1. What happens if the body background color differs from your table's background color? (See "The Home Page's Bottom Table.")

2. What part of the Barkley's home page best lends itself to using frames? (See "The Navigation Bar.")

3. True or False: The more fonts you use, the fancier and more rich your Web page looks. (See "Simplicity Is the Key.")

4. Why is Arial a safe font to use a lot? (See "Simplicity Is the Key.")

5. Although the center column is primarily for graphic images, why do the Barkleys store some text in that column? (See "The Final Two Columns: Images and Text.")

Creating and Connecting the Web Site's Pages

Session Checklist

✔ Get the Barkleys' Web site noticed by search engines

✔ Turn the Barkleys' logo into a hyperlink to their home page

✔ Link the Barkleys' thumbnail images to larger images

✔ Add hyperlinks to the Barkley home page's navigation bar and create subsequent Web pages

**30 Min.
To Go**

In this session, you continue to hone the Barkleys' home page by embedding meta tags to gain the attention of search engines and activating the home page's links to the logo and navigation bar. You also learn how to create the links from the thumbnails to larger images as well as how to create the linked pages for the Barkley Mom's and Dad's Web pages.

Getting the Barkleys' Site Noticed by Search Engines

The Barkleys obviously intend that their friends and family view their site. In fact, they want their hard work to be seen by as many people as possible. Therefore, they would like for their Web site to appear inside search engine listings if possible. Although a family Web site usually does not warrant payment to a firm to advertise among many search engines, and although such a Web site often does not even warrant registering with a *single* search engine if the registration costs money, you're free to use meta tags in your site's HTML code so that the site's content can be picked up and indexed by any search engine that notices the site.

To get the site seen by roaming search engines and inform them of its content, the Barkleys embedded the meta tags (<meta>) shown in Listing 25-1 into their home page at the top of their site. The meta tags appear after the </title> end tag but before the header table begins, as Listing 25-1 shows.

Listing 25-1
Creating meta tags to get the site noticed by roaming search engines

```
<!--------------------------->
<!-- The header begins here -->
<!--------------------------->
<head>

<title>The Barkley Family Web Page</title>

<!-- The search engine tags appear next -->
<meta name="description"
 content="Barkley Family Web Site">
<meta name="keywords"
 content="Barkley, Barkleys, Scott Barkley, Gail Barkley,
    Rachel Barkley, Annie Barkley, new home, we've moved,
 Kid's Playground">

<table width=100% cellpadding=0 cellspacing=0 border=0
bgcolor=#009900>
```

The search engines, if they locate the Barkley Web site, will list the site as Barkley Family Web Site due to the meta tag name and content attributes (meta name="description" content). The meta tag keyword attributes (<meta name="keywords">) and the keywords themselves, such as Scott Barkley and Annie Barkley, will help move the site up in the ranks of the search engine.

Turning the Logo into a Hyperlink

Should the site's logo appear over a hyperlink that takes users to the home page? In other words, if a user clicks the logo on the home page, should the home page reload, or should the link be dead and nothing happen? Likewise, if the user clicks the logo in subsequently linked pages, should the link return the user to the home page? This concept is similar to that of the Home link covered in Session 23. As with home-page links, the answer is debatable; some think that same-page references are a waste of the user's time. Others feel that by making the logo a link back to the home page on *every one of the site's pages,* you train the user to notice that a quick jump back to the home page is simple and available on every page bearing the logo.

The Barkleys decided to turn the logo into a hyperlink to the home page. To help the user get back to the home page, they will retain this hyperlink every-where they use the header. Listing 25-2 shows the modified header code that links the logo appropriately.

Listing 25-2
Allowing the logo to always link back to the home page

```
<tr align=left>  <!-- Logo -->
<td align=left width="179" height="24">
<!-- The logo links to the home page -->
 <a href="http://www.BarkleyFamilyPage.com/">
  <img src="barkleys.gif" width=149 height=66
align="absmiddle" border=0 alt="Family Home Page">
 </a>
</td>   <!-- Rest of header follows -->
```

The `<a href>` and `<img src>` tags that follow the `<!-- The logo links to the home page -->` comment turn the image into a link back to the home page. Therefore, if the user clicks the logo, on any Barkley page on which the logo appears, the home page will display.

You have not created any of the Barkleys' linked pages so the links on the home page won't work yet. You will need to adjust the links to point to your own disk drive to try these examples. In addition, you will need to change the location of the images. Load this text's files from the CD-ROM, locate the image files used in this example, such as the thumbnail image named ourhousT.jpg, and substitute that pathname for the references in the HTML code listings.

**20 Min.
To Go**

Linking the Thumbnails to Larger Images

The Barkley Web site's home page contains two thumbnail pictures: a family photo and a home photo. Those thumbnails produce larger images that will take longer to load if the user chooses to view the larger pictures. The Barkleys loaded their digital camera with film and captured the photos they use on their site directly to their hard disk.

When you locate photos for your Web site, you can either use a digital camera or scan regular pictures. A quick scan of any search engine for stock, royalty-free photographs produces several sites from which you can purchase any of thousands of photos or download free photos.

Given the site's nature, the Barkley home page benefits especially from personal photographs that are fresh. A corporate home page, however, may use a single photo of the business or primary product and not always use many other pictures throughout the site.

When you place image thumbnails on your page, your users decide, by clicking the thumbnails or not, whether they want to wait for the larger image downloads. You should provide accurate loading information for the user by listing the picture's file size below the thumbnail or in the alternative text of the thumbnail.

When the user clicks the thumbnail, it can produce a larger image in one of three ways:

1. It can open a new window that displays the larger picture. The title bar doesn't display a nice title, and when the user finishes viewing the picture, the user must close the new window to return to your Web page.

2. It can hyperlink to display the picture inside the same window. When the user finishes viewing the picture, the user can press the Back button to return to the thumbnail page.

3. In thumbnail pages such as the Barkley home page, it can hyperlink to a new page inside the browser, showing the Web site's usual navigation bar and header with the picture in the content area. The user can then press the Back button to return to the thumbnail page or click any other link to go elsewhere on the site.

Usability studies show that the Back button is vital to the beginning, intermediate, and advanced Internet user. HTML programmers generally agree that by opening a new window and so leaving the source page on the screen, they leave the user less tempted to go elsewhere once done with the new window. Yet, with the second window on the screen at the same time as the first, the user cannot press the Back button to close the second and return to the first; the user must instead *close* the new window to see the first one that launched the new window. Little is more frustrating than pressing Back and having nothing happen.

Therefore, you are more likely to keep your users at ease if you link to new content within the current window (option #2 in the preceding list) than if you open a new window for the thumbnail (option #1). The question then becomes, do you show only the larger image, or do you wrap the header and navigation bar around the larger image so that your user views just another page on your site when looking at the picture (option #3)?

By wrapping the header and navigation bar around the picture, you increase the window's load time and the amount of work you must perform every time you create the new page that's linked from a thumbnail picture. You must not only add the picture but also the header and navigation bar to the page. Because of this, the Barkleys decided to link only to pictures within the same browser window. Listing 25-3 shows the added hyperlink code needed to display the large photo (outfam.jpg) from the thumbnail (outfamT.jpg). The comments will help you pinpoint the hyperlink.

Listing 25-3
Adding the hyperlink for the first thumbnail picture

```
<td width=114 height=1 bgcolor=white valign=top align=right>
<p align=right>
<font face=Arial size=3 color=#CC9900>
<b>Welcome to o</b>
<!-- The thumbnail image links to a larger photo -->
<a href="http://www.BarkleyFamilyPage.com/ourfam.jpg">
   <img border=0 src="ourfamT.jpg" align=top width=105
   height=82 alt="Our Family (24Kb)">
</a>
</font>
</p>
</td>
```

Notice that the alternative text attribute in the `<a href>` tag (the attribute `alt="Our Family"`) enables the user to see the size of the pictures before clicking the thumbnail. Because the larger photos are not opened in a new window, the user can press the Back button to return to the Barkley home page cleanly.

Listing 25-4 shows the hyperlink for the second photo (`ourhouse.jpg`) from the thumbnail (`ourhousT.jpg`).

Both Listing 25-3 and Listing 25-4 contain new code as well as code you entered in previous sessions.

Listing 25-4
Adding the hyperlink for the second thumbnail picture

```
<td width="114" height=80 bgcolor=white valign=top align=right>
  <font face=Arial size=3 color=#CC9900>
   <b>We're movin</b>
   <!-- The thumbnail image links to a larger photo -->
     <a href=" http://www.BarkleyFamilyPage.com/ourhouse.jpg">
      <img border="0" src="ourhousT.jpg" align=top
       width=105 height=82 alt="Our New Home (33 Kb)">
     </a>
  </font>
</td>
```

Linking the Navigation Bar and Creating Subsequent Pages

**10 Min.
To Go**

When do you add the hyperlinks to your home page's navigation bar? After each individual Web page is created? Perhaps you omit the links completely until after you create the home page and the subsequent pages that link to the home page.

The latter option is actually the best. To put up a Web site with bad links invites trouble. Your users will think the site is incomplete because it is incomplete. You will lose trust among users. Although trust is not as important for a family Web site like the Barkleys', good HTML and Web page design habits are always appreciated by users and rewarded by more frequent returns to your sites.

In creating a session-by-session Web site, as this Weekend Crash Course does, the rules must be broken somewhat. At the end of the previous session, you saw the Barkleys' entire home page in its final form, sans links, and without the subsequent Web pages created yet. If this book had waited for the subsequent pages to be developed, you wouldn't have seen the home page in its entirety early on, and its production would not have made as much sense. In this session, I continue this approach and first show you how to link the entire home page's navigation bar before creating any subsequent pages for those links.

Adding the links

Listing 25-5 shows the start of the home page's HTML code where the navigation bar links need to reside. You've seen most of this code already without the embedded hyperlinks. The navigation bar links are simple hyperlinks anchored with the `<a>` and `</a>` anchor tag pair. The navigation bar items (as outlined in Session 21) are linked to the subsequent Web pages.

Substitute your own hard disk location for the Web page addresses that you create here so that the Barkley site works as you follow along.

Listing 25-5
Creating the navigation bar links

```
<!------------------------->
<!-- The body begins here -->
<!------------------------->
<body bgcolor=009900>

<table border=0 width=2000 height=3 cellspacing=0 cellpadding=0>
 <tr>
  <td width=140 height=382 bgcolor=#009900 align=center valign=top
rowspan=3>
  <font face=Arial size=2 color=#FFFFFF>
  <b><i>Welcome</i>
  <hr>
  <a href="http://www.BarkleyFamilyPage.com/Mom.htm/">
   Mom's Corner
  </a><br>
  <a href="http://www.BarkleyFamilyPage.com/Dad.htm/">
   Dad's Corner
  </a><br>
  <a href="http://www.BarkleyFamilyPage.com/Kids.htm/">
```

Continued

Listing 25-5

Continued

```
Kid's Playground
</a><br>
<a href="http://www.BarkleyFamilyPage.com/Pics.htm/">
 Family Pictures
</a><br>
<a href="http://www.BarkleyFamilyPage.com/Movies.htm/">
 Favorite Movies
</a><br>
<hr><hr>
 <i>Special
 <br>Bulletins</i>
<hr>
<a href="http://www.BarkleyFamilyPage.com/Travels.htm/">
 Family Travels</b>
</a>
</font>
</td>
```

As soon as you load the home page, you will notice that the page looks the same as before except that the navigation bar's links now appear. The problem is that the links' default color is blue, which does not look good on the page's green background. White text looks much better. Change the color of the unvisited links on the page by changing the single <body> tag as follows:

```
<body bgcolor=009900 link=white>
```

All the links now appear in white, and their underlining makes it clear that they are links to other places. The initial home page is now finished. If this were a true home page to load onto a Web server, you would name the home page index.htm or index.html (your Web host will tell you the preferred name for that host's servers).

You will have to create each linked page in a separate .html file. Once you upload such linked files to the Web, your home page can access them by their addresses. To follow along here, you can create each page and store the page on your hard disk or copy the CD-ROM's completed Web pages to your hard disk and connect the links to them. A Web site is often little more than several HTML text files and graphic images located on the same server, referencing each other through hyperlinks.

Making Mom's Corner

Now that you've completed the home page, try your hand at one of the secondary pages. The first link, Mom's Corner, is a good place to start. Keep the following considerations in mind that the Barkleys made when they designed their site:

- The header and navigation bar are to appear on most of the site's pages for consistency.
- Only the large white content area changes from page to page.

The best way to begin creating Mom's page is to make a copy of the home page because the home page serves as a good prototype for the remaining pages. Call the copy Mom.htm and save the file in the same folder as the home page. If the Barkley site was a registered domain name, you would upload the mother's HTML file onto the server in the same directory as the home page. Given that your sample files are not on a Web server, adjust the links in the code mentioned here. The adjustments are simple to make because you change them to refer to your own hard disk.

Most of Mom's Web page follows the pattern of the home page. After making the copy, edit Mom.htm and change the comments (`<!>`) and the title (`<title>`) to reflect the new page. Leave the meta tags the same for all the site's pages. The meta tags (`<meta>`) are general for the site, and the higher the number of Web pages on which they appear, the more attention a search engine will give your site. Listing 25-6 shows the first part of the HTML file with the comments and title and a place for the meta tags.

Listing 25-6
Creating the comments and title for Mom's Web page

```
<!------------------------------------------------->
<!-- Mom's Page                            -->
<!-- Linked to www.BarkleyFamilyPage.com   -->
<!-- Created: June 9, 2003                  -->
<!-- Last modified: June 30, 2003           -->
<!-- Write Barkley@ourweb.net if            -->
<!-- you have questions.                     -->
<!------------------------------------------------->

<!--------------------------->
<!-- The header begins here -->
<!--------------------------->
```

Continued

Listing 25-6   *Continued*

```
<head>

<title>Mom's Home Page</title>

<!-- The search engine tags appear next -->
```

The next step is to create the content portion of Mom's Web page. Figure 25-1 shows that Mom prefers a simple content area that she can quickly update with notes and messages to friends and with her news of the family. She doesn't want to put pictures on her page. The entire page looks and acts just as the home page does except for the white content area.

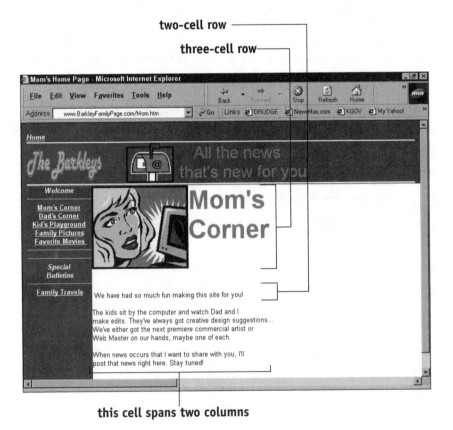

Figure 25-1
Mom's Corner holds a simple content area.

The content area is part of the lower table that includes the navigation bar in its first column. *Only the first row with the picture contains all three columns.* The first row holds the navigation bar, Mom's graphic image (located on this tutorial's CD-ROM just as all the site's images are), and her large welcome message ("Mom's Corner"). The cell below is large and spans two column widths. This large area holds all the text that Mom wants to add, making it easier for Mom to add, edit, and remove text from inside her HTML page. As Mom adds to the text, the white content area grows without affecting the rest of the page. If Mom adds enough content to fill the entire page and more, the page lengthens and scroll bars appear to the right of the browser window so that users can scroll to read more.

Listing 25-7 shows the HTML section of Mom's page that holds the content. All the other code matches that of the home page with the exception of the title and comment modifications made in Listing 25-6. Look through the code to see how Figure 25-1's content appears.

Listing 25-7
Creating the content table for Mom's Web page

```
<!-- Mom's logo and Welcome message -->
<td width=114 height=1 bgcolor=white valign=top align=right>
 <img border=0 src="Mom.jpg" align=top width=190
      height=157 alt="Our Dear Mom">
</td>

<td width=2000 height=1 bgcolor=white valign=top align=left>
 <p>
 <font face=Arial size=7 color=#CC9900>
  <b>Mom's
  <br>Corner</b>
 </font>
</td>
</tr>

<!-- The final row spans both columns and falls vertically
     as long as Mom has something to write -->
<td width=2000 height=80 bgcolor=white valign=top align=left
    colspan=2>
```

Continued

Listing 25-7   *Continued*

```
<font face=Arial size=2 color=black>
<!-- Mom updates the text after this -->
 We have had so much fun making this site for you!
<br><br>The kids sit by the computer and watch Dad and I
<br>make edits. They've always got creative design
suggestions...
<br>We've either got the next premiere commercial artist or
<br>Web Master on our hands, maybe one of each.
<br><br>When news occurs that I want to share with you, I'll
<br>post that news right here. Stay tuned!
<!-- Mom's text updates stop here -->
</font>
</td>
</tr>
```

The length of Mom's page is not as critical as the length of the home page. Home pages should fit inside the user's browser screen and load fast. However, once a user clicks to another page on the site, the user is digging deeper and will not mind waiting a little longer for the page to load and will not mind reading more text that requires some scrolling.

Making Dad's Corner

Figure 25-2 shows Dad's web page. Dad wants his page to be shorter snippets of his own worldly words of wisdom (Dad's version of the *WWW!*). Therefore, Dad uses a list to format his page's text, but the format of the content is identical to that of Mom's.

To create Dad's page, make a copy of Mom's page and change the `<title>` tag and comments appropriately. Then insert Dad's graphic image (named Dad.jpg), change the title to the right of the image, and add the list in the bottom table cell. Listing 25-8 shows the content area of Dad's table. This text's CD-ROM contains the entire HTML listing, as it does all listings in the book, but the code other than the content, title, and comments is identical to Mom's Web page.

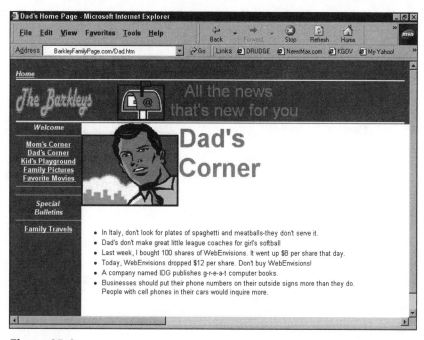

Figure 25-2
Dad's Corner contains a list-based content area.

Listing 25-8
Creating the content table for Dad's Web page

```
<!-- Dad's logo and Welcome message -->
<td width=114 height=1 bgcolor=white valign=top align=right>
 <img border=0 src="Dad.jpg" align=top width=190
  height=157 alt="Good Ole Dad">
</td>

<td width=2000 height=1 bgcolor=white valign=top align=left>
 <p>
 <font face=Arial size=7 color=#CC9900>
 <b>Dad's
 <br>Corner</b>
 </font>
```

Continued

Listing 25-8 *Continued*

```
</td>
</tr>

<!-- The final row spans both columns and falls vertically
     as long as Dad has items for his lists -->
<td width=2000 height=80 bgcolor=white valign=top align=left
    colspan=2>
 <font face=Arial size=2 color=black>
 <!-- Dad updates the text after this -->
 <ul>
 <li>In Italy, don't look for plates of spaghetti
 and meatballs-they don't serve it.
 <li>Dad's don't make great little league coaches for girl's
 softball
 <li>Last week, I bought 100 shares of WebEnvisions. It
 went up $8 per share that day.
 <li>Today, WebEnvisions dropped $12 per share. Don't buy
 WebEnvisions!
 <li>A company named IDG publishes g-r-e-a-t computer books.
 <li>Businesses should put their phone numbers on their outside
 signs more than they do.
 <br>People with cell phones in their cars
 would inquire more.
 </ul>
 <!-- Dad's text updates stop here -->
 </font>
 </td>
 </tr>
```

Done!

REVIEW

- Add linked pages to your home page to complete your site.
- You'll reuse HTML code as you create your site's pages.
- A general and consistent Web site design makes the creation of secondary pages simple.

QUIZ YOURSELF

1. True or False: Embedded meta tags help get your site noticed by search engines. (See "Getting the Barkleys' Site Noticed by Search Engines.")

2. What is the advantage of allowing the home page to reload when users click the logo rather than letting the logo be a dead link, in which case, when users click it, nothing happens? (See "Turning the Logo Into a Hyperlink.")

3. Describe three ways to render thumbnail pictures into their larger pictures. (See "Linking the Thumbnails to Larger Images.")

4. Why should you keep from opening a new window when the user clicks a link on your page, such as a thumbnail's larger image? (See "Linking the Thumbnails to Larger Images.")

5. Why would you want to keep the same meta tags throughout your site? (See "Making Mom's Corner.")

6. Where can you find HTML code to use as the starting point for secondary pages on your site? (See "Making Mom's Corner.")

Adding Special Elements to the Web Site

Session Checklist

✔ Optimize the placement of graphics on the Barkley Family
   Picture page

✔ Create the Barkley Family Picture page and the pictures

✔ Create the Barkley Kids' page with frames, drawings, and sound

**30 Min.
To Go**

I n this session, you will create two new Barkley Family Web pages: the Family
Picture page and the Kid's Playground page. As you create these pages, you
will apply some of the tools covered in the previous sessions for adding special
elements. This section focuses on handling graphics-intensive Web pages and
adding frames and sound. The next session will cover additional special elements.

Deciding How to Place Pictures on the Family Web Pages

In a graphics-intensive page, such as the Kid's Playground page, you must consider
how to present the graphics so that your audience enjoys the pictures while not
thinking too much about the load time. The Kid's Playground page is linked from
the home page site, so the load time is not as critical as on the home page; users

have specifically requested the Kid's Playground page and will wait for the page to load. Nevertheless, you need to present the graphics in a manner that is pleasing.

Even though your users show they are more hooked when they request a secondary page than they do by just visiting the home page, you should still consider how long your user must wait when visiting a graphics-intensive page. When putting pictures on a site, you must decide on one or more of the following options:

- Use thumbnails that link to larger images such as those that appear on the Barkley Web home page (see Session 10 for thumbnail information).

- Use a low-resolution set of pictures that the user can view with the option of viewing a higher-resolution set of the same pictures (see Session 8 for graphics placement information).

- Use interlaced images that appear quickly but blurry and then slowly get crisper as more of the image loads (some graphics programs can convert regular images to interlaced images that load as described here).

- Use the lowsrc= attribute when you place graphics on a Web page; this attribute can quickly load a low-resolution version of the image while the browser loads the higher-resolution version in the background. When the background image finishes loading, the browser replaces the lower-resolution image with the higher-resolution image. The load time increases, but the user doesn't notice it because the pictures can be viewed immediately (see Session 15 for resolution information).

The Barkleys have decided not to put too many pictures on their Family Picture page at any one time. If they happen to have several photos to show, as may happen at a successful birthday party, they will create a two- or three-page set of pictures that the user can click to with a Next hyperlink placed on the page. Keeping only three or four photos on the page, and replacing those regularly with fresh pictures, enables the Barkleys to keep their Web site's HTML simple to maintain.

The Barkleys did use frames for this particular page just to keep the special children's heading on the screen no matter what the user does to scroll the page. The pictures are clear and large for easy viewing. For a family Web site, that is probably an appropriate decision. If you develop a site for a more professional audience, however, you will have to give weight to each of the options just mentioned.

**20 Min.
To Go**

Creating the Family Picture Page with Graphics

Naturally, the first step is to create the Barkleys' Family Picture page's file. The bulk of the file is nothing more than the pages that you've already seen in the previous sessions. The HTML code will provide the header and navigation bar for consistency. Only the initial comments and `<title>` tag will differ. Listing 26-1 provides the code that is specific for the Family Pictures page.

Listing 26-1
Creating the comments and title for the Family Pictures page

```
<!------------------------------------------->
<!-- Family Picture Page               -->
<!-- Linked to www.BarkleyFamilyPage.com  -->
<!-- Created: June 12, 2003            -->
<!-- Last modified: June 14, 2003      -->
<!-- Write Barkley@ourweb.net if       -->
<!-- you have questions.               -->
<!------------------------------------------->

<!--------------------------->
<!-- The header begins here -->
<!--------------------------->
<head>

  <title>Barkley Family Picture page</title>

  <!-- The search engine tags appear next -->
```

Copy the header HTML from the home page to the family picture page down through the navigation bar area. The final lines to copy are:

```
<a href="http://www.BarkleyFamilyPage.com/Travels.htm/">
  Family Travels</b>
</a>
</font>
</td>
```

Before tackling the specific HTML code that's left on the page, consider how you would lay out the pictures on the page. Figure 26-1 shows one of the most obvious ways to lay out pictures. Just place the pictures in table cells, one per cell with a caption below each picture. With this method, the pictures fill the page. Don't worry about the user having to scroll to see all the photos, because on a page such as this, the user expects to scroll.

Figure 26-1
The pictures fill the page.

Listing 26-2 shows the code needed to produce Figure 26-1. (The code for the header and navigation bar is not shown.) The code is simple, using simple <img> tags (that were introduced in Session 8) to display the pictures in four table cells, each with a caption. The pictures all use alt= attributes so that the pop-up descriptions appear in the user's browser even when the images do not.

Listing 26-2
Creating the photos, captions, and pop-up descriptions

```
<td width=315 bgcolor=white valign=top align=left>
 <img src=images\thegirls.jpg valign=top align=left width=266
height=230
```

```
   alt="Horseback riding">
 <br clear=left><font face=Arial size=4>
  <b>The girls are riding the range...</b></font>
</td>
<td width=2155 height=271 bgcolor=white valign=top align=left>
 <img src=images\rachel.jpg valign=top align=left width=220
height=189
 alt="Sweet Rachel">
 <br clear=left><font face=Arial size=4><b>She's sweet...when
asleep!</b></font>
</td>
</tr>

<tr>
<td width=315  bgcolor=white valign=top align=left>
 <img src=images\reading.jpg valign=top align=left width=266
height=230
  alt="Annie's Reading to Dad">
 <br clear=left><font face=Arial size=4><b>Annie's teaching Dad to
read</b></font>
</td>
<td width=2155 height=2000 bgcolor=white valign=top align=left>
 <img src=images\watson.jpg valign=top align=left width=271
height=231
  alt="Yum!">
 <br clear=left><font face=Arial size=4><b>Watson has Dad's Bar-B-
Que again!</b></font>
</td>
</tr>
</table>

 <!-------------------------->
 <!-- Any footer goes here -->
 <!-------------------------->
 </body>
</html>
```

*10 Min.
To Go*

Creating the Kids' Page with Frames, Graphics, and Sound

Web sites need consistency. But too much consistency, especially on a family Web site, can get to be too stuffy. Just to vary things some, the children's page, referred to as the Kid's Playground in the navigation bar, will look different from the rest of the site. The Kid's Playground will consist of a frame-based Web page with a background image, chimes that play when the page first opens, and drawings.

Creating the frames

The frame may not be the most appropriate Web page design in most cases, but adding a frame across the top of the children's page allows visitors to scroll down to see the children's drawings without losing the top window. Therefore, users will be able to return to the home page quickly and at any time no matter how far down the page they scroll.

The use of the two-frame page will give you some hands-on practice with frames. Figure 26-2 shows the completed page that you will now code in HTML. Note how it is dramatically different from the others. The header does not contrast well against its background, and the page is less structured compared to the previous pages that were created, but the kids like it. Your Web site's client may not always be correct, but you must ultimately make the client happy when you design Web sites.

As you know from Session 18, frames require more than one Web page because the frameset defines the frame, and each window inside a framed area requires its own Web page. The Barkley children's frameset page defines two frames. Listing 26-3 shows the code. As usual, the HTML code begins with comments and meta tags.

Listing 26-3
Creating the children's frameset Web page with two frames

```
<html>

<!------------------------------------------->
<!-- Kid's Playground Page              -->
<!-- Linked to www.BarkleyFamilyPage.com -->
<!-- Created: June 12, 2003             -->
<!-- Last modified: June 14, 2003       -->
```

```
<!-- Write Barkley@ourweb.net if          -->
<!-- you have questions.                   -->
<!------------------------------------------>


<!--------------------------->
<!-- The header begins here -->
<!--------------------------->
<head>

 <title>Kid's Playground</title>

 <!-- The search engine tags appear next -->
 <meta name="description"
  content="Barkley Family Web Site">
 <meta name="keywords"
  content="Barkley, Barkleys, Scott Barkley, Gail Barkley,
    Rachel Barkley, Annie Barkley, new home, we've moved,
    Kid's Playground">
</head>

<frameset rows="135,*">
 <frame name=header scrolling=no noresize target=main
src=KidHeader.htm>
 <frame name=main src=KidBody.htm>
 <noframes>
 <body>
   <p>This page uses frames, but your browser doesn't support
them.</p>
  </body>
 </noframes>
</frameset>

</html>
```

Figure 26-2
The kids' page uses a frame and less structure than the other pages.

Creating the header frame, sound, and drawings

The next step is to create the header frame, sound, and drawings. The header frame contains three graphics:

- The background image
- The title created as graphic text
- The link box graphic that takes the user back to the Barkley home page

All three graphic images reside on this book's CD-ROM.

The Barkley children want a little more pizzazz for their visitors, so they have requested that a chime play welcoming the user. Therefore, their Web site will play a WAV file that chimes when the user views the page. Session 19 described how to add sound to Web pages with the use of the <a> anchor tag. The <a> tag is perfect for sounds because it only plays at the user's request. It is better to have the sound set up so that it must be requested by users, because sounds take long to load.

However, here's the problem: The kids want the sound to play as soon as the page opens, instead of only after users click to hear the sound. To do this, you must use a new tag called the <bgsound> tag. The <bgsound> tag always plays an audio file when the page background loads. The syntax of <bgsound> is:

```
<bgsound src="source.wav" loop=
```

The loop= attribute is optional and specifies how many times the audio file plays. If you must use a background sound, don't repeat the sound too many times. The sounds begin to wear quickly on the user.

Listing 26-4 shows the header frame's HTML with the three graphic images outlined previously and with the <bgsound> tag. The name of the HTML file must be KidHeader.htm because that's the name the frameset, Kids.htm, expects. The name of the chime file is chimes.wav. The <bgsound> tag plays the WAV file only one time.

Listing 26-4
Creating the children's header and WAV file

```
<html>
  <!-- Header frame for the kids' page -->
<head>
  <base target="main">
</head>

<body background="KidsBack.gif">
  <!-- Add soung file -->
  <bgsound src=chimes.wav>
 <p><img border="0" src="images\kidtitle.gif" width=560 height=96>
 <!-- Non-breaking spaces to separate text properly -->
         

  <a href="http://barkleyFamilyPage.htm/">
    <img border=0 src="images\HomeB.gif" width=127 height=86>
  </a>
</p>

</body>

</html>
```

Finally, the kids' drawings consume the lower window. Scroll bars appear if too many drawings reside on the page and will not all fit at once. The frame ensures that the header remains on the screen at all times while the body frame scrolls. Listing 26-5 contains the code for the drawings that use <img> tags to place the images on the page.

Listing 26-5
Creating the kids' drawings

```
<html>
  <!-- Body frame for the kids' page -->
  <head>
  </head>

<body>

  <!-- Annie has two pictures side-by-side -->
  <p><img border=0 src="images\kid1.gif" width=123 height=148>
      <img border=0 src="images\kid2.gif" width=141 height=148>
  <img border=0 src="images\Kid3.jpg" width=331 height=414>
  </p>
  <p>
  <font face=Arial size=5>Annie's animals
    and Rachel's Blue-Ribbon Painting!
  </font>
  </p>

</body>

</html>
```

Done!

REVIEW

- Use frames if you want to ensure the heading stays on the page at all times.

- Use caution when creating pages with many graphics so as not to make your Web page too busy.

- Place sounds on your page that play when the user views the page to make the site fun.

QUIZ YOURSELF

1. What are four common methods you can use to present graphic images on your Web page? (See "Deciding How to Place Pictures on the Family Web Pages.")

2. True or False: Using the `lowsec=` attribute speeds up a page's load time. (See "Deciding How to Place Pictures on the Family Web Pages.")

3. How can you be sure that a description will appear even if the user has graphics turned off? (See "Creating the Family Picture Page with Graphics.")

4. What tag enables you to start a WAV sound file as soon as the user loads the page? (See "Creating the Header Frame, Sound, and Drawings.")

5. How does a scroll bar keep the header on a framed page? (See "Creating the Header Frame, Sound, and Drawings.")

PART

V

Sunday Morning
Part Review

1. What role does a Web site's Project Leader play?
2. Why is the Web site's client not always the Web site's user?
3. Describe the purpose for a B2B company.
4. Why are logos so important?
5. True or False: Your logo can load slowly without penalty.
6. What is the first Web page you should develop for your site?
7. Why does the home page set the design stage for the rest of the site?
8. Describe the prototype's job.
9. What tools can help you design a prototype?
10. Generally, why are tables better Web page tools than frames?
11. How can you use a prototype to determine table cell lines?
12. What advantages does an HTML template provide?
13. What is the purpose of HTML documentation?
14. True or False: A Web page can contain, at most, one table although that table can be large.
15. What special string of special characters indicates a nonbreaking space?
16. What can happen if your table's background colors differ from your Web page's body color?
17. Why does text headlines sometimes span two cells in a table?
18. Which pages on your Web site should contain the meta tags that search engines use?

19. What advantage does the closing forward slash add to hyperlinks (for example, `http://www.idg.com/` as opposed to `http://www.idg.com`)?

20. What does framing pictures on a page do for the page's overall look?

PART

VI

Sunday Afternoon

Adding Other Special Elements to the Web Site

Session Checklist

✔ Create the Barkleys' Favorite Movies page

✔ Add a form to the Favorite Movies page

✔ Create an image map for the Barkleys' Family Travels page

**30 Min.
To Go**

I n this session, you will create the Barkley Family Movies page and then add a new special element to it: a form. The Barkleys want their friends and family to rate movies on the form, which the Barkleys will use to update their movie review page. This session will also show how to add another special element, an *image map,* to the Barkleys' Family Travels page. This session provides only a simple overview of image maps, since image maps bring with them problems as well as solutions.

Creating the Favorite Movies Page

Figure 27-1 shows the top of the Barkleys' Favorite Movies page. The page is straightforward, reusing the header and navigation bar used on the Barkleys' other Web pages. The first two rows of the bottom table contain the bulk of the movie review content. The middle cell (the left cell holding the navigation bar) holds the camera image, and horizontal lines created with <hr> tags separate these cell rows.

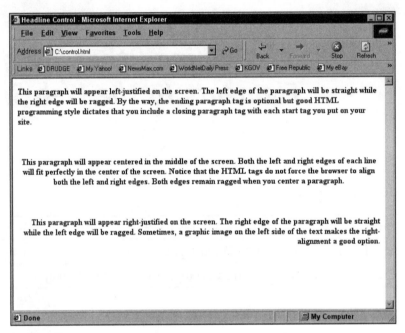

Figure 27-1
The complete Favorite Movies page is now easy to create.

As with the other Barkley Web pages, the movie page contains the standard comments and meta tags. Listing 27-1 shows the middle portion of the HTML code for the navigation bar and content. It does not show the introductory comments, meta tags, and header HTML that you've already seen in the previous two sessions. The listing contains the HTML down to the end of the ratings page section. The listing is lengthy, but nothing new exists in it.

Listing 27-1
Creating the navigation bar and content area of the Favorite Movies page

```
<body bgcolor=009900 link=white>

<!--------------------------->
<!-- The body begins here -->
<!--------------------------->
```

```
    <table border=0 width=1169 height=157 cellspacing=0 cellpadding=0>
      <tr>
        <td width=140 height=469 bgcolor=#009900 align=center
valign=top rowspan=4>
          <font face=Arial size=2 color=#FFFFFF>
          <b><i>Welcome</i>
          <hr>
          <a href="http://www.BarkleyFamilyPage.com/Mom.htm/">
            Mom's Corner
          </a><br>
          <a href="http://www.BarkleyFamilyPage.com/Dad.htm/">
           Dad's Corner
          </a><br>
          <a href="http://www.BarkleyFamilyPage.com/Kids.htm/">
           Kid's Playground
          </a><br>
          <a href="http://www.BarkleyFamilyPage.com/Pics.htm/">
           Family Pictures
          </a><br>
          <a href="http://www.BarkleyFamilyPage.com/Movies.htm/">
           Favorite Movies
          </a><br>
          <hr><hr>
          <i>Special
          <br>Bulletins</i>
          <hr>
          <a href="http://www.BarkleyFamilyPage.com/Travels.htm/">
           Family Travels</b>
          </a>
        </font>
      </td>

    <!-- The We Love Movies Row -->
    <td width=170 height=1 bgcolor=white valign=top align=right>
     <p align=right>
     <font face=Arial size=3 color=#CC9900>
       <b>We Love Movies!</b>
     </p>
     <p align=right>
```

Continued

Listing 27-1 *Continued*

```
    <img border=0 src="Movie.gif" width=88 height=81>
     
   </font>
   </p>
  </td>


   <!-- Right side of We Love Movies Row -->
   <td width=1113 height=1 bgcolor=white valign=top align=left
colspan=2>
    <p align=left>
    <font face=Arial size=2 color=black>
     <br>   </font>
    <font color="#000000" face=Arial>On this page,
     we'll review the movies we enjoy so much. Each of us<br>
     ranks the week's movie. We'll then give you our official
Barkley <br>
     Family Rating! You can trust us, we're pros!
    <p align=left>
        If you want to add input,
     tell us what you thought about the movie<br>
     by filling out the form.</font>
   </td>
  </tr>


   <!-- The week's Movie description row -->
   <td width=170 height=98 bgcolor=#FFFFFF valign=top align=right>
    <hr>
    <p align=center>
    <b><font face=Arial size=3 color=#CC9900>
     This week's flick:
    </font></b>
    <font color=#009900><b>
    <font face=Arial size=4>
     <i>Saving the Moon</i>
    </b> </font></font></p>
   </td>
```

```
<!-- Second cell in Movie description row -->
<td width=1113 height=98 bgcolor=#FFFFFF valign=top colspan=2>
<hr>
<p align=left>
<font color=#000000 face=Arial>
   Capsule: A vacationing family learns that love comes only
from
   <br>  commitment, responsibility, and concern.
</font></P>
</td>
<tr> <!-- End of the first two rows of content -->

<!-- Continue the second row... -->
<td width=170 height=106 bgcolor=#FFFFFF valign=top align=right>
   <p align=center>
     <a href="http://www.xyzMovies.com/STMoon.htm/">
      <font face=Arial size=3 color=#009900>
        Movie's Web site
     </a></p>
   <p align=center>Barkley
   Family Rating:<br>
   </font>
   <font face="Arial" color=#009900 size=4>
    3.5 of 5 Stars</font>
</td>

<!-- The right cell of the second row -->
<td width=1113 height=106 bgcolor=#FFFFFF valign=top colspan=2>
   <p align=left>
    <font face=Arial>  Mom: 4 - <i>Finally, a realistic
    solution for family troubles!</i><br>
      Dad: 3 -
     <i>Slow in places, overall good, needs more action.</i><br>
       Rachel: 4 - <i>I liked it!</i><br>
       Annie: 3 - <i>I didn't see any horses...
   </i></font></P>
  <p>
   <font color=#000000 face=Arial>
     Friends' compiled rating: 3.25 Stars - Add yours below!
```

Continued

Listing 27-1   *Continued*

```
      </font>
   </td>
 </tr>

 <tr>
  <!-- The bottom row of the content page begins here -->
  <td width="170" height=290 bgcolor=white valign=top
align=right>
     <hr>
  </td>

  <td width=494 height=290 bgcolor=white valign=top>
   <hr>
  </td>

  <td width=397 height=290 bgcolor=white valign=top>
    
  </td>
 </tr>
</table>

 <!------------------------->
 <!-- Any footer goes here -->
 <!------------------------->
 </body>
</html>
```

Adding the Form to the Favorite Movies Page

**20 Min.
To Go**

The special part of the movie page — the rating form — occurs in the table's third row. Figure 27-2 shows the form that appears at the bottom of the page. Again, this entire Web page will not fit on most user monitors, but that's okay. The page is not the home page, and the user won't mind scrolling.

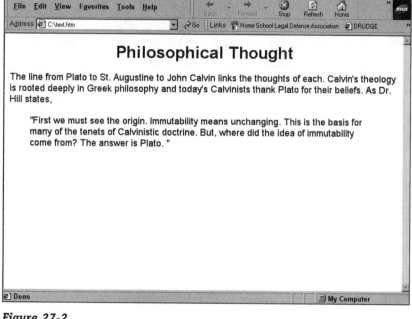

Figure 27-2
The bottom of the movie page holds a form the user can submit.

The Barkleys are keeping the form simple. They want results e-mailed to them. Notice that the form contains these controls:

- A description in the left cell
- Five radio buttons for the star-rating system
- A multiline text box
- A Submit button that triggers e-mailing the form's contents
- A Reset button that resets the user's entries

The Barkleys do not use check boxes for the star-rating system. If the form contained check boxes, users would be able to select multiple ratings for the same movies. The radio buttons keep the choices down to one.

In Session 14, you learned how to add form elements to your page. Forms are relatively simple to add. The Barkleys could have had the form answers submitted to the Web host, via a CGI script. E-mailing of the answers, however, is a much simpler solution. It brings the form data to the Barkleys on an individual basis so that each e-mail message from the form brings a new set of form results.

Listing 27-2 shows the rest of the code that completes the page and displays the form. The HTML code for the form is simple, but it does the job.

Listing 27-2
Creating the form

```
    <td width=170 height=290 bgcolor=white valign=top align=right>
    <hr>
    <p align=center><font color=#000000 face="Arial">Submit this
form and we'll update our Friends' compiled rating</font>
    </td>

    <td width=494 height=290 bgcolor=white valign=top>
    <hr>
    <form method=post name="MovieSTM"
action="mailto:Barkleys@email.mn.net">
      <p align=center>
      <i><font face=Arial size=4 color=#009900>
      <b>Saving the Moon</b>
      </font><br>
      </i><font color=#000000 face=Arial>
        Your Rating:<br>
      </font>        
       *<input type=radio name=R1 value=V1>
      <br>      
       **<input type=radio name=R1 value=V2>
      <br>    
       ***<input type=radio name=R1 value=V3>
      <br>  
       ****<input type=radio name=R1 value=V4>
      <br> 
       <!-- Last button is selected due to 'checked' option -->
       *****<input type=radio name=R1 value=V5 checked></p>
      <p align=left> <font color=#000000 face=Arial>
      Enter any comments: </font>
      <textarea rows=2 name=S1 cols=20>
      </textarea>
      <input type=submit value=Submit name=B1>
```

```
      <input type=reset value=Reset name=B2>
    </p>
  </form>
  <p> 
</td>

  <td width=397 height=290 bgcolor=white valign=top>
   
</td>
    </tr>
</table>

  <!------------------------->
  <!-- Any footer goes here -->
  <!------------------------->
  </body>
</html>
```

When the form contents are mailed to the Barkley family, the V1 through V5 variables contain 1 or 0 based on the user's selection (1 if the user checks the radio button, 0 if the button is unchecked). By default, the five-star radio button is selected when the form first appears on the screen; this is true because of the checked option in the fifth button's <input type=radio> attribute.

**10 Min.
To Go**

Creating the Image Map for the Family Travels Page

An *image map* is a graphic image that contains multiple links. It forms a backdrop for the hyperlinks forming the image map. Depending on where the user clicks, the image map takes the user to a different location. You should load the graphic image that you'll use as the image map into your graphics program and note the pixel coordinates (both width and height) for the entire image and the coordinates of the areas you want to use as hot spots for the links.

An image map's links can fall into the following kinds of hot-spot areas:

- A rectangle defined by the upper-left and the bottom-right coordinate pairs

- A triangle defined by three coordinate pairs, one at each of the three angles

- A circle defined by two coordinate pairs: the center and the right-edge coordinate point

Two pixel measurements always define a pair of coordinate points: the starting pixel row width and the starting pixel column height of the point. Therefore, a coordinate pair of 130, 245 specifies a point exactly 130 pixels to the right and 245 pixels down from the upper-left corner of an image. The upper-left corner is considered to be the starting point.

The Barkleys' recent vacation spots will serve as hot spots on the map. They have visited the following places in the past three years, and they want to share pictures and memories of those places on their site's Family Travels page:

- San Diego, California
- New York City
- Miami, Florida
- Toronto, Canada

The Family Travels page contains the usual header and navigation bar used for the other primary pages of the site. The body of the page contains only a map of the United States, as shown in Figure 27-3.

Although only enough time exists to cover the use of the image map briefly, your HTML education would not be complete without an example. Given that the vacation spots are so far apart, the Barkleys decide to use simple rectangular hot-spot areas to mark their four vacation locations. The image is only 285 x 295 pixels wide.

When you use an image map, you place the image on the Web page as usual using the <img> tag. Inside the <img> tag, use the usemap= attribute to name the map in case the page has, or will have, multiple image maps. Either immediately following the <img> tag or last in the HTML code, you should specify the coordinate points for every hot spot in the image.

Consider the following section of an HTML file that uses an image map:

```
<img border=0 src="US.gif" usemap="#states" width=285 height=295>
<map name="states">
<area shape=rect coords="26, 167, 56, 197"
href="http://www.BarkleyFamilyPage.com/LA.htm">
<!-- More coordinates and link references would follow -->
</map>
```

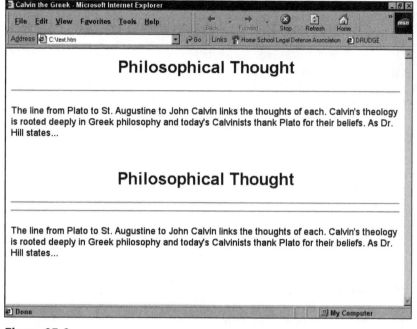

Figure 27-3
The map provides a backdrop for hyperlinks forming an image map.

The image is named US.gif, and the image contains mapped coordinates named "states". The <area> tag tells the browser the coordinates that define the rectangle (26, 167, 56, and 197, in this case); when the user clicks anywhere within that coordinate range, the hyperlink takes over. You specify as many coordinates and links as the image requires, and then you terminate the coordinates with a </map> tag.

A triangular hot spot would require six values, making a total of three coordinate pairs. A circle requires only four values, making a total of two coordinate pairs (the circle's center and its right edge).

The Barkleys use code just like this to map the four hot spots onto their map named, not coincidentally, US.gif. The code in Listing 27-3 shows the entire image mapping for the states. The image map requires very little HTML code. (This crash course does not create any of the image map's linked pages.)

Listing 27-3
Creating the entire image map with the four hot spots

```
<!-- Image map comes next for travels -->
<td width=1864 height=290 bgcolor=#FFFFFF valign=top>
 <font face=Arial size=4>
  These are the areas of our travel pages.
  <br>  Point to the map and when the pointer
  <br>
    becomes a hand, click that area and
  <br>  we'll show you our travel pictures and
  <br> stories from there!<br>
 </font>

 <img border=0 src="US.gif" usemap="#states" width=285 height=295>
 <map name="states">
 <!-- Each coordinate pair links to its own page for that city -->
 <!-- San Diego -->
 <area shape=rect coords="26, 167, 56, 197" href="http://www.
BarkleyFamilyPage.com/Sd.htm">
 <!-- New York City -->
 <area shape=rect coords="239, 107, 268, 135" href="http://www.
BarkleyFamilyPage.com/NYC.htm">
 <!-- Miami, FL -->
 <area shape=rect coords="227, 209, 262, 239" href="http://www.
BarkleyFamilyPage.com/MI.htm">
 <!-- Toronto -->
 <area shape=rect coords="207, 93, 235, 118" href="http://www.
BarkleyFamilyPage.com/TO.htm">

 </map>
 </td>
```

Image maps have drawbacks, such as the lack of support for alternative text that pops up descriptions of the hot spot. For simple matters, they work well, and for some Web page applications where maps and diagrams provide an overview for Web pages that follow, image maps are good to use.

Cross-Ref

Session 28 lists limitations of image maps.

Done!

If you've followed along for the past 27 sessions, you are much farther along than a newcomer to HTML! You are on your way to becoming an HTML programmer.

REVIEW

- Add forms to get user feedback on your site.
- Use image maps in those situations where a graphic image makes an effective navigation tool.
- Use coordinate pairs to recognize where the user clicks on your page's image maps.

QUIZ YOURSELF

1. What happens when the user clicks the Barkleys' form's Reset button? (See "Adding the Form to the Favorite Movies Page.")

2. What happens when the user clicks the Barkleys' form's Submit button? (See "Adding the Form to the Favorite Movies Page.")

3. What are two disadvantages to sending a form's answers to yourself via e-mail? (See "Adding the Form to the Favorite Movies Page.")

4. What is the difference between an image used as a hyperlink and an image map? (See "Creating the Image Map for the Family Travels Page.")

5. What is one drawback to image maps? (See "Creating the Image Map for the Family Travels Page.")

Correcting Web Site Problems

Session Checklist

✔ Understand potential site problems and how to obtain site statistics

✔ Determine the cause of the Barkleys' site problems with a usability study

✔ Learn the problems associated with image maps and how the Barkleys chose to handle its image map

**30 Min.
To Go**

I n this session, you learn how Web page designers and HTML programmers (often the same group!) perform usability studies to find out about any problems with their Web sites. This session includes an example of a usability study performed by the Barkleys for their Kid's Playground Web page. During these studies, you will see where users shine and where your site makes the user stumble. This session also covers the problems associated with image maps and how to get around them.

Potential Usability Problems and Statistics

Your users might be having difficulties accessing certain parts of your site without your even realizing it. The Web contains billions of Web pages, each just as easily accessed as another. When a page doesn't suit a user, when a page confuses a user, when a page doesn't work, or when a page takes too long to download, the user moves on to something else. Users, even friends and family (*especially* friends and family), have little to no incentive to tell you about problems with your site. Too many sites are competing with yours, and they all reside at the user's fingertips.

Of course, you can turn such competition around to your advantage. Many popular Web sites, just like Microsoft itself, began in someone's home. Other examples include The Drudge Report and eBay, both of which were considered *home-brew* until they made international fame by providing simple and fast services of one kind or another.

One of the most important tasks you should perform monthly is to get a copy of your Web host's usage reports for your site. Almost all Web hosts provide usability reports. These reports show statistics such as the following:

- The number of *hits*, or people who click on your site or times your site has been accessed
- A page-by-page hit count, showing hit numbers per page
- *Click-through* numbers showing how many times a user went to your home page and then clicked through to at least one other page
- The average amount of time spent on your site
- The average amount of time spent on each page

Different Web hosts provide different statistics. Yours may provide more or fewer.

These statistics are imprecise. For example, it is difficult to determine how long someone spends at your site. A user may click to your page and then walk away from his or her computer until the Internet Service Provider (ISP) shuts off the Web connection. Even worse, if the user has a Digital Subscriber Line (DSL) or cable modem access, he or she is considered to be "always on" and may not return to the computers until the next day — only to find that your site still happens to be on the screen.

In spite of the inaccuracy of these values, their general nature and especially their trends are vital for you to track. Keep accurate records of your site's visits and use. Determine which secondary pages are looked at the most and the least. For example, you'll want to eliminate some pages on your site that do not interest your users as much as you first thought.

The Barkley family noticed after several months that their Family Web site's home page received many hits (and "many" for a personal Web site may be ten a month, depending on the number of people who know about your site, whether you've registered the site, and how many others link to your site). The family also noticed that their Favorite Movies page also enjoyed a high hit rate. Far down on the list were the Family Travels and Kid's Playground pages.

Does that mean people have much less interest in those pages than in the other pages on the site? Perhaps, but perhaps not. The usability issue comes into play when you consider site hits. Never forget that your site may look and work great for you and your immediate family but that to the outside world, something may be keeping users from doing what you expect them to do. Perhaps you don't have technical problems but have designed a section that users don't want to revisit. The following things can cause users to stay away from individual pages after the first time:

- The page loads too slowly.
- The page's color contrast makes the text difficult to read.
- A multimedia element requires a plug-in.
- The page looks bad on common resolutions that you didn't test.
- The page fails to load properly on some versions of some browsers still in popular use.

Never require a plug-in that's been out on the market less than 18 months. If your users want to see a video clip you've provided but the clip requires a new plug-in format that's just been released, you may link to the download site for that plug-in, but your users will virtually never wait for the download. Too many other sites await them, and those sites don't require new technology to visit.

Nobody expects you to make your site compatible with Netscape and Internet Explorer browser versions 1.0. However, if you take advantage of the *latest* versions of these products and don't test on the *slightly older versions still in use,* you will lose audience.

20 Min. To Go

Performing a Usability Study to Determine Cause

As you learned in the previous section, the Web host's statistics are only half of the picture. The cause of user visitation problems may very well be your site's design or implementation.

As an example, you learned in the previous section that the Barkley site's Kid's Playground page and the Family Travels page are not getting the hits that the family expects. Actually, the children's page gets extremely few hits. The Family Travel page gets hits but little click-through, meaning few people click on the image map to read about the Barkleys' travels.

The Barkleys decided to perform a little market analysis of their own, inside their home, by inviting some of Rachel's friends over and watching how they access the site. The Barkleys know the importance of a usability study and decided to test their site with the actual users of the Kid's Playground page, the children, since they are the ones who are not hitting this page. In addition, *children are far more technically savvy than adults who might visit the site!* At least, that's what the Barkleys think, and it is possibly true.

How do you perform a usability study? Stand back and watch users work your site. Don't guide them! Rather, see how long they take to figure things out for themselves. Next, gather the answers to the following questions in regard to the users' behavior:

- Where do they click?
- What expressions are on their faces?
- Do they smile or sneer when trying a new feature?
- Do they access half the home page often but rarely get to the other?
- What seems to keep them from the other half of the page? Are elements not visible enough or not simple to use?
- Do they click the text hyperlinks?
- Do they ignore graphic hyperlinks?

- Do they click on pictures that don't have hyperlinks?
- Do they read your text carefully or just scan it rapidly?

The way you format text makes a dramatic difference in what the user reads. The next session offers tips that you can use to get visitors reading your text instead of scanning for headlines.

As the Barkleys watched the kids, they learned quickly why the Kid's Playground page was getting very few hits. The home page bored the kids! When the children visited the home page, they looked at the pictures, clicked on a thumbnail, and saw the larger image. At this point, they either looked away for something else to do, looked bored, or clicked other areas of the site. These children were old enough to read, and some would click on Kid's Playground and seem interested if they ever went there.

The answer for the Barkleys' Kid's Playground page seems to be that children simply don't want to mess with the home page before getting there. They are willing to give the site a chance, but they won't stay long if nothing quickly interests them. Even with Rachel's encouragement, few of her friends visited the Kid's Playground page on their own.

The Barkleys solved the solution in two ways. First, they added an icon next to the Kid's Playground button that would attract the interest of the children's friends but was small enough not to detract from the page. Figure 28-1 shows the figure. Without exception, the kids who then went to the page saw the fireworks graphic and clicked it. At first, the image was not a hyperlink to the Kid's Playground page but only a non-linked image *next* to the link. Just a few seconds with the new image, during a usability study, taught the Barkleys that both the image and the page title needed the same hyperlink in the navigation bar.

Second, they had Rachel give out the address of the actual Kid's Playground page to her friends. They could then surf directly to the Kid's Playground page. Although they had to type more characters (the /kid.htm/ at the end of the site address), they seemed more likely to do that with Rachel's encouragement. Sure enough, the Kid's Playground page, within a month, was getting more hits than the other secondary pages.

The Barkley family's simplistic site and children's usability study is not an answer for you, but a start. Obviously, your usability studies and concerns will differ greatly. Yet your approach should be similar.

icon doesn't overpower rest of page

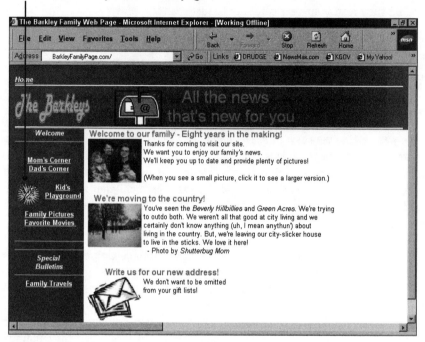

Figure 28-1
The small icon was enough to get children clicking through.

When you improve your site, as the Barkleys did with the icon, study the effects of that improvement on the entire site. Will improving the children's ability to surf to the Kid's Playground hinder, in any way, the adults who surf the site? In this page's case, the fireworks graphic *may negatively affect the adults' ability to surf the site as easily*. The graphic is not obtrusive, but the placement of the graphic next to the Kid's Playground label changes the top of the navigation bar considerably (look back to Figure 28-1). The new text spacing on the navigation bar makes one think that the top of the navigation bar contains *three* and not *five* items! The grouping, in pairs of lines, does not distinguish among the five menu elements. A user might click in the middle, between Mom's Corner and Dad's Corner, thinking that both are part of a link to the same page. Depending on where the users click, the link will take them to only one of those two pages. The Barkleys will find, in their next usability study, that some microspacing between Mom's Corner and Dad's Corner, as well as between Family Pictures and Favorite Movies, corrects this possible user error.

**10 Min.
To Go**

Image Map Problems and Solutions

In the previous session, you saw that the Barkleys' Family Travels page contained an image map that linked the user to the places the Barkleys had visited. Many Web sites use image maps. Their very names indicate one of the best uses for them: mapping situations when you want your users to be able to surf to a variety of places depending on where they click on the map. Unfortunately, image maps come with a set of problems that HTML programmers do not always easily overcome. With this in mind, make sure your site benefits more from an image map, in spite of the drawbacks that you're about to learn, than from a more traditional selection, such as a menu.

Image map problems

One problem is that text menus load dramatically faster than image maps. Your users will be selecting from a text menu and reading the subsequent page long before the users' image maps finishe loading. Even worse, browsers cannot scale an image map due to the map's fixed pixel coordinate system. A small resolution-based browser will not be able to display all of a large image map at one time. The user must resort to scrolling just to be able to click all parts of the map.

Another drawback is that image maps are invisible to text-only browsers. When a user turns off the display of graphics, he or she will not be able to understand the purpose of an image map and will be unable to benefit from anything about the map. If the user uses a modem-based connection, even today in the new millennium, he or she is likely to turn off graphics instead of waiting for every site's graphic images to download.

Image maps also bring a fixed aspect to Web pages. For example, users with accessibility problems cannot change the colors on an image map to suit themselves as they can other colors on the screen. In addition, users cannot change the text that appears, if any, on an image map, because the text is part of the image and is not rendered from a browser font.

Another problem is that the user cannot always see the image map's clickable areas. Figure 28-2 once again shows the Barkleys' Family Travels page with the image map. Where on the map are the hot spots? Your users will not know until they point to the map, and many areas won't be hot spots. With an unused hot-spot area, such as this map provides in the central portion of the United States where the Barkleys have never visited, a user might actually click a few places inside the map and *not* happen to hit a hot spot, then leave the page thinking something's wrong. But the only wrong thing was the image's design.

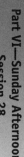

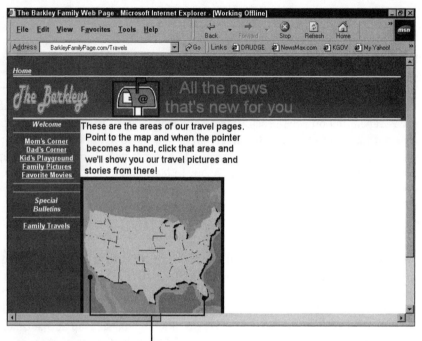

The hot spots are here somewhere

Figure 28-2
Where in the image map are users supposed to click?

The Barkleys' Solution

One common way to avoid the where-do-I-click problem is to shade areas of the image map with different colors. Shaded areas that distinguish one hot spot from another are great ways to distinguish the spots and give the user more hints of the image's purpose. Shading works well on maps that geographically divide into similar-sized sections, as might be the case for a divisional map of a company. The company's image map might show the south, east, north, and west divisions, each colored by their own hot-spot sections, and each boxed with a rectangular hot spot for the image mapping coordinates.

The Barkleys chose another way to increase the click-through on the Family Travels map. Shading does not work well because their site has only four travel pages linked to four cities on the map, and most of the map is therefore not clickable. The Barkleys decided to put circular beacons on the map in the four clickable areas, as Figure 28-3 shows. No HTML editing is required; the only edit needed is to place the four circled areas onto the map with a graphics program.

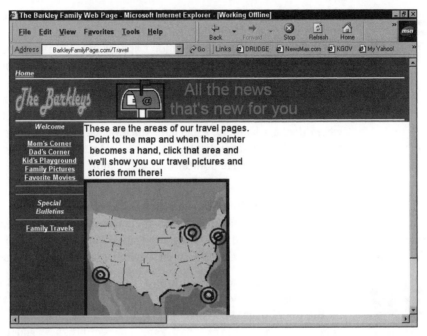

Figure 28-3
The circular beacons represent the image map's four hot spots.

Note

Notice that the Barkleys' navigation bar on the Family Travels page does not have the Kid's Playground icon that they put on the home page. Should the icon remain on each page or stay on the home page? Such a question is the kind you should ask yourself as you develop your site. Always question your site's details. If the Barkleys keep the navigation bar consistent, they can cut and paste the same code every time they create a new page. Each page will get the same navigation bar. The drawback is that the children's icon really doesn't need to be on each page. Users looking through Mom's Corner or the Family Travels pages probably aren't the ones who need to go straight to the children's page.

Not only are the hot spots now indicated, but the user's mouse pointer will change to the hyperlink shape when the user points to any of the hot spots, giving the user a kind of rollover effect that goes even further toward pinpointing the hot spots.

To help further, recent browsers display the URL address of the hot spot in the user's status bar. Earlier browsers did support image maps, but the connecting URL didn't appear in the status bar at the bottom of the browser's screen. Therefore, the users had no idea what was going to happen when they clicked an image map's hot spot. Although the site address doesn't always tell users much more than they already know, at least they have a better clue to where they are heading, especially since image maps don't provide a universal method for displaying a pop-up text message when the user hovers the mouse pointer over a hot spot.

Once you master your JavaScript skills, you can create some interesting rollover effects with image maps that modify other elements on the screen as the user guides the mouse pointer over the map. Of course, too much rollover animation detracts from a site, but generally, if your site's application begs for the use of an image map, do all you can to make that map more obvious for your users to use.

Done!

If you use image maps, provide your users extra instructions in all but the most obvious of cases. The Barkleys put this message on the travel page: Point to the map and when the pointer becomes a hand, click that area and we'll show you our travel pictures and stories from there! You do not have to put such a message on a command button or text hyperlink because those controls are so common users already know what to do.

REVIEW

- Watch users who access your site to learn where the site's weaknesses lie.
- Make your site as simple to use as possible.
- Image maps can be confusing, but they also provide a fairly advanced way to access particular information.
- Label your image maps well to help your users navigate them.

QUIZ YOURSELF

1. What kinds of information about your site's visitors can your Web Host provide? (See "Potential Usability Problems and Statistics.")

2. What is the difference between a hit and a click-through? (See "Potential Usability Problems and Statistics.")

3. What are some things you do during a usability study on your site? (See "Potential Usability Problems and Statistics.")

4. What alternative to image maps can you use? (See "Image Map Problems.")

5. What are two ways to guide your users to an image map's hot spots? (See "Image Map Problems and Solutions.")

Keeping the Family Web Site Fresh

Session Checklist

✔ Learn how the Barkleys keep their Web site fresh

✔ Document your site with future maintenance in mind

✔ Study the well-documented Barkley home page HTML for documentation tips you can use on your page

✔ Improve the readability of the text on the site

✔ Don't write long, flowing streams of text but keep your site moving rapidly, breaking up thoughts along the way with headings and hyperlinks

✔ Let your users scan your site for the information *they* want to read; don't push too much text onto the user all at once

**30 Min.
To Go**

I n this session, you begin to wrap up your HTML learning! You'll master some pointers about HTML feedback, site documentation, and text flow to help keep your Web site fresh. Here, you learn how the Barkleys keep their family Web site fresh. In addition, the Barkleys' fully documented home page is provided so that you can study it and then practice revising the HTML code and documentation.

Freshness Is the Key

This session describes how to keep your site fresh by making your site easy to update. You already know that freshness is the key to return Web users, and this session spends some time wrapping up your HTML knowledge by offering hints on Web site maintenance. What are the best ways to keep your site fresh? You'll learn some here.

Get quick HTML feedback

HTML code is simple to maintain. When you make an HTML mistake, you instantly see that mistake in your browser and a change that you make shows up immediately. Years ago, programmers had to wait, sometimes 24 hours, before their *batch programs* would compile, and if they fixed a mistake in the code, another long round was required. One way that you get extremely fast HTML feedback is to create and edit HTML using this routine:

1. Open your HTML text editor.
2. Open your browser.
3. Maximize both in full-screen mode.
4. Enter or edit your HTML code in the editor and save the file to the appropriate directory.
5. Switch to your browser screen and open the HTML file. Most browsers provide a menu option that opens a file, such as File ➪ Open. Instead of selecting a Web page, you select the HTML file from your own disk drive. The HTML code appears inside your browser, and you see the results.
6. Without closing the browser, move back to your HTML editor and make some changes.
7. Without closing the editor, move to your browser and click your browser's Refresh button. Instantly, the browser loads the fresh copy of the file, and you see the results of your change.
8. Keep moving back and forth between your editor and browser, saving the HTML file every time you make changes and then immediately looking at those changes after clicking Refresh on your browser's menu or toolbar.

If your monitor is large enough, you can keep both the HTML text window and your browser window open at the same time. You can make a change in the HTML code and see the change's effect as soon as you click your browser's Refresh button.

With the HTML code still on the screen in the other window, you can more easily locate where in the code the HTML still has a problem.

Write the documentation

In spite of the speed and simplicity of HTML described in the previous section, you must add some documentation to your site. Throughout earlier sessions, you saw some of the ways that documentation eases your maintenance burden as well as helps to provide contact information and a change log for all HTML coders on a team who maintain the same site.

As you add comments, you must consider the time you'll spend changing and adding content to your site later. Just because you create a site does not mean that you will be the one who changes the content. If you're out of town, someone else on your team or in your family may need to make changes. Another reason for the comments is that *you* will be adding and changing content and sometimes the HTML code gets confusing without comments.

Consider the Mom's Corner section of the Barkleys' Web site. On the page where her contents appear, the Barkleys must use ample documentation that explains which areas of the Web page's HTML don't change when the content changes. Of course, a change to the navigation bar or heading may be needed as well, but the day-to-day maintenance of the site more often requires changing only the fixed content and not the structure that surrounds the content.

Throughout the entire Barkley home page, comments explain what each section does. You've already seen most of those. But more comments are needed that explain exactly how to change the various elements that appear on the page. Even the logo or the large message, All the news that's new for you, may need to change, depending on the circumstance and depending on how much the Barkleys want to spruce up their site.

You should spend some time studying the Barkley family home page HTML code in its final form because that page contains the full set of comments. The entire ten-minute section that follows displays the home page's HTML code in a program listing.

**20 Min.
To Go**

The Barkleys' Fully Documented Home Page

Listing 29-1 contains the entire Barkley family Web site's home page with a full round of comments that explain the code. You've seen many of the comments before in the code in the earlier sessions. The comments are represented by the `<!>` tag.

Once you complete your initial site's development, spend time studying the effective comments in the Barkley code. The comments describe every aspect of the code that the Barkleys might want to change. Then go back and edit the places in the code in Listing 29-1 that are described by the comments.

Listing 29-1

The final Barkley home page's HTML code with maintenance comments throughout

```
<html>
  <!------------------------------------->
  <!-- The Barkley Family Web site    -->
  <!-- To relate news to family and   -->
  <!-- friends around the world.      -->
  <!-- Created: June 4, 2003          -->
  <!-- Last modified: August 15, 2003 -->
  <!-- Write wBarkley@ourweb.net if   -->
  <!-- you have questions.            -->
  <!------------------------------------->

  <!--------------------------->
  <!-- The header begins here -->
  <!--------------------------->
  <head>

    <!-- Change the following title whenever
         the window title bar needs changing -->
    <title>The Barkley Family Web Page</title>

    <!-- The search engine tags appear next -->
    <meta name="description"
     content="Barkley Family Web Site">
    <!-- Add to the keywords below if we have more
         children or add features to our Web site
         that we want search engines to pick up. -->
    <meta name="keywords"
     content="Barkley, Barkleys, Scott Barkley, Gail Barkley,
       Rachel Barkley, Annie Barkley, new home, we've moved,
       Kid's Playground">
```

```
<!-- This table is the header portion of our site -->
<table width=100% cellpadding=0 cellspacing=0 border=0
bgcolor=#008000>

    <!-- First row only contains a Home link
         No need to change it unless our Web
         address changes and we want the Home
         link to point to a different address -->
    <tr>
      <td height=21 width=179 align=left>
         <font face=Arial size=2>
         <a href="http://www.BarkleyFamilyPage.com/">
         <b><i>Home</i></b></font></a>
      </td>
      <!-- Table needs two more cells defined -->
      <td width=169 height=21>
      </td>
      <td width=788 height=21>
      </td>
    </tr>

    <tr>   <!-- Blank Line as a thin row -->
      <td colspan=3 bgcolor=white width=100% height=2
       align=left>
      </td>
    </tr>

      <!-- This begins the logo band of the header.
           No need to change anything here unless we
           change our logo image file name and/or its
           size. We'll also want to change the logo's
           link if our Web address ever changes -->
      <tr align=left>  <!-- Logo -->
      <td align=left width=179 height=24>
       <!-- The logo links to the home page -->
         <a href="http://www.BarkleyFamilyPage.com/">
         <img src="barkleys.gif" width=149 height=66
align="absmiddle"
         border=0 alt="Family Home Page">
```

Continued

Listing 29-1 *Continued*

```
      </a>
    </td>

      <!-- The mailbox image and email link is here.
           No need to change unless we change the mail
           image and/or its size. We'll also want to
           change the link if our email address ever
           changes. -->
    <td width=169 height=24>
    <p align=center>
           
    <a href="mailto:Barkleys@email.mn.net">
     <img border=0 src="mailbox.gif" align=middle
     width=120 height=77 alt="Mailbox">
    </a>
    </td>

      <!-- The following <td> through </td> simply define the
           large gold text that appears to the right of the
           email graphic image. If we change the text, we
           will probably need to change the number of non-
           breaking spaces that help center the text inside
           the cell but still keep the text on the left edge
           portion of the cell. -->
    <td height=24>
    <font face=Arial size=6 color=#CC9900>
         All the news<br>
      that's new for you</font>
    </td>

  <!-- The remaining code between here and the body defines
       only colored, separating lines that separate the header
       area from the body. -->
  <tr>  <!-- Blank Line as a thin row -->
    <td colspan=3 bgcolor=white width=100% height=2 align=left>
    </td>
  </tr>
```

```
    <tr>    <!-- Golden Line as a thin row -->
      <td colspan=3 bgcolor=#CC9900 width=100% height=2
      align=left>
      </td>
    </tr>
</table>
</head>

<!------------------------->
<!-- The body begins here -->
<!------------------------->
<!-- The body's background color should match the header's
      and the navigation bar's color -->
<body bgcolor=008000 link=white>

  <!-- The following code defines the navigation bar that
        falls down the left side of the Web site. The
        navigation bar is actually the first of three columns
        in the table at the bottom of the site. We'll
        have to change the navigation bar once in a while.
        The navigation bar primarily consists of a link followed by
        the text that the user will click to go to that link.
        We'll usually not change the the primary, top section,
        but we'll be adding and removing the special bulletins
        from time to time. Also, we may be changing the icon
        we use for the link to the Kid's Playground. -->
  <!-- *** If we make any changes to this navigation bar,
        except for the Kid's Playground, we must replicate this
        change throughout all pages on our site because we
        want each page to display a consistent navigation bar.
        If we tire of copying all code EXCEPT the Kid's
        Playground icon, we may begin to put the icon on the
        other pages also to keep things easier
        instead of maintaining two separate versions
        of the same navigation bar. -->
  <table border=0 width=2000 height=3 cellspacing=0
        cellpadding=0>
    <tr>
      <td width=140 height=382 bgcolor=#008000 align=center
```

Continued

Listing 29-1 *Continued*

```
valign=top rowspan=3>
  <font face=Arial size=2 color=#FFFFFF>
  <b><i>Welcome</i>
  <hr>
  <a href="http://www.BarkleyFamilyPage.com/Mom.htm/">
    Mom's Corner
  </a><br>
  <a href="http://www.BarkleyFamilyPage.com/Dad.htm/">
   Dad's Corner
  </a><br>
  <p align=center>
  <!-- The next <img> tag defines the graphic we use
       for the Kid's Playground. Routinely, we should
       change this graphic to keep the image fresh,
       but maintain the same pixel size measurements
       or we'll throw off the size of the navigation
       bar -->
  <img border=0 src="Kids.gif" width=49 height=44
   align=left>
  <a href="http://www.BarkleyFamilyPage.com/Kids.htm/">
   Kid's Playground
  </a><br><br>
  <a href="http://www.BarkleyFamilyPage.com/Pics.htm/">
   Family Pictures
  </a><br>
  <a href="http://www.BarkleyFamilyPage.com/Movies.htm/">
   Favorite Movies
  </a><br>
   <hr><hr>
   <i>Special
   <br>Bulletins</i>
  <hr>
  <a href="http://www.BarkleyFamilyPage.com/Travels.htm/">
   Family Travels</b>
  </a>
 </font>
</td>
```

```
<!-- This begins the second and third columns, the white
     area, of the site's body content. Most of the
     second column cells hold the first few letters
     of our gold headline text and a graphic image.
     Keep any replacement images the same width and
     height (105x82) so as not to disturb the table's
     width. -->
<td width=114 height=1 bgcolor=white valign=top align=right>
 <p align=right>
 <font face=Arial size=3 color=#CC9900>
 <b>Welcome to o</b>
 <!-- The thumbnail image links to a larger photo -->
 <!-- The first JPG image is the large photo and the
      second is the smaller, thumbnail version. Make both
      available in our images folder. Update the size
      of the larger image when the picture changes. -->
 <a href="http://www.BarkleyFamilyPage.com/ourfam.jpg">
   <img border=0 src="ourfamT.jpg" align=top width=105
   height=82 alt="Our Family (24 Kb)">
 </a>
 </font>
 </p>
</td>


<!-- This is the continuation of the first row's 3rd column.
     Put continuing headline text here and follow that with
     black text that details the headline. Add links to any
     story that requires more room and open those in a second
     window created for that specific story only. -->
<td width=2000 height=1 bgcolor=white valign=top align=left>
 <p>
 <font face=Arial size=3 color=#CC9900>
  <b>ur family - Eight years in the making!</b>
 </font>
 <font face=Arial size=2 color=black>
  <br> Thanks for coming to visit our site.
  <br> We want you to enjoy our family's news.
```

Continued

Listing 29-1 *Continued*

```
      <br> We'll keep you up to date and provide plenty
      of pictures!
      <br><br> (When you see a small picture, click it
      to see a larger version.)
    </font>
   </td>
 </tr>

 <!-- Here is the second row of the large, white, middle and
      rightcolumns that form the body of content. As before,
      this cell holds the left part of our gold headline text
      along with a thumbnail image linked to a
      larger one. -->
 <td width="114" height=80 bgcolor=white valign=top align=right>
   <font face=Arial size=3 color=#CC9900>
    <b>We're movin</b>
    <!-- The thumbnail image links to a larger photo -->
    <!-- The first JPG image is the large photo and the
         second is the smaller, thumbnail version. Make both
         available in our images folder. Update the size
         of the larger image when the picture changes. -->
     <a href="http://www.BarkleyFamilyPage.com/ourhouse.gif">
      <img border=0 src="ourhousT.jpg" align=top
      width=105 height=82 alt="Our New Home (168 Kb)">
     </a>
   </font>
 </td>

 <!-- The continuation of the text from the middle column. -->
 <td width=2000 height=80 bgcolor=white valign=top>
   <p align="left">
   <font face=Arial size=3 color=#CC9900>
    <b>g to the country!</b>
   </font>
   <font face=Arial size=2 color=black>
   <font face=Arial size=2>
    <br> You've seen the
```

```
            <i>Beverly Hillbillies</i> and <i>Green Acres</i>. We're
                trying
<br> to outdo both. We weren't all that good at
                city living and we
            <br> certainly don't know anything (uh, I mean
                anythun') about
            <br> living in the country. But, we're leaving our
                city-slicker house
            <br> to live in the sticks. We love it
                here!
            <br>   - Photo by <I>Shutterbug
                Mom</I></FONT></P>
        </font>
    </td>
    </tr>

    <!-- The final row on the home page that enables the user to
            send us email. We will have to change the email link if
            our email address ever changes. -->
    <tr>
    <td width=114 height=80 bgcolor=white valign=top align=right>
        <font face=Arial size=3 color=#CC9900>
        <b>Write us f</b><img border=0 src="lettersT.gif"
            align=top width=105
            height=82 alt="Send us mail!">
        </font>
    </td>
    <td width=2000 height=80 bgcolor=white valign=top>
        <p align="left">
        <font face=Arial size=3 color=#CC9900>
        <b>or our new address!</b>
        </font>
        <font face=Arial size=2><br> We don't want to be
        omitted
        <br> from your gift lists!</FONT></P>
    </td>
    </tr>
</table>
```

Continued

Listing 29-1   *Continued*

```
<!----------------------------------------->
<!-- We don't use footers at this time -->
<!----------------------------------------->
</body>
</html>
```

Whew! Listing 29-1 is certainly long. If you went through the code analyzing the comments to learn how well-documented the code is, you are almost to the end of your 30-minute session already.

Improving the Way Text Is Presented

**10 Min.
To Go**

Before finishing this session, you must understand one final aspect of a Web page that this tutorial has not yet had the opportunity to address. You must understand that text on a Web page does not translate well into a book's format, and more important, a book doesn't translate well into Web text. This section explains the flow of the text on your site. How does your message come across? If you have a lot to say, how do you go about presenting all those words using a medium that shuns wordiness?

The Web and printed media are two completely different kinds of reading vehicles. One does not replace the other. Users read text from the two kinds of media differently. Skimming the headlines is the normal way for a user to view a Web page. Too much text will not confuse the user, but the user has more than a billion pages out there vying for his or her attention, and you must assume that your user's attention is more fleeting than the newspaper reader's attention. If you don't make your text scannable by including numerous headlines and divisions, your user won't read the text.

Users aren't shortsighted or unable to read your site's text, but screen resolutions are not yet clear enough to substitute well for printed type, and the user's browser provides far more jump options than the printed page. With a book, the user can jump to any page in that book; with a Web site, the user can jump to any page in the world.

The following three rules should dictate the text layout on your site:

1. Less is better. Always put off the detailed text until later on in the page. Preferably, place the text on another page requested by the user when the user wants to see the text.

2. Break up long articles into multiple pages, referring to articles with hyperlinks.

3. Break up long paragraphs into bulleted lists or small, multiple paragraphs with a heading once in a while.

Done!

Consider the news sites that you visit. They don't work at all like the newspapers and magazines you read. The Web sites provide headlines and, at most, just a few words from the major articles on the site. Even the banner ads don't waste room with text. Very little appears except a handful of headlines. Not even all the headlines show: The rest are elsewhere, off the page somewhere. Only the top stories are given. The top headlines are the push content; the user can be pushed into selecting one, can look around the site and grab a less prominent article that appears later, or can go somewhere else. Mr. Barkley understands that even though he has a lot to say, his Dad's Corner needs to present his views in short snippets of information instead of in a manuscript format.

REVIEW

- Maintain your site regularly to keep it fresh.
- Document your site to make maintenance easier.
- Use shorter snippets of text instead of long, flowing paragraphs to keep your user's attention.

QUIZ YOURSELF

1. What's the difference between the way batch programmers used to work and today's HTML programmers? (See "Get quick HTML feedback.")

2. How can you quickly see what your HTML code is doing? (See "Get Quick HTML feedback.")

3. Name the purposes for HTML documentation. (See "Write the documentation.")

4. How does reading a Web page differ from reading a newspaper? (See "Improving the Way Text is Presented.")

5. What are some of the ways you can improve the readability of text on your site? (See "Improving the Way Text is Presented.")

The Future of HTML

Session Checklist

✔ Learn that the Internet is not static but a growing entity

✔ Understand that new hardware will support HTML

✔ Keep up with HTML-related technologies related to your job

✔ Focus on securing your systems with HTML in the near future

✔ Learn about two future technologies — WebTV and PDAs — now in their infancies

**30 Min.
To Go**

Congratulations! You now know how to code with HTML. To close out your weekend crash course, this final session brushes off the magic eight-ball somewhat to discuss the future of HTML. HTML's future will affect *your* future. This session describes some of the ways that the growth of the Internet, new hardware changes, and security issues will affect HTML coding and your job as an HTML programmer.

Growth Increases Demand for HTML

Nobody sells the Internet. In 1994, before most people knew what the Internet was, no company made it their goal to "make the Internet the greatest innovation of the next ten years." The Internet's huge growth came about as the result of technology coming together at the right time. The Internet happened; it was not planned. In 1994, companies wanted to be a part of this thing called "the Internet," and they formulated business strategies to jump onto the expected growth, and they did everything they could think of to increase the growth, but they would not and could not fathom that more than one billion Web pages would be in use at the turn of the next century.

One cannot fathom what the next ten years will bring. You do know that growth in the Internet will occur, that most of the world is not yet connected to the Internet, and that technology is getting faster and less expensive. The Internet will continue to grow, and given the past, it's safe to assume that its growth will far surpass today's expectations. Where does that growth leave you, the newcomer to HTML programming? Exactly where you want to be: in the middle of things!

New Hardware Brings HTML Challenges

If you program with HTML, then actually you are in a better position than anyone to respond to changes in technology. Look at the newest versions of Windows. The online help system, for ten years, remained fairly stable and manifested itself in a uniform format across all Windows applications. A collapsible tree-structured list of topics presented you with an overview or with detail about a specific item.

When the Web came along, much of it was not being designed to suit Windows. Although the Web page's command buttons, scroll bars, and browser designs were borrowed from Windows and the Mac (and ultimately, from Sun, which developed a Mac-like prototype, with mouse, years before the first Mac hit the streets), the browser's language, HTML, was intended to proliferate text across networked computers, linking the computers and documents with hyperlinks embedded inside the HTML code.

As time wore on, Windows became more like the Web; the Web did not become more like Windows! Think about the help system you now have on your Windows machine. The help system works inside a browser with a scroll bar and hyperlinks. In addition, almost all of today's help systems are written in HTML. The designers chose the simplicity of HTML to change the entire nature of online help systems.

In spite of the proliferation of powerful and useful language tools such as JavaScript, XML, and DHTML, HTML remains at the core. The new languages build on top of HTML. It seems as though HTML remains in the forefront even as other tools take hold. The more people who write JavaScript code, the more they write HTML code to go along with the JavaScript. The more people who write XML code, the more they write HTML code to go along with the XML code.

But software is not the best result of HTML; hardware is. HTML has leapt out of the software arena now and finds itself controlling hardware. Browsers are HTML-based, and Internet-aware hardware devices are just seeing the light of day.

Smart appliances, with computers inside them that connect to the outside world, are in our vision. One example is a refrigerator that updates a screen in the door with items you're low on and then automatically sends a request to the local grocer's Web site. Another example is a washing machine that sends an automatic e-mail message to the repair site when it begins to fail. These devices are cute in theory, but they are not yet practical enough to make the mainstream. Some consumers don't want the bother or expense of having a phone line or a network cable running to every appliance in their houses.

Many rural areas are years away from being fully wired for high-speed Internet access provided by Digital Subscriber Lines (DSL) or cable modems. But high-speed, wide-area wireless technology such as *bluetooth* (which is discussed in more detail in the next section) is blooming to offer a hint of how our homes and environments will be connected without the hassle of wires. Two-way Internet satellite technology is supposed to be right around the corner so our homes won't have to be wired any-where. Whether we're on the road or in the desert, we'll have the same high-speed access that we have in our offices. Each of these in-home *information appliances* currently in the design and prototype stage supports some form of HTML.

Your Job Is to Keep Up with HTML-Related Technologies

20 Min. To Go

It is incumbent upon you to learn as much as you can about the way the Internet connects to the world. The hardware will be taken care of, but without software, it cannot be smart enough. Your code will be transported to new kinds of hardware.

To be such a base language for hardware devices nobody has even thought of yet, HTML will have to change along the way, just as it has since version 1.0. A new device of some sort will force the World Wide Web Consortium to develop new command tags or attributes that can take advantage of the new hardware.

Your job is to keep learning the technologies related to HTML. The HTML program-ming foundation you now have will springboard you into the newer technologies. You are more than ready to tackle DHTML and JavaScript now and use those tools to accent your HTML coding experience. You might even try your hand at actual Java programming, a task that differs greatly from JavaScript in nature. Trust your instincts. If you like HTML coding, and another Web language catches your interest, that new Web language may be the next big language that uses HTML as a stepping stone to take hold of an area of online service.

As online access expands, as it will continue to do, and as wireless technologies grow, people will no longer be tethered to a desktop PC for online access or a laptop-to-phone connection. The Bluetooth kinds of technology mentioned earlier provide a niche that offers short-range, wide-access, wireless technology. In a nutshell, such technology enables devices within short distances of each other to communicate with each other at high speeds. This technology enables organizations with several warehouses spread across a few square miles, such as airports, to connect their computers, phones, and other video and audio communications without wires, meaning that the on-the-ground personnel have as much information available to them as the corporate office workers.

Even though such technology will dramatically change the way people use computers and connect to the World Wide Web's resources, the goal is the same as it's always been: provide fast access to information. That's what you will be doing more of. These new technologies work just as today's modem-based PCs work, in that your HTML code browses for the information the user wants to see. The HTML must change, however, not in nature but in expansion of new connections. You won't be limited to screen pixels because tomorrow's technologies will output to controlling modules inside jets as well as to voice-enabled devices that answer a user's request in spoken language instead of showing the user the simple data. You will be writing to a giant array of output devices, and HTML will have to adapt to new devices for output. Other languages will adapt as well, such as DHTML, JavaScript, XML, and whatever other HTML-based languages appear on the horizon.

The Future: WebTV and PDAs

**10 Min.
To Go**

To give you a taste of current forward-thinking uses for HTML code, the next two short sections demonstrate WebTV and PDAs (personal data assistants). These technologies are in their infancies. The WebTV as it exists today will probably change dramatically in the next few years, perhaps even disappearing when another, more general, Internet appliance takes it place. Nevertheless, the considerations you'll take into account with regard to WebTV device-based HTML are similar to some of the considerations you'll have to take into account with regard to future technologies you'll write for. By looking at PDA device-based HDML (an offshoot of HTML), you will see how one must adjust HTML thinking so the pages display on small devices.

WebTV device-based HTML

Slow response hinders current WebTV users. WebTV connected to DSL or cable-modem services promises to help, but the large majority of WebTV users are modem-based. In addition, those with modems often experience slower connection speeds than similar-speed modems connected to computers. Therefore, you must do what you can to keep WebTV viewers browsing as fast as the technology allows.

One way to accomplish this speed-up is via a WebTV extension to HTML 4.01 called the <link> tag. Although <link> does seem to support future enhancements, its primary use now is for WebTV users. The <link> tag speeds performance of WebTV browsing by pre-fetching (or pre-loading) a Web page. The format follows this general pattern:

```
<link rel=next href="http://www.idg.com/">
```

Never attempt to pre-load pages for regular browsers. Often, WebTV users visit sites designed for them, and these sites take advantage of the pre-fetching feature. Often, a site will offer both a WebTV version and a non-WebTV version so that the pre-fetch instructions are never handled by the regular browsing environments. However, through ample use of JavaScript, you can pre-load images into a user's non-WebTV browser. No regular browser-aware HTML instructions can pre-load Web pages or images in the same way available to WebTV viewers.

The WebTV browsers come with memory cache pages that store the pre-fetched pages until the user displays those pages. In theory, pre-fetching is extremely appealing, and one wonders why regular browsers don't support the <link> tag's ability to pre-load pages. In practice, pre-fetching works only marginally, in special cases, to speed up the loading process. Only Web sites that produce a series of sequential Web pages work well with such a pre-load system. Often, WebTV users display program guide information through the WebTV browser. While the user browses one program listing, the next can be fetching. If the user continues, therefore, to scroll through the program listings, those listings will already be loaded into the user's cache.

PDA device-based HDML

HDML stands for *Handheld Device Markup Language,* and it refers to an HTML offshoot that developers use for small PDAs (personal data assistants) such as browser-ready cell phones and large-screen pocket organizers. The public's demand for pocket-sized Internet-ready devices far outpaces the supply of good technologies.

PDAs require only an eight-line, one-color (and that color is gray) screen. When you write HTML code that produces Web pages for the world to see, you know after 30 sessions that you don't write to the lowest-common-denominating system, but you certainly do not implement the latest browser and monitor bells and whistles if you want your site to be revisited. Yet, the proliferation of PDAs makes the demand for small Web content too great to ignore. You cannot create Web pages that satisfy one-color, 8-line screens and also send those pages out onto the Web and expect millions of desktop and laptop computer users to enjoy the page.

You have three choices:

1. Write HTML for a niche audience — either the non-PDA market (with HTML) or the PDA market (with HDML) — and your pages will be marketed towards that niche only.

2. Write two versions of your site: one for non-PDA (with HTML) and one for PDA (with HDML). Good luck; nobody envies your market channeling nightmares.

3. Use a combination of HTML and HDML that somehow sends the proper content of the Web page to the proper kinds of devices.

The reality is that many are using combinations of all three choices. The market will change as the hardware changes and as people better determine what they really want to do with such devices. In the meantime, the W3C (World Wide Web Consortium) is honing an already popular proposed standard for the HDML language that HTML programmers can use today.

A Brief Introduction to HDML

HDML is enough like HTML that you won't have to learn a whole new command set. It works on the smaller devices whereas HTML falls apart because of its inability to work well on smaller hardware screens. As an introductory taste of HDML, consider its concept: HDML is *card-based* and not *page-based*. Obviously, the entire focus of HTML code is the Web page. HDML shrinks that focus to a card analogy, squeezing the programming focus down at the outset. These cards appear on the

PDA screen, whether the screen is a telephone device or a pocket organizer. Within the card analogy, programmers have the same considerations they have on the larger-scaled Web page: Not all PDA screens are large enough to hold the same size of card as some of the other PDA screens. One shoots for the normal card size and does as good a job as possible at making PDA users happy and motivating them to revisit the card-sized site.

The cards are organized into a *deck,* just as Web pages are organized into a Web site. The cards hold data and *actions.* The actions do things with the cards in the deck, perhaps displaying a card or manipulating information on a card so that the change appears on the user's handheld screen. The actions are often brought about by unique hardware interfaces: One user might push the buttons on the cell phone to access a site, while another might use a stylus to point to an icon that brings up the site. The actual user-to-hardware interface is often masked to the HDML programmer. If you program with HDML, you won't care if a card's display is requested by a user holding a pen, pushing a button, or working a rolling track ball. Likewise, if you program with HTML, you won't care if the user clicks a form's button with a mouse or by pressing Enter.

HDML code example

Listing 30-1 contains a short set of HDML code. Look through the comments to understand the code's purpose. The key tags used in the code listing are the start tag `<hdml>`, the display tag `<display>`, and the action tags `<action>`. Although this session only had time to scratch the surface, you will see that you are already sufficiently grounded in HTML to tackle offshoots such as HDML.

Listing 30-1
Creating a short set of HDML code

```
<!-- Display the version in the start tag.
     This tag might be embedded inside HTML
     code for a site. In theory, both the
     full-screen user as well as the PDA
     user can access the same site. -->
<hdml version=3.4>
  <!-- The display tag sends a tag with the
       name attribute to the screen. -->
  <display name=sales>
    <!-- The action tag locates the next card to
```

Continued

Listing 30-1　　　　　　　　　　　　　　　　　　　　　　*Continued*

```
        display based on the display tag's relative
        location. costs is the name of the next card
        to display. -->
   <action type=accept label=costs task=go dest=#costs>
   <!-- Text appears on the PDA as a result of the
        following line as it would in HTML. -->
   Last year's figures are spectacular.
   <BR><br>
   We expect a 7% increase in profits this year.
   </display>
</HDML>
```

Done!

REVIEW

- You will learn various forms of HTML as hardware evolves.

- When writing for WebTV, take advantage of the image pre-loading instruction.

- Use HDML on small hardware devices whose screens do not allow for full-featured browsing.

QUIZ YOURSELF

---

1. Who designed the Internet so that it would grow to the size it has become? (See "Growth Increases Demand for HTML.")

2. What is an information appliance? (See "New Hardware Brings HTML Challenges.")

3. Name at least one benefit of an Internet appliance. (See "New Hardware Brings HTML Challenges.")

4. Where do WebTV devices store the pre-fetched papers? (See "WebTV device-based HTML.")

5. What is HDML and why must you use it and not HTML for pocket-sized browsing devices? (See "The Future: WebTV and PDAs.)

1. What protocol do you use to request e-mailed form results?

2. What kind of script is required when you want your Web host to gather form data?

3. What security concerns arise when you request the e-mail of form data directly to you?

4. What is the difference between an image and an image map?

5. True or False: At most, image maps support two hyperlink locations.

6. Describe the three ways to specify coordinate pair values for the image map's hot spots.

7. What is the best way to learn if users can understand and use your site the way you expect them to?

8. What are things to look for during a usability study?

9. What does the click-through rate indicate?

10. What usability issues arise with image maps?

11. How can you help narrow the user to image map hot spots?

12. True or False: Procedural programming offers quicker feedback than HTML programming.

13. How can you help ease the burden required by routine updates to your pages' HTML-based content?

14. How can you improve the odds that visitors will read all the text you place on your site?

15. True or False: Hardware breakthroughs make HTML less important every day.

16. What kinds of devices are now becoming Internet-aware that were not just a few years ago?

17. What technology does the Bluetooth specification describe?

18. Why will security become increasingly important for the HTML programmer?

19. How does the `<link>` tag improve the way WebTV users surf the Internet?

20. Finish this sentence: HTML is to Web pages and Web sites as HDML is to cards and:

Answers to Part Reviews

Following are the answers to the part review questions at the end of each Part in this Weekend Crash Course. Think of these reviews as mini-tests that are designed to help you prepare for the final — the Skills Assessment Test on the CD.

Friday Evening Review Answers

1. HyperText Markup Language
2. Web pages must change often to keep users coming back.
3. Tags are HTML commands.
4. Angled brackets enclose HTML tags.
5. The browser ignores the tag.
6. True
7. The text appears back-to-back and not on different lines.
8. The resolution determines how much of your page the user can see at one time.
9. The user will first see the upper-left corner of the page.
10. Placeholders appear in place of graphics sometimes.

11. You may want to offer low- and high-resolution sites, as well as sites that load quickly and more slowly to please all users. Such multi-layered sites can be difficult to market properly, however.

12. HTML validators analyze your site for loading speed and color correctness.

13. Sequential, hierarchical, and Web

14. The Web Host owns the server that provides the site to the rest of the Internet users.

15. The images folder holds all the site's images.

16. Name all HTML files with the htm or html filename extension.

17. You have full control over the serving of the pages.

18. DHTML includes JavaScript that enable rollover effects and other special elements that activate your site better than stand-alone HTML can do.

19. True; CGI scripts appear on the Web Host's server.

20. Rollover effects can be used to make buttons change shape and color as the user points to the buttons with the mouse.

Saturday Morning Review Answers

1. The <title> tag resides in the header.

2. Lowercase keeps your tags consistent and helps distinguish them from values that you use as attributes.

3. The browser substitutes other fonts.

4. Use the <h1> tag.

5. True (some browsers do not render the <p> tag perfectly, however)

6. Use the align=left attribute.

7. <center>

8. Use the <blockquote> and </blockquote> tags.

9. A horizontal rule is a line or bar across a Web page and the <hr> and </hr> tags specify the horizontal rule.

10. An ordered list retains its order as you add and remove items from the list.

11. Definition lists also work well for address books.

12. 216

13. A hexadecimal value is a base-16 number that specifies the RGB value of a color combination.

14. Red, Green, and Blue

15. The image appears too grainy.

16. False

17. A location on the screen where the user can click to link to another page.

18. An active link is a link the user has clicked but that has not loaded yet.

19. Use a hyperlink with the `target="_blank"` attribute.

20. False

Saturday Afternoon Review Answers

1. The mailto: protocol opens the user's email message window.

2. The HTML code displays an error message in this rare instance.

3. `<!-->` and `<-->` enclose comments.

4. Either of these lines will work:

   The `&#60;p&#62;` tag is an HTML paragraph tag

   The `&lt;p&gt;` tag is an HTML paragraph tag

5. False; tables form from top-to-bottom and left-to-right.

6. `<tr>` and `<td>`

7. The `<th>` defines a header cell that is boldfaced.

8. Cellpadding determines the space between table cell contents and the cell's edge while cellspacing determines the space between table cells.

9. False; 100 percent makes the cell span the *rest* of the screen's width after the first few cells appear.

10. By table percentage and by pixel width

11. The field holds a value and the field label adds a title to the field.

12. By email and via the server's CGI script

13. Use the `type=text` attribute inside an `<input>` tag.

14. The asterisk, *

15. A text area is a multi-lined text field.

16. Scroll bars appear if the contents of the text field do not fit within the pre-defined space of the field on the screen.

17. The user can check more than one check box but only one radio button at a time.

18. Antialiasing adds a grainy background to images.

19. The `lowsrc=` attribute sends a fast-loading, low-resolution image to the user's Web page while a larger resolution image loads in the background more slowly.

20. A navigation bar helps the use traverse the pages of the Web site.

Saturday Evening Review Answers

1. The meta tag displays nothing on your Web page.

2. Place meta tags in the header section.

3. The `name=` and `description=` attributes determine the placement of the site on a search engine and the text that appears in that search engine listing.

4. True

5. The header, navigation, and detail frames

6. The user cannot reside table borders.

7. Frames are difficult to use and often consume too much screen space.

8. The frameset holds the individual frame pages and acts as the page's structure.

9. The `<noframes>` and `</noframes>` tags enclose content for users without frame-enabled browsers.

10. Sound

11. Multimedia content takes an extremely long time to load.

12. The streaming video begins playing as soon as the user connects to the video's multimedia element.

13. An external video clip displays controls with which the user can control the playback of the video.

14. The `<embed>` tag is better supported than `<object>`.

15. Rollover effects produce a color or shape change as the user moves the mouse pointer over Web page elements such as buttons.

16. An event is something that happens in a graphical user interface, such as the user clicking a mouse.

17. The user will not be able to resize your Web page text if you've specified exact font sizes.

18. The margin: characteristic substitutes for both the margin-left and margin-right attributes.

19. Embed styles in the header section of a Web page or link to a centralized Web page of styles.

20. a {text-decoration: none;} a:visited {color: #ff0000 }

Sunday Morning Review Answers

1. The Project Leader coordinates the Web Team, manages the design and production of the site, and acts as the liaison between the team and the client.

2. The client may be a business who wants a Web site for customers to use.

3. A B2B company provides Web services for other companies doing business on the Web (B2B means "Business to Business").

4. Logos generate brand recognition.

5. False

6. Develop your home page before any other page on the site.

7. The user should gain a feel for your site from your home page.

8. The prototype acts as a model for the Web site's pages.

9. Graphics programs are great for creating prototypes.

10. Tables hide their structure from users more easily than frames do.

11. Use the prototype and graphics program to draw lines that form the table cells.

12. The template ensures that you include the proper sections for the page.

13. Documentation lists the site creators and editors, explains what HTML code does, and describes how changes can be made to the page.

14. False

15.

16. The table will have a border that does not match the table's color and the table will appear more obvious.

17. The table cells may need to appear between a headline's wording for graphic image placement.

18. All pages on your Web site, with the exception of non-frameset frame pages, should contain meta tags.

19. The closing forward slash can speed the connection to hyperlinked Web pages.

20. Framing graphics helps to accent the images.

Sunday Afternoon Review Answers

1. The mailto: protocol

2. CGI script

3. The email is not encrypted and the email address is obvious.

4. An image might be used as a hyperlink and an image map can be used to support multiple hyperlinks.

5. False

6. Specify image map coordinate values as rectangular, triangular, or circular coordinates.

7. Perform a usability study.

8. Look for the user's ability to traverse the site without trouble, study the user's face as the user surfs the site, notice what the user thinks is easy and what the user seems to miss.

9. The click-through rate indicates how deep into your site users tend to surf.

10. Image maps do not always make the clickable areas obvious to the users.

11. Use shading colors or mark image map hot spots so the user knows where to click.

12. False

13. Document Web pages well so that you and others can update the site easily.

14. Break long passages of text into shorter passage, span text across several pages, break text articles into short subjects.

15. False

16. Information appliances

17. Bluetooth offers suppoer for wireless communication between devices.

18. More connections to the Internet will appear as technology is used more and more.

19. The `<link>` tag pre-fetches WebTV Web pages.

20. decks

APPENDIX

What's On the CD-ROM

This book's CD-ROM includes the source code from all the examples in this book, the HTML 4.01 Weekend Crash Course Assessment Test, and a few supplemental programs that may be of interest to you as you program with HTML. The following sections briefly explain each component of the CD-ROM.

To display one of your own files, such as the Web pages you create in this weekend crash course, don't use the `http://` **prefix followed by a Web page address in your browser's address bar. Instead, simply type your own computer's disk and directory. You might type** `C:\html\Barkley.htm` **to view the Barkleys' Web page that you've created, assuming the page resides in the HTML directory of drive C and that you've named the file Barkley.htm.**

Source Code Listings

The sample source code for the book is included on the CD-ROM. There is a folder for each session in the book that contains an HTML code listing. Each folder contains the HTML file listing that you can load directly into your Web browser by issuing the File ➪ Open command. The images used throughout this book are stored in the images folder. The Barkley Family Web Site's pages are also included in its entirety in the folder named Barkley, with its own images folder. The Barkley home page is named index.htm.

As you work through the sessions that explore the Barkley Web site, you must adjust any file locations referenced in the code to match the location where you copy the Barkley Family Web page.

HTML 4.01 Weekend Crash Course Assessment Test

The CD-ROM contains 60 multiple-choice questions with answers. These questions serve two purposes. You can use these test questions to assess how much HTML knowledge you already have and thereby determine what sessions you can skip. You can also go through them after reading individual sessions or this book in its entirety to assess how much you have learned. The questions are organized by session; therefore they follow the order of topics discussed in this book. The session that each question corresponds with is noted next to each question.

Color Chart

To accent your HTML programming as you explore this weekend crash course, use the CD-ROM's color chart to help you locate the exact color codes you want to place on your Web pages. Inside the CD-ROM folder named Colors, is an HTML file named Color Chart.htm that you can load into your browser. The color chart displays the 216 Web-safe colors as well as their hexadecimal values.

Internet Explorer 5.5

Microsoft's Internet Explorer 5.5 is one of the most feature-rich Internet browsers on the market today. Internet Explorer 5.5 supports all major aspects of HTML 4.01 and is the most popular browser on the PC platform. Internet Explorer 5.5 includes FrontPage Express, a WYSIWYG (What You See is What You Get) Web page builder with which you can graphically design your Web site.

Netscape Navigator

Netscape Navigator is a direct competitor to Internet Explorer. Netscape Navigator is also feature-rich and supports the HTML 4.01 covered in this text. With both

Navigator and Internet Explorer 5.5, you can try your HTML code in both interfaces to determine how your Web pages look to users of both browsers.

HotDog Express

HotDog Express is a snazzy editor that provides visual feedback as you work and the tools to help you do the job you need to do. You can drag and drop HTML components onto a Web page screen to build the HTML file without knowing a lot of HTML. Unlike regular text editors, HotDog's designers created HotDog Express specifically to aid the newcomer to HTML programming.

BBEdit

BBEdit is one of the finest text editors available for the Mac today. BBEdit defines the editing standards by which all other editors are described. You can use BBEdit for both HTML and other text file work.

WebPage Wizard

You can create, edit, and publish your own Web pages with the online WebPage Wizard software. Unlike traditional hosting services, WebPage Wizard guides you through the steps needed to publish a site quickly and easily. As you enhance your HTML skills, you can take advantage of the WebPage Wizard's more powerful features.

ULead's GIF Animator

The Ulead's Gif Animator provides everything you need to create, edit, and manage your animated GIF images. You can liven your Web pages with these animated images. The frame-by-frame editing feature set is perhaps the simplest and most clear-cut avenue towards generating animated GIF images today.

HomeSite

Homesite is an editor designed specifically for the HTML programmer. Homesite provides editing options rarely found in text editors, such as a spelling checker, color-coded tags, estimated page download times, pop-up font selection dialog boxes, and automatic insertion of common code and ActiveX controls when requested.

Index

Continued

Continued

Continued

IDG Books Worldwide, Inc.
End-User License Agreement

READ THIS. You should carefully read these terms and conditions before opening the software packet(s) included with this book ("Book"). This is a license agreement ("Agreement") between you and IDG Books Worldwide, Inc. ("IDGB"). By opening the accompanying software packet(s), you acknowledge that you have read and accept the following terms and conditions. If you do not agree and do not want to be bound by such terms and conditions, promptly return the Book and the unopened software packet(s) to the place you obtained them for a full refund.

1. **License Grant.** IDGB grants to you (either an individual or entity) a nonexclusive license to use one copy of the enclosed software program(s) (collectively, the "Software") solely for your own personal or business purposes on a single computer (whether a standard computer or a work-station component of a multiuser network). The Software is in use on a computer when it is loaded into temporary memory (RAM) or installed into permanent memory (hard disk, CD-ROM, or other storage device). IDGB reserves all rights not expressly granted herein.

2. **Ownership.** IDGB is the owner of all right, title, and interest, including copyright, in and to the compilation of the Software recorded on the disk(s) or CD-ROM ("Software Media"). Copyright to the individual programs recorded on the Software Media is owned by the author or other authorized copyright owner of each program. Ownership of the Software and all proprietary rights relating thereto remain with IDGB and its licensers.

3. **Restrictions On Use and Transfer.**

   (a) You may only (i) make one copy of the Software for backup or archival purposes, or (ii) transfer the Software to a single hard disk, provided that you keep the original for backup or archival purposes. You may not (i) rent or lease the Software, (ii) copy or reproduce the Software through a LAN or other network system or through any computer subscriber system or bulletin-board system, or (iii) modify, adapt, or create derivative works based on the Software.

(b) You may not reverse engineer, decompile, or disassemble the Software. You may transfer the Software and user documentation on a permanent basis, provided that the transferee agrees to accept the terms and conditions of this Agreement and you retain no copies. If the Software is an update or has been updated, any transfer must include the most recent update and all prior versions.

4. **<u>Restrictions on Use of Individual Programs</u>.** You must follow the individual requirements and restrictions detailed for each individual program in Appendix B of this Book. These limitations are also contained in the individual license agreements recorded on the Software Media. These limitations may include a requirement that after using the program for a specified period of time, the user must pay a registration fee or discontinue use. By opening the Software packet(s), you will be agreeing to abide by the licenses and restrictions for these individual programs that are detailed in Appendix X and on the Software Media. None of the material on this Software Media or listed in this Book may ever be redistributed, in original or modified form, for commercial purposes.

5. **<u>Limited Warranty</u>.**

   (a) IDGB warrants that the Software and Software Media are free from defects in materials and workmanship under normal use for a period of sixty (60) days from the date of purchase of this Book. If IDGB receives notification within the warranty period of defects in materials or workmanship, IDGB will replace the defective Software Media.

   (b) IDGB AND THE AUTHOR OF THE BOOK DISCLAIM ALL OTHER WARRANTIES, EXPRESS OR IMPLIED, INCLUDING WITHOUT LIMITATION IMPLIED WARRANTIES OF MERCHANTABILITY AND FITNESS FOR A PARTICULAR PURPOSE, WITH RESPECT TO THE SOFTWARE, THE PROGRAMS, THE SOURCE CODE CONTAINED THEREIN, AND/OR THE TECHNIQUES DESCRIBED IN THIS BOOK. IDGB DOES NOT WARRANT THAT THE FUNCTIONS CONTAINED IN THE SOFTWARE WILL MEET YOUR REQUIREMENTS OR THAT THE OPERATION OF THE SOFTWARE WILL BE ERROR FREE.

   (c) This limited warranty gives you specific legal rights, and you may have other rights that vary from jurisdiction to jurisdiction.

6. **Remedies.**

   (a) IDGB's entire liability and your exclusive remedy for defects in materials and workmanship shall be limited to replacement of the Software Media, which may be returned to IDGB with a copy of your receipt at the following address: Software Media Fulfillment Department, Attn.: *HTML 4.01 Weekend Crash Course(tm)*, IDG Books Worldwide, Inc., 10475 Crosspoint Blvd., Indianapolis, IN 46256, or call 1-800-762-2974. Please allow three to four weeks for delivery. This Limited Warranty is void if failure of the Software Media has resulted from accident, abuse, or misapplication. Any replacement Software Media will be warranted for the remainder of the original warranty period or thirty (30) days, whichever is longer.

   (b) In no event shall IDGB or the author be liable for any damages whatsoever (including without limitation damages for loss of business profits, business interruption, loss of business information, or any other pecuniary loss) arising from the use of or inability to use the Book or the Software, even if IDGB has been advised of the possibility of such damages.

   (c) Because some jurisdictions do not allow the exclusion or limitation of liability for consequential or incidental damages, the above limitation or exclusion may not apply to you.

7. **U.S. Government Restricted Rights.** Use, duplication, or disclosure of the Software by the U.S. Government is subject to restrictions stated in paragraph (c)(1)(ii) of the Rights in Technical Data and Computer Software clause of DFARS 252.227-7013, and in subparagraphs (a) through (d) of the Commercial Computer — Restricted Rights clause at FAR 52.227-19, and in similar clauses in the NASA FAR supplement, when applicable.

8. **General.** This Agreement constitutes the entire understanding of the parties and revokes and supersedes all prior agreements, oral or written, between them and may not be modified or amended except in a writing signed by both parties hereto that specifically refers to this Agreement. This Agreement shall take precedence over any other documents that may be in conflict herewith. If any one or more provisions contained in this Agreement are held by any court or tribunal to be invalid, illegal, or otherwise unenforceable, each and every other provision shall remain in full force and effect.

my2cents.idgbooks.com

Register This Book — And Win!

Visit **http://my2cents.idgbooks.com** to register this book and we'll automatically enter you in our fantastic monthly prize giveaway. It's also your opportunity to give us feedback: let us know what you thought of this book and how you would like to see other topics covered.

Discover IDG Books Online!

The IDG Books Online Web site is your online resource for tackling technology — at home and at the office. Frequently updated, the IDG Books Online Web site features exclusive software, insider information, online books, and live events!

10 Productive & Career-Enhancing Things You Can Do at www.idgbooks.com

- Nab source code for your own programming projects.
- Download software.
- Read Web exclusives: special articles and book excerpts by IDG Books Worldwide authors.
- Take advantage of resources to help you advance your career as a Novell or Microsoft professional.
- Buy IDG Books Worldwide titles or find a convenient bookstore that carries them.
- Register your book and win a prize.
- Chat live online with authors.
- Sign up for regular e-mail updates about our latest books.
- Suggest a book you'd like to read or write.
- Give us your 2¢ about our books and about our Web site.

You say you're not on the Web yet? It's easy to get started with IDG Books' *Discover the Internet,* available at local retailers everywhere.

CD-ROM Installation Instructions

The CD-ROM that accompanies this book contains the complete code examples from the text as well as evaluation versions of various HTML-based tools, which are described in Appendix B.

The code and tools are stored on the CD-ROM in their own subfolders. To install, open each vendor's folder and run the installation program. See Appendix B for further information on the programs' specifics.